Data Analysis
for the
Helping
Professions

SAGE SOURCEBOOKS FOR THE HUMAN SERVICES SERIES

Series Editors: ARMAND LAUFFER and CHARLES GARVIN

A source is a starting point, a place of origin, information, or payoff. The volumes in this series reflect these themes. For readers they will serve as starting points for new programs, as the place of origin of advanced skills, or as a source for information that can be used in the pursuit of professional and organizational goals.

Sage Sourcebooks are written to provide multiple benefits for both professionals and advanced students. Authors and contributors are recognized authorities in their fields or at the cutting edge of new knowledge and technique. Sourcebooks deal with new and emerging practice tools and current and anticipated policy issues, transforming knowledge from allied professions and the social sciences into information applicable to the human services.

THE TRAPPED WOMAN: Catch-22 in Deviance and Control
edited by JOSEFINA FIGUEIRA-McDONOUGH & ROSEMARY SARRI

FAMILY THERAPY WITH ETHNIC MINORITIES
by MAN KEUNG HO

WORKING IN SOCIAL WORK: Growing and Thriving in Human Services Practice
by ARMAND LAUFFER

MIDLIFE MYTHS: Issues, Findings, and Practice Implications
edited by SKI HUNTER & MARTIN SUNDEL

SOCIAL WORK IN PRIMARY CARE
edited by MATTHEW L. HENK

PRACTICAL PROGRAM EVALUATION: Examples from Child Abuse Prevention
by JEANNE PIETRZAK, MALIA RAMLER, TANYA RENNER, LUCY FORD & NEIL GILBERT

DATA ANALYSIS FOR THE HELPING PROFESSIONS: A Practical Guide
by DONALD M. PILCHER

DESIGNING AND MANAGING PROGRAMS: An Effectiveness Based Approach
by PETER M. KETTNER, ROBERT K. MORONEY, & LAWRENCE L. MARTIN

GROUP WORK: A Humanistic Approach
by URANIA GLASSMAN & LEN KATES

Donald M. Pilcher

Data Analysis for the Helping Professions

A Practical Guide

SAGE SOURCEBOOKS FOR THE HUMAN SERVICES SERIES 10

SAGE PUBLICATIONS
The International Professional Publishers
Newbury Park   London   New Delhi

For information address:

SAGE Publications, Inc.
2111 West Hillcrest Drive
Newbury Park, California 91320

SAGE Publications Ltd.
28 Banner Street
London EC1Y 8QE
England

SAGE Publications India Pvt. Ltd.
M-32 Market
Greater Kailash I
New Delhi 110 048 India

Printed in the United States of America

Library of Congress Cataloging-in-Publication Data

Pilcher, Donald M.
  Data analysis for the helping professions : a practical guide
/ Donald M. Pilcher.
      p.   cm. — (Sage sourcebooks for the human services series ;
  v. 10)
  Includes bibliographical references.
  ISBN 0-8039-3724-5. — ISBN 0-8039-3061-5 (pbk.)
  1. Social sciences—Statistical methods. 2. Statistics.
I. Title. II. Series.
HA29.H622   1990
519.5—dc20

                                                      89-28109
                                                           CIP

FIRST PRINTING, 1990

CONTENTS

ACKNOWLEDGMENTS

This book is dedicated to my wife, Ann, in appreciation of her support and encouragement and to the many students at San Diego State University, La Trobe University, and Melbourne University, who taught me how to make data analysis meaningful in the face of diffidence and skepticism about the relevance of statistics for the helping professions.

The patience and dedication of the editors at Sage Publications and the skill of the typesetter is also appreciated. I am indebted to Terry Hendrix and to the Series Editors for their encouragement throughout. I am also indebted to Bruce Lagay for his helpful suggestions and comments on the original manuscript.

I am grateful to the Literary Executor of the late Sir Ronald A. Fisher, F.R.S. to Dr. Frank Yates, F.R.S. and the Longman Group Ltd., London for permission to reprint Tables A, C, & D from their book *Statistical Tables for Biological, Agricultural and Medical Research* (6th Edition 1974).

PREFACE

The presentation of statistics in this book reflects an approach developed over twenty years of teaching statistics to a few enthusiastic students, but more often to reluctant and apprehensive students, in one of the helping professions. This approach emphasizes guiding principles for the use of statistical procedures. The organization and emphasis on guiding principles is unusual but reflects my experience in leading students to an appreciation and understanding of the place of statistics in social and behavioral research.

The book is organized in two parts. Part I sets forth guidelines and principles used in selecting statistical procedures and reducing data to meaningful indices. Application of these procedures to research issues from the world of the helping professions provides the illustrations and examples. Data from the professional journals and theses are used throughout to provide meaningful examples of the use of statistics in research.

Part II provides the reader with illustrations on how data can be set up for analysis and computation of statistical indices, whether by hand, by calculator, or by computer. Examples are used to show the actual mathematics involved.

The reason for this somewhat unusual separation is to allow the reader an opportunity to examine the principles involved in selecting statistical procedures and the application to research data without the interruption required when calculations and formulas are introduced.

For readers who find themselves cowed by equations and mathematical symbols, this format provides a logical transition from the principles to meaningful applications.

The chapters in Part II can be read in sequence after completing Part I or in conjunction with matching chapters from Part I: Chapters 2 and 6, Chapters 3 and 7, Chapters 4 and 8, and Chapters 5 and 9.

Technical terminology is used throughout but attention is paid to providing definitions as new concepts are introduced. In addition, a glossary of terms is provided in Appendix A. Statistical terminology will be new to some readers, but the text and glossary should facilitate understanding. It is important for the reader to be familiar with statistical terminology if statistical procedures are to be used in research.

In Part I formulas and mathematical symbols are kept to a minimum, and in Part II these are given in the simplest style possible, assuming little mathematical sophistication on the part of the reader. It is also emphasized throughout that formulas need not be memorized at a time when they can be programmed into the memories of calculators and computers. It is, nevertheless, important for the reader to grasp the meaning behind the formulas.

This book is intended as a practical guide to baccalaureate and master's students in nursing, education, social work, and related professions and to nurses, social workers, and teachers in their practice and teaching situations. It is concerned with the application of statistical procedures to their research data.

University and college faculty and doctoral-level students with little statistical experience may wish to use the book to review statistical concepts because it does provide basic principles and guidelines for use of statistical procedures. As an introductory text, it is not intended for those who are looking for esoteric applications of statistical procedures to their research. Rather, it is a bridge to more advanced statistical texts.

This book contains the basic statistical procedures needed for the analysis of many, if not most, situations encountered by the student or the practitioner. For advanced statistical procedures and more elaborate discussion of issues, readers will wish to pursue the references provided throughout.

Part One

FINDING THE RIGHT STATISTICAL PROCEDURE

In the first chapter, principles and guidelines are presented that enable the reader to find the appropriate statistical procedures congruent with the purpose of the researcher and the purpose of the analysis, the number of variables in the analysis, the nature of the data, and the source of the data.

In the next four chapters, these principles are applied to data from the professional literature, and statistical procedures are identified that are appropriate for the analysis. Various statistical measures and devices will be discussed in terms of their use and usefulness and how they are interpreted.

The emphasis in these five chapters will not be on actual computation of statistical procedures; this is left to the last four chapters in which statistical procedures are applied to data from the literature to illustrate how data are organized and processed. Chapters 2 to 5 have matching chapters in Part II, and these can be studied as a unit.

The guiding principles are the linchpin for the reader because they provide the context for determining what statistical procedures are appropriate for the analysis and for determining how the procedures can be used in decision making in the development of knowledge.

Chapter 1

INTRODUCTION

USE OF STATISTICAL PROCEDURES IN DECISION MAKING

It will be obvious to most readers that modern calculators, computers, and microcomputers take the tedium out of data analysis and reduce the time needed for computation, enabling the researcher to concentrate on the substance of the analysis. Ready access to statistical procedures by naive users makes it all the more imperative that guiding principles be equally accessible. It is a mixed blessing that computers can be used to manipulate and grind out masses of data at lightning speed, because this can happen without regard to the appropriateness of statistical procedures used for a given set of data or the indices they yield.

The Statistical Package for Social Science (SPSS [Nie, Hull, Jenkins, Steinbrenner & Bent, 1975] or the new version SPSS-X [Nie, 1983) and SPSS/PC) program, for instance, may yield a dozen measures of association for a given pair of variables, but the researcher must know which of these indices is most appropriate to the problem at hand and to the characteristics of the data.

There are at least twenty common measures of association that might be used in social and behavioral research and as many tests of significance. We must be aware of certain guiding principles in order to select the most appropriate statistical procedures and avoid others. Once the researcher is familiar with these guiding principles, the decision about statistical procedures to be used can be narrowed to a few options.

Usually, each statistical procedure has several assumptions or requirements tied to it. These assumptions must be reviewed to determine whether the set of data at hand meets the requirements for the selected procedure. If your data do not meet all of the assumptions, you will need to make that explicit when presenting your analysis. The aim should be to violate as few assumptions as possible when using a particular statistical procedure.

The selection of measures should be made early in the planning of research because the way in which data are collected will limit the range of procedures available and may rule out the possibility of using more precise and definitive measures. In other words, the way you conceptualize your variables and the way you set about obtaining data will determine what range of statistical measures are possible.

Professionals in the helping professions constantly deal with observations about the variation in characteristics of students, patients, clients, or groups with which they are concerned. The degree of variation, as we observe it, makes it possible to compare one person, patient, or family with another or to compare their characteristics or attributes from one time to another. The focus of research is on these attributes. The attribute might be temperature (of a patient), level of anxiety, academic achievement, aggressive behavior, frequency of bed-wetting, social class, or leadership style.

Because these attributes vary from person to person and also from time to time with one person, they can be termed variables. We assign categories to these variables—degrees, intensity, frequency, scores, scales, values—and these categories may or may not be expressed in numbers. When expressed in numerical terms, we often call them measurements. Whether or not expressed in numerical terms, these categories make up the "data" for research.

From systematic observation of characteristics or attributes, we collect, accumulate, and assemble data into frequency distributions in order to analyze differences, variations, and relationships between individuals, or variations from one time to another for the same individual. Assembling, describing, and analyzing observed data is what research is all about, and statistical description and analysis are parts of this process. Our observations result in the accumulation of data on temperature, frequency of aggressive behavior, or test results. The recorded temperature of a patient at any one time would be a datum. The researcher collects data on phenomena or variables that appear to be important or relevant, and the values of these variables can be compared to see if they are closely related, e.g. (level of anxiety and frequency of bed-wetting). Statistics used for this purpose are termed measures of association.

Observations may be derived from a population of students, patients, or clients, or they may be derived by taking a sample of these groups. Statistical procedures used to describe or analyze these populations are called *descriptive statistics*. If we wish to infer characteristics of the population from the observations made on a sample of that population, the procedures used are called *inferential statistics*. In other words, we are making an inference about the population from the sample we have taken from that population. The common practice in research is to determine the level of confidence in making that inference by a test of significance. Descriptive and inferential statistics are the substance of this book.

In summary we use statistics for several purposes:

(1) To reduce distributions of research data to meaningful indices for quick reference and comparison

(2) To make decisions about how closely two or more variables are related or how well one can predict the value of one variable, the dependent variable, by knowing the value of another variable, the independent variable

(3) To make decisions about the confidence one can have in generalizing about a population from information about a sample of that population

(4) To determine whether or not a set of research findings may be due to chance.

In a general sense we use statistics to help us make decisions about the distribution of phenomena as represented by empirical (observed) data and the relationships between phenomena. We cannot let the results of statistical procedures make decisions for us; these results can only guide decisions grounded on an understanding of the underlying phenomena.

Some studies will not require the use of statistics at all; others will require several procedures, sometimes quite complicated and intricate statistical procedures. We will not explore the more complicated and intricate statistical procedures in this book, but will concentrate on fundamental, essential, and pragmatic statistical procedures, which are, for the most part, adequate for analyzing most sets of data. This book is designed to assist the reader in learning how to determine the most appropriate set of statistical procedures for the data at hand or the data to be obtained. It makes no claims to an exhaustive, technical treatment of the procedures outlined. The references provided will enable students to extend their knowledge as desired.

Students and practitioners in the helping professions often shy away from statistics because they see it as mathematical and mechanical. The word *statistics* may evoke an image of equations and formulas unfamiliar and strange to the uninitiated. This need not be a stumbling block. It is not necessary to memorize formulas; in fact it is foolish to try to do so when they are available in statistics books and are in computer and calculator memories (or can be programmed into the memories). It is important to understand what the formulas represent, and this requires concentrated study about the specific procedures you are using. With few exceptions, the equations that you will examine involve no mathematics beyond the four basic arithmetic operations — addition, subtraction, division, and multiplication (with squaring as a special case of multiplication) — and extracting square roots, which can all be done readily by calculator or computer.

Once decisions are made about appropriate statistical procedures, programs exist in statistical packages and manuals for computers and calculators to perform the actual calculations. The reader may, however, wish to make the calculations by hand in order to acquire a better understanding of what the calculations are all about. Later chapters provide an opportunity to do so.

We have noted several uses of statistics in the helping services related to differing purposes and goals. Some elaboration of these applications may be useful to the reader in understanding the importance of the guiding principles to be presented.

In general, statistical procedures are techniques for assembling, describing, and inferring from numerical or categorical data. More specifically, statistical techniques are often used to provide indices of distributions so that we can compare one distribution with another. We can use the mean, for instance, to describe the ages of two groups and to compare them. The mean is not the only statistical device for this purpose, but it is one useful index of central tendency for a distribution. Nevertheless, as we shall see, the mean cannot be used with certain types of data.

Statistical procedures are used to reduce complex data to indices that can be used as variables or as constructs. For instance, Wiehe (1986) used two scales to compare abusing and nonabusing parents on level of empathy (using the Hogan Empathy Scale) and locus of control (using the Nowicki Strickland Internal-External Locus of Control Scales). The scores on these two scales are used as variables in examining the relationship between the two concepts and with other variables. The two variables are constructed from responses on items making up the scale.

Reduction of complex data is common in organizational research as well. For instance, fragmentation or cohesion in a legislative body can be reduced to a fractionalization ratio that is a measure of the likelihood on a standardized scale that any two randomly selected members will be of the same party. This is a useful index in political research. It can be used to determine the effect of legislative cohesion on ability to pass legislation.

A third example of reducing complex data to indices comes from literature on income distribution. Suppose we divide the total number of income earners into ten groups, ranging from the 10% with the least income (the bottom decile) to the top 10% of income earners (the top decile). If we total the amount of income going to each of the deciles, we can make statements like, "the bottom 10% of the population (of income earners) receives 2% of the national income, and the top 10% of the population receives 30% of the national income."

The data on amount of income going to each income group are difficult to compare from one year to the next. If the distribution is reduced to a Gini coefficient (an index of the unequal distribution of income) or, alternatively, the share going to each population decile (decile share), comparisons from year to year are then possible. These two indices are important in comparing various nations on levels of income equality or following the trends in any given country. Thus data reduction and the development of indices can be useful in research, either in making comparisons or in finding shorthand ways of describing a distribution or in representing a concept.

Statistical procedures are sometimes used in social research to make inferences about a larger population from a random sample of people and to calculate the level of confidence we can have in generalizing about the population from the sample. We may use one of a number of inferential statistics to make this decision. The trick is to know which one is most appropriate. At other times in social research, we study the population itself directly, rather than making inferences from a random sample about the population we are studying.

Most frequently we want to make decisions about how closely two variables are related to each other, and we may even want to predict the values of one variable from the values of the other. Or perhaps, we want to know the effects or predictive power of a number of independent variables on a dependent variable. Our decisions about the strength of the relationships might be informed by a dozen or more statistical techniques. Which one will be most useful and appropriate in making these decisions?

The fact that there are literally dozens of statistical techniques and procedures that could be used in social and behavioral research need not daunt us. Guiding principles can help us narrow our choice of possible techniques which we can then assess individually by reference to textbooks until we select the most appropriate one. The focus of the chapters that follow will be on these principles and their application to sets of data, along with relevant references for further reading. Before these principles are stated, some definitions must be provided.

NUMBER OF VARIABLES

Often we are concerned with only one variable and we want to see how data are distributed across its categories. For instance, we may want to know the source of referral of youngsters referred to the probation department: were they referred primarily by the police, by the school, or by parents? We can then sort the cases into these three categories and describe the distribution in a number of ways: proportional statements, percentage statements, or in terms of modal category.

Thus we can say about the distribution in Table 1.1 (Pope & Feyerherm, 1982) that only 935 of the 8,479 youngsters were referred by the school, whereas 7,258 were referred by the police. Or we can say that nearly 86% were referred by the police, 11% were referred by the school, and only 3% were referred by parents of the youngsters. We could also say that the modal category of referral was law enforcement officials.

On another occasion, our interest might be centered on age at the time of referral. We might want to use a summary index of central tendency, the mean, for instance to describe the age of the youngsters. To compute the mean age, however, we would need to have the raw data or we would need to have small discrete categories to make an estimate of the mean. The article by Pope and Feyerherm (1982) does not provide the raw data to compute the mean, but it does give us some information

Table 1.1

Number and Percentage of Youngsters Referred to the Probation Department,
by Source of Referral

Referral Source	Number	Percentage
Law Enforcement Agency	7,258	85.6
School	935	11.0
Parents	286	3.4
Total	8,479	100.0

SOURCE: Derived from Pope & Feyerherm (1982).
NOTES: Number of offenders was computed from the percentages given in the source article. Rounding
may have created some error in the number of offenders.
Number of variables: One (referral source)
Level of measurement: Nominal
Sample or population: Sample
Statistical procedures: Frequency distribution & percentages

about age composition. In Table 1.2, we see that 3,873 of the 8,863 youngsters in the distribution were 17 years of age and over, nearly 44% of the total.

One-variable statistics include proportions, percentages, and ratios, various measures of central tendency (mean, median, and mode), measures of dispersion (e.g., standard deviation), and tests of significance such as the Chi Square Test of the Goodness of Fit or the t Test. We will discuss these in the next chapter.

Again our concern may be on the relationship between two or more variables. Is source of referral related to gender? How strong is this relationship? Are boys more likely to be referred by the school than girls? Are boys more likely than girls to be referred by police? Now we are dealing with two variables. In such instances we may wish to know how closely the categories of the two variables are related and look for a measure of the degree of association. We usually cross-tabulate the variables to depict such data (see Table 1.2). The reader should note that gender is a dichotomous variable, (i.e., it has only two categories, male and female). This will be important when we consider our options in statistical procedures.

We can use percentages to analyze the data in Table 1.2, examining one variable in its relationship to the other. Looking at the total column, we see that nearly 44% of all of these youngsters fall in the "older" category, but less than 37% of the females fall in that category. By

Table 1.2

Number and Percentage of Offenders by Gender and Age

Age of Offender	Gender of Offender		Total
	Male	Female	
Older (17 and older)	2,967 (46.4)	906 (36.7)	3,873 (43.7)
Younger (under 17)	3,428 (53.6)	1,562 (63.3)	4,990 (56.3)
Total	6,395 (100.0)	2,468 (100.0)	8,863 (100.0)

Derived from Pope & Feyerherm (1982).
NOTES: Number of offenders was computed from the percentages given in the article. Rounding may have created some error in the number of offenders.
Number of variables: Two (gender and age)
Level of measurement: Gender – nominal dichotomous; age – ordinal or nominal dichotomous
Sample or population: Sample
Statistical procedures: Cross-tabulation & percentages

examining the percentages in the right-hand column, we can determine whether females or males are overrepresented or underrepresented in the older and younger age groups. In this case females are under-represented in the older group; however, they predominate in the youn-ger category. We could also perform a test of significance on the distribution and compute an index of the strength of relationship, but let us leave that for a later chapter.

If we suspect that source of referral is also affected by gender as well as age, we could construct a three-variable table to examine the data from that perspective (a multivariate distribution). The purpose of a three-way table could be to determine what mediating effects a third variable has on the relationship between the other two variables. Table 1.3 presents a three-way table showing the relationship between gender, age, and use of detention by the probation department.

From Table 1.3, one can see that in status cases females were much more likely to be given detention than males at the time of initial referral; this was even more likely with the younger offenders. In other words, the relationship between gender and detention is mediated by age.

Bivariate and multivariate distributions lend themselves to various statistical procedures: tests of significance, measures of the strength of association, and predictive indices. Just which of these we use depends primarily on level of measurement, but also on other factors to be discussed below.

Table 1.3

Number and Percentage of Offenders by Gender, Age, and Whether
or Not Offender was Held in Detention at Time of Initial Referral
(status offenses only)

Detention at Time of Initial Referral	Male Age		Female Age		Total
	17 +	< 17	17 +	< 17	
Yes	293 (61.7)	512 (58.0)	177 (65.8)	498 (71.2)	1,480 (63.7)
No	182 (38.3)	370 (42.0)	92 (34.2)	201 (28.8)	845 (36.3)
Total	475	882	269	699	2,325

SOURCE: Derived from Pope & Feyerherm (1982).
NOTES: Number of offenders was computed from the percentages given in the source article. Rounding may have created some error in the number of offenders.
Number of variables: Three (gender, age, and detention)
Level of measurement: Detention — nominal dichotomous; gender — nominal dichotomous; age — ordinal or nominal dichotomous
Sample or population: Sample
Statistical procedures: Cross-tabulation and percentages

LEVEL OF MEASUREMENT

In research, as in nursing, social work, education, and other human service practice, we are concerned with variables. Because a variable must, by definition, be able to vary from case to case, it always has two or more categories or values. It is the characteristics or qualities of categories attributed to a variable that determine its level of measurement: nominal, ordinal, or interval.

The simplest level of measurement is nominal (also called categorical). The values are named (nominal) categories and lack the feature of order and rank; they are essentially qualitative rather than quantitative. Common nominal-level variables are gender, religious affiliation, country of birth, marital status, source of referral, diagnostic classification, and educational classification (e.g., junior, senior). Many of the variables we are concerned with in the human and social services have nominal-level categories. They are gross and sometimes crude classifications of qualitatively different categories with no order or measurable dimension. Male is not "greater" or "lesser" than female. Christians are not "more" or "less" than Moslems. Inpatients are not "more" or "less" than outpatients. Truanting children are not "more" or "less" than nontruanting children, although their frequency of school attendance may be. Nominal-level variables usually have exhaustive and mutually exclusive categories but they are not ordered nor are they in standard units of measurement. (See Table 2.6 in Chapter 2 for an example of nominal-level data.)

Some variables have categories that do have an intrinsic order but without being measured in standardized units. Our use of the terms *first*, *second*, and *third*, an ordinal use of numbers, illustrates the ordinal-level variable. When social workers or nurses rank by order of importance or priority the types of functions that they carry out in their work, this is an ordinal use of numbers and an ordinal-level variable. The categories have a definite sequence but the difference between first and second has no necessary equivalence to the difference between second and third. Ranking by size of population makes this clear.

If we rank China, India, the USSR, the United States, Pakistan, Indonesia, and Japan by population size, we have an ordered sequence by population, but the differences between ranks are not equivalent. The difference between the population of China and India is not the same as the difference between India and the Soviet Union. (See Tables 4.7 and 4.8 in Chapter 4 for examples of ranked ordinal-level data.)

There is another type of ordinal category that does not make use of ranks but orders categories along a continuum of more or less. For instance, the typical scale of *high*, *medium*, and *low* presents ordered categories. Scales that make use of such terms as *often__*, *infrequent__*, and *never__*, or *strongly agree__*, *agree__*, *disagree__*, and *strongly disagree__*, are ordinal scales. Patients might be classified as non-ambulatory, semi-ambulatory, and ambulatory; this could be considered an ordinal classification. Students might be classified as having a high, medium, or low level of aptitude on computer use; this would be an ordinal-level variable. However, if this classification were made on the basis of an actual score on a test of aptitude, it could be an interval-level variable. (See Tables 4.10 and 4.11 in Chapter 4 for examples of categorical ordinal data.)

You will note that with ordinal data, the distance between one pair of adjacent categories and the distance between another adjacent pair has no necessary equivalence: the categories are ordered but not in quantitative terms of precise measurement. Some researchers confound this fact by arbitrarily assigning numbers to the categories as if they represented amount of difference instead of mere labels on an ordered sequence. Further, it should be noted that we cannot be sure that two people whose respective incomes, for example, are both categorized as high have the *same* income in monetary units. In other words, there is variation within the categories.

The cardinal (i.e., quantitative) use of numbers, as opposed to an ordinal use, gives rise to the interval level of measurement. In this instance, numbers stand for quantity expressed in standard units: feet, years, months, temperature in degrees, blood pressure, intelligence quotient, score on a test, number of people, or number of elements. Statistics textbooks often distinguish between interval and ratio scales, but then go on to discuss both types of scales as if they were interval scales. These two levels of measurement make use of standardized scales but a ratio scale has a defined and absolute zero point (e.g., age) whereas interval scales have an arbitrary zero point (e.g., temperature).

Because we use the same statistical procedures for both interval and ratio scales, the distinction is not terribly important for us, although it might be in engineering or physics. Thus, most social science statistics books make the distinction but then treat the two types of variables as if they were the same and designate both as interval. The reader should be alert to this anomaly in the statistical literature but keep in mind that for all practical purposes we use the same statistical procedures for both types of scales.

With interval-level data, each unit has equal quantitative significance. Each unit is equal to each other unit. However, interval-level data can be reduced to ordinal data and both interval and ordinal data can be reduced to nominal data but the process cannot be reversed. If you obtain data by nominal categories (in interviews for example), you cannot construct ordinal or interval categories from them (although some researchers argue that you can treat a dichotomy as a simple interval scale).

As an illustration, level of education as a variable can be obtained on an interval scale (i.e., "How many years of school have you completed?"). One could reduce this to an ordinal variable by developing categories corresponding to completion of tertiary degree, some tertiary education, completion of secondary, some secondary, completion of elementary school, some elementary, and no schooling. These would be ordinal categories but not equal units and should, therefore, be treated with statistics appropriate for the ordinal level of measurement. One could also develop qualitative categories and consider educational level to be a nominal-level variable: school attenders and nonschool attenders. Thus we have reduced interval data to ordinal data and to nominal data. Note that if we collected the original data above in nominal or ordinal categories, we could not transform them into interval categories.

In many instances the level of measurement is quite clear. However, it may be your conceptualization of the variable that determines whether or not it is a nominal-level or ordinal-level variable. You must ask whether the categories are qualitatively different or quantitatively different in the ordinal (more — less) sense? If educational level were conceptualized in such categories as tertiary graduates, secondary graduates, early school leavers, and nonschool attenders, what level of measurement would you assign to it, nominal or ordinal? The answer is not always apparent, and it is up to the researcher to determine how the variable is to be viewed.

While there is some flexibility in applying a statistical procedure to various levels of measurement, it would be generally true that the statistical procedure that fully reflects the level of measurement applied to the variable will give you a better index for decision making than one that does not. Furthermore, the statistical measures that can be applied to interval-level data tend to provide more powerful tools for analysis than do those applicable to ordinal-level data (and the same is true for ordinal-level data in relation to nominal-level measures). This is partly because the higher levels of measurement make fuller use of the more precise attributes of the phenomena being studied. Nevertheless, some phenomena cannot or should not be categorized in ordered or standardized units, and we need not apologize for using the nominal level of measurement in such cases.

In statistical terminology, level of measurement refers to different types of scales: nominal, ordinal, and interval. Thus the question can be asked "what type of scale are you using?" or "what type of data do you have?". The answer should be nominal, ordinal, interval, or combinations of these. The answer to this question is extremely important because it is a key to choosing the statistical procedure that is most appropriate for the analysis of data.

This does not mean that the three levels of measurement cannot be involved in the same analysis. As an example, the Task Force on Teaching as a Profession prepared a useful table comparing SAT scores

Table 1.4

Combined SAT Scores for College-Bound High School Seniors by Intended Field of Study

Major	Blacks Percentile 25th	75th	Mexican-Americans Percentile 25th	75th	Puerto Ricans Percentile 25th	75th	Whites Percentile 25th	75th
Arts and humanities	556	810	622	913	594	892	763	1,068
Biological science	633	929	698	992	715	1023	863	1,162
Health & medicine	579	833	651	933	588	904	774	1,073
Business	551	785	612	873	578	823	736	1,012
Computer science	571	813	641	927	583	890	795	1,093
Engineering	648	954	730	1,021	707	1047	885	1,180
Social sciences	562	818	651	943	627	916	762	1,060
Education	511	722	587	835	543	819	702	973
Mean	715		796		766		932	

SOURCE: Adapted from Hawley (Feb. 1987, table 1, p. 306).
NOTES: Number of variables: Three (ethnicity, major, and SAT score)
Level of measurement: Ethnic group — nominal; major — nominal; SAT scores — ordinal
Sample or population: Unknown, but probably sample
Statistical procedures: Cross-tabulation, percentiles, and mean

for high school students planning to enter tertiary education by ethnic groups and intended field of study (see Table 1.4). The basic data on the SAT scores are interval level and they have been put into an ordinal classification (percentiles) for comparative purposes among various ethnic groups (a nominal classification) and among various majors (another nominal classification).

DISTINCTION BETWEEN DEPENDENT AND INDEPENDENT VARIABLES

Another key to finding the appropriate statistical procedure to use in examining the relationship between two variables is whether or not a distinction is made between a dependent and an independent variable. An independent variable is conceived as one that influences or brings about change in the dependent variable. Some illustrations may provide the student with a clear understanding of this distinction.

If pulse rate fluctuates, what variable or variables seem to account for the fluctuations? We may look at the intake of nicotine as a possible "cause," a variable that conceivably influences pulse rate. The fluctuation in pulse rate is the dependent variable, and the amount of nicotine intake is the independent variable.

Or consider the voting behavior in families. Is voting preference of daughter or son seen to be determined or conditioned by parental voting preference? If so, daughter's or son's voting preference is dependent and parental voting preference is independent, and the relationship is presumed to be asymmetric (i.e., one variable — the independent — influences the other variable — dependent — in some way).

In looking at the relationship between two variables, it is not always apparent that one variable is independent and the other dependent. In the example given above, one could provocatively, but perhaps illogically, argue that young people are more persuasive than older people, so that parental voting preference is presumed to be dependent, and daughter's or son's voting preference is presumed to be causal or independent. It is the researcher who makes this decision on the basis of logic, knowledge of the phenomenon, and knowledge of previous research.

On the other hand one could assume that variables other than familial ones influence voting preferences and that there is no causal or determining presumption to be made. In such instances the relationship would be considered symmetrical and no distinction between dependent and independent variables would be made.

Some researchers describe these relationships as directional (asymmetric) or nondirectional (symmetric). Thus we sometimes speak of a directional or nondirectional hypothesis. If the relationship is considered to be asymmetric or directional, a distinction is being made between an independent and dependent variable. The researcher must decide, in analyzing data, whether or not it is logical and meaningful to consider the relationship to be symmetric or asymmetric. This decision will determine how the relationship is discussed in the analysis and it will also determine what statistical procedures are appropriate.

SOURCE OF DATA: POPULATION OR SAMPLE

In studying a population or sample involving two variables, we usually want to determine the strength of association between variables (i.e., the degree to which two variables are associated with each other). With population data, our primary concern is with the strength of association between two variables, although we may want to ask questions about the probability of the distribution arising from chance. But with sample data on two variables, we are necessarily concerned with both: tests of significance because we are generalizing to the population from which the sample was drawn; and with a measure of association because we want to know how closely two variables are related, particularly if the relationship is found to be significant, but even if it is not (Cowger, 1984, p. 369).

The statistics associated with populations are often called descriptive statistics; the statistics associated with generalizing to a population from a sample are called inferential statistics because we are inferring to the population from the sample. However, there may be a case for using tests of significance (an inferential statistic) with population data, and certainly a case can be made for using descriptive statistics with sample data in a bivariate table. A test of significance may be used with a population as well as a sample but for somewhat different purposes (see Blalock, 1981, pp. 251–243; Henkel, 1976, pp. 85–87) which we will discuss in Chapter 3.

GUIDING PRINCIPLES

The guiding principles of primary interest to the social researcher concern the number of variables included in the distribution, the level of measurement, the expected symmetry of a relationship, source of data (population or sample), the assumptions behind the measure under consideration, and any unusual properties of the indices being used. The first five of these principles will be discussed in some detail in the chapters that follow; the remaining principle will receive only cursory consideration and will be left to the reader for further study. The six principles can be stated simply:

(1) First, distinguish between one-variable (univariate) and two-variable or three-or-more variable (bivariate or multivariate) distributions in determining which statistical procedures are to be used. How many variables are you analyzing in the distribution?

(2) Second, determine the level of measurement of the variables in the distribution and use statistical procedures compatible with that level of measurement.

(3) For two-variable (bivariate) and three-or-more-variable (multivariate) distributions, the researcher must decide whether or not there is a distinction between dependent and independent variables and select procedures designed for measuring either symmetric or asymmetric relationships.

(4) With population data in the two-or-more-variable situations, measures of association will be the primary concern; with data from a random sample, both a measure of association and a test of significance are important for decisions about the existence and degree of relationship and about the representativeness of data.

(5) The researcher should become familiar with any unusual properties or characteristics of a given measure that may distort its value as an index. Such distortions can arise because of concentration of values or dispersion of values, number of units in the categories of a distribution, the definition of perfect association, lack of standardization of the index, ties in rank-ordered data, or lack of clarity in interpretation.

(6) The reader should become familiar with the assumptions behind the measure under consideration and, within the constraints of principles (1) through (5), should select the one that violates the fewest possible assumptions. Violations of assumptions should be specifically noted in the analysis.

Although these six principles must be kept in mind in selecting statistical procedures for your distribution(s), they provide only the first step in making decisions about your variables and the relationships between variables. Intensive study of the selected measure(s) cannot be avoided. Each chapter will suggest sources relevant for each measure.

In Chapters 2 through 5, these principles will be applied to three types of data sets: univariate, bivariate, and multivariate problems with various levels of measurement. Statistical indices will be discussed, and the principles outlined above will be used to suggest how the student or practitioner might go about determining what procedures are appropriate for different sets of data. Chapters 6 to 9 provide an explanation and illustrations of how these various measures are calculated and how data are organized for analysis and computation.

Chapter 2

THE UNIVARIATE DISTRIBUTION

ORGANIZING DATA:
ARRAYS AND FREQUENCY DISTRIBUTIONS

Whether one has a sample or a population, descriptive statistics enables us to compare distributions, discern trends, or describe in a more or less definitive way the distributions obtained. When only one variable is being considered (univariate analysis), the most prominent descriptive statistics in use are percentages, proportions, ratios, measures of central tendency, and measures of dispersion (see Chapter 6 for examples of calculating percentages and ratios). All of these measures and indices can be used not only to describe single variable distributions but also to compare distributions from year to year or from group to group. Occasionally, with a sample, one may also wish to test the known distribution of a variable obtained from a sample against a hypothetical (or "expected") distribution. The Chi Square Test of Goodness of Fit is one procedure designed for this purpose.

We have already discussed in the introductory chapter the use of proportions, percentages, and ratios. Let us take a set of raw data and see what we can do to make sense of it, using various indices and organizing the data in different ways.

If someone should ask about the ages of students admitted to your professional school or department, you realize that there is no simple answer that will capture the variability of age unless you have an

Table 2.1

Age of Students Admitted to the University of Melbourne Social Work
Program in 1984 (*N* = 102)

23	26	21	22	21	25	34	34	21	45	25	21	26	23	34	23
26	33	20	42	20	20	25	27	26	34	22	27	27	24	47	23
29	21	25	21	22	21	36	26	22	21	21	21	22	32	22	45
19	32	20	34	27	22	22	44	21	21	43	37	22	22	52	26
33	31	43	39	23	23	38	31	46	20	20	39	21	34	40	25
37	22	21	27	29	22	37	38	31	22	23	21	22	31	24	33
22	40	19	21	33	24										

NOTES: Number of variables: One (age)
Level of measurement: Interval
Sample or population: Population
Statistical procedure: Distribution of raw data

extremely homogeneous age group. You could give any questioners the
raw data and let them see the distribution for themselves; but that is not
very satisfactory as the set of data in Table 2.1 will illustrate.

One can examine the raw data carefully, but they do not make much
sense until arranged or organized systematically or until indices are
derived which summarize the data. There are a number of ways we can
discuss distribution of age, none of which is completely satisfactory
because any index one uses will lose some of the attributes of the
distribution. We could talk about range, a crude measure of dispersion.
The oldest student is 52, the youngest is 19, a span of 33 years. But that
is not too helpful.

Table 2.2 organizes the data in a frequency distribution by age,
listing all of the ages and indicating the number of students that fall in
each age group. This is called an array; values are arranged from lowest
to highest in the distribution. Now we can begin to see some characteristics that might be important to note. There are more 21 and 22-year-
old students than any other age categories; not many younger than that
but quite a few older who are spread discontinuously through the late
twenties, the thirties, and the forties; and only one that is over 50.

Perhaps if we put the students in age groups it would help us visualize
the distribution more clearly (see Table 2.3). With this grouped frequency distribution there are a number of ways we can characterize the
population by age. We can note that nearly 66% (or two-thirds) are
under 30, nearly 24% are in their thirties, and only about 11% are 40
and over. We can describe the distribution in terms of central tendency,
clustering, concentration, or dispersion. Thus we can say that the pop-

Table 2.2

Frequency Distribution by Age of Students Admitted to the University of
Melbourne Social Work Program in 1984

Age	Fre-quency	Age	Fre-quency	Age	Fre-quency	Age	Fre-quency	Age	Fre-quency
19	2	20	6	30	0	40	2	50	0
		21	16	31	4	41	0	51	0
		22	15	32	3	42	1	52	1
		23	7	33	4	43	2		
		24	2	34	6	44	1		
		25	5	35	0	45	2		
		26	6	36	1	46	1		
		27	5	37	3	47	1		
		28	0	38	2	48	0		
		29	2	39	1	49	0		

Mean (μ) = 27.87   Median (Md.) = 25   Mode = 21

NOTES: The symbol for mean of a population is the Greek letter μ (mu).
Number of variables: One (age)
Level of measurement: Interval
Sample or oopulation: Population
Statistical procedure: An array; frequency distribution

Table 2.3

Number and Percentage of Students Admitted to the University of Melbourne
Social Work Program in 1984, by Age Group

Age Groups	Number	Percentage (rounded)	
19	2	2.0	
20–24	47	46.1	65.7
25–29	18	17.6	
30–34	16	15.7	
35–39	8	7.8	23.5
40–44	6	5.9	
45–49	4	3.9	10.8
50–54	1	1.0	
Total	102	100.0	

NOTES: Number of variables: One (age)
Level of measurement: Ordinal (all units are not equal)
Sample or population: Population
Statistical procedure: Grouped frequency distribution

ulation is clustered tightly around the twenties and early thirties. It would also be accurate to say that the modal age is 20 to 24. The mode is one index of central tendency. There are two other indices of central tendency we could use with this distribution: the median and the mean. The most common is the arithmetic mean, usually referred to simply as the mean or the average.

MEASURES OF CENTRAL TENDENCY: MEAN, MEDIAN, AND MODE

Mean and Mode

The mean age of this distribution is 27.87. Thus if we add all of the ages together and divide that sum by 102 (the total number in the distribution), we obtain a mean age of nearly 28. The mean takes into consideration all of the values in the distribution and uses more attributes of the data than does the mode. Note that the mode is determined only by the most frequent occurrence in a given category. The modal figure given above was in terms of an age range. The actual mode (most frequent age) is 21 (see Table 2.2).

Median

There is another common index of central tendency that makes use of the halfway point in the distribution (or the 50th percentile), the median. After putting the ages in some kind of an array (Table 2.2), we can determine the median easily. We simply count from either end of the distribution until we come to the 51st case. The midpoint falls between the 51st and the 52nd cases. These cases clearly fall in the 25-year-old-age category. Therefore the midpoint or median of the distribution is age 25.

Discussion of Mean, Median, and Mode

Now we have three indices of *central tendency*, all different; the mode is 21, the median is 25 and the mean is 28. Which are we to use? Which index best typifies the distribution of ages in this population? Each index has distinct properties. The mean takes into consideration all of the ages; the median uses only the position of one age (i.e., the midpoint of the distribution when ages are ranked from lowest to highest); and the mode is the most frequently occurring value.

Table 2.4

Age of a 10% Sample of Students Admitted to the University of Melbourne
Social Work Program in 1984, Illustrating Types of Distributions
(purposive sample)

Ages	Array	Frequency Distribution		Cumulative Frequency Distribution	
		Age	f	Age	f
23	20				
26	21	20	1	20	1
25	22	21	1	21	2
22	22	22	3	22	5
22	22	23	1	23	6
52	23[1]	25	1	25	7
21	25	26	1	26	8
31	26	31	2	31	10
20	31	52	1	52	11
22	31				
31	52				

$$\overline{X} = 26.82 \qquad N = 11$$
Med. = 23
Mode = 22

NOTES: The symbol for the mean of a sample is $\overline{X}$, (X-bar).
Number of variables: One (age)
Level of measurement: Interval
Sample or population: Purposive sample
Statistical procedures: Array, frequency distribution, and cumulative frequency distribution
[1]There are five individuals above this age and five below; this is the midpoint in the distribution.

Suppose we remove the 52-year-old student from the distribution.
How would the *central tendency* indices of the distribution be changed?
The mode and median would remain the same, but the mean would
change to 27.63. This is not much of a change, but it illustrates the effect
of extreme values in a distribution on the mean. This can be seen much
better if we use fewer cases. Table 2.4 lists a 10% purposive sample of
the distribution in Table 2.1. That is to say, we have deliberately
selected specific cases to include the variation and distribution required
to illustrate some of the attributes of measurements of central tendency.

If we delete the most extreme unit from the sample, the 52-year-old
student, the mean changes to 24.30, an increment of 2.5 years, illustrating the effect on the index of an extreme value in the distribution. If we
had removed one of the students in the center of the distribution, it
would have little effect on the mean. For instance, removing one of the

Table 2.5

Age of a 10% Sample of Students Admitted to the University of Melbourne
Social Work Program in 1984, Illustrating Types of Distributions
(actual random sample)

Ages	Array	Frequency Distribution Age	f	Cumulative Frequency Distribution Age	f
21	21				
42	22	21	1	21	1
22	22	22	4	21	5
22	22	31	1	31	6
22	22[1]	33	2	33	8
31	31[1]	42	1	42	9
46	33	46	1	46	10
33	33				
33	42				
22	46				

$$\overline{X} = 29.40 \qquad N = 10$$
$$\text{Med.} = 26.5$$
$$\text{Mode} = 22$$

NOTES: Number of variables: One (age)
Level of measurement: Interval
Sample or population: Random sample
Statistical procedure: Frequency distribution of raw data
[1]There is no actual midpoint in this distribution so the hypothetical midpoint becomes 26.5.

22-year-old students changes the mean very little, from 26.82 to 27.30, an increment of less than half a year.

The median in the sample distribution is 23. Note that this age divides the distribution in half. If we delete the 52-year-old student, the median becomes 22.5; if instead, we delete the 22-year-old student, the median becomes 23.5. When there is no value that precisely divides the distribution in two equal parts, the convention is to take a value halfway between the two values that includes the center of the distribution to represent the median.

The mode in this distribution does not change with the deletion of the older individual above, but with the deletion of one 22-year-old student, the distribution becomes bimodal (i.e., there are two ages that have equal frequencies, age 22 and age 31).

In Table 2.5 we have taken another sample, this time a 10% random sample of the data in Table 2.1; that is, we selected cases at random from the distribution. Note that the median in this distribution is 26.5. If one case is removed, let's say the 46-year-old student, the median now becomes 22; or if we remove one of the 22-year-old students, the median becomes 31. This illustrates the potential instability of the median arising from the fact that it defines the midpoint in relation to its position in the distribution. Thus the median changes by an increment of 4.5 years by the deletion of one case.

The mean, on the other hand, is changed very little in this distribution by the deletion of the oldest, from 29.40 to 27.56 (less than 2 years) or by the deletion of one of the 22-year-old students, from 29.40 to 30.22 (less than one year).

Thus one can see that there can be great instability in these indices under certain circumstances, but considerable stability in other circumstances. If the mean is not derived from a symmetrical distribution, it is strongly influenced by extreme values, whereas the median and the mode are not. The mean varies less from sample to sample and is generally a more stable index than the median, unless you have a skewed distribution. The mean also uses more information than either the median or the mode. In summary, the mean is a preferable index except when dealing with skewed distributions.

Researchers analyzing data on income, for instance, usually make use of the median because of the extreme effect on the mean of a small number of very high incomes. The median is particularly useful when distributions are skewed; the mean is distorted in such distributions.

In the samples above, the mode is not very useful; however, in Table 2.2 with a population of 102, it provides a useful index, although more so when age groups are used, as in Table 2.3. The mode is used primarily in describing nominal-level categories. This is illustrated in Table 1.1 (see Chapter 1), which presents categorical (nominal) data on source of referral to the probation department. In general, the mode is most useful when the dispersion is low or if there are only two or three categories in the variable. The reader will not find the mode very useful in Table 2.9. As we shall see later, used in conjunction with a measure of dispersion, the interpretation of the mode becomes more useful.

The three measures of central tendency are related to the three levels of measurement. The mode is associated with nominal-level categories, the median with ordinal-level data, and the mean with interval-level data. One can only compute a mean with interval data, but one can also determine the median and mode with interval data. However, one cannot compute a mean from nominal data or ordinal distributions. (For

Table 2.6

Number and Percentage of Youngsters Referred to the Probation Department
by Type of Offense, by Gender

Type of Offense	Males		Gender Females		Total	
	No.	%	No.	%	No.	%
Violent	505	7.9	97	3.9	602	6.8
Property	2,272	35.5	437	17.7	2,709	30.5
Drugs	1,382	21.6	415	16.8	1,797	20.3
Status	1,984	31.0	1,405	56.9	3,389	38.2
Other	256	4.0	116	4.7	372	4.2
Total	6,399	100.0	2,470	100.0	8,869	100.0

SOURCE: Derived from Pope & Feyerherm (1982).
NOTES: Number of variables: Two (gender and type of offense)
Level of measurement: Nominal and nominal dichotomous
Sample or population: Sample
Statistical procedure: Cross-tabulation with percentages

examples of determining the median in a distribution and of calculating means and medians with grouped data, see Chapter 6.) Let us now examine some additional data from the Pope-Feyerherm (1982) study to illustrate this fact, but for comparative purposes at this time (see Table 2.6).

Of the three measures of central tendency, only the mode can be used to describe this distribution. We can say that the modal type of offenses for males are property offenses while the modal type of offenses for females are status offenses. Neither a mean nor a median can be computed or determined for type of offense. The mode is useful in comparing the two groups, but the percentages allow us a more definitive view of the categories with a proportional perspective. We can examine the total column to determine that nearly two-fifths (38.2%) of the offenses were status offenses, and then we can examine the same category for males and females to determine how they differ from this proportion. We find that females are overrepresented in this category, compared with males.

Use of Percentages

Sometimes percentages are used directly for comparative purposes, as in Table 2.7. In this instance Sampson (1987) has reduced the raw data to percentages to make a more concise table, demonstrating the

Table 2.7

Participation of Teachers in In-Service Activities

Type of Activity[1]	Percentage of Those Doing any In-Service Activity		Level of Significance
	Females	Males	
Administration	17.8	33.1	.001
Pastoral care	35.5	30.5	.01
Computers	22.1	30.7	.01
Curriculum	79.3	74.4	ns[2]
Other (TUTA)	0.46	0.26	ns[2]
Total no. persons	1,073	744	
Total as percentage of all respondents who had undertaken in-service training in last 5 years	73.8	80.1	

SOURCE: Adapted from Sampson (1987, table 1, p. 33).
NOTES: Number of variables: Two (gender and type of activity)
Level of measurement: Percentages applied to interval data on in-service activity; type of activity — nominal
Sample or population: Sample
Statistical procedures: Cross-tabulation and percentages
[1] 1,817 respondents had undertaken two days or more of in-service training in the last five years; however many had been involved in more than one type of activity.
[2] ns = not significant at .05 level.

difference between male and female teachers in various types of in-service training. She has also determined the probability and found three of the in-service training variables to be significant. We will discuss probability and significance in more detail in later chapters.

MEASURES OF DISPERSION

In addition to examining the central tendencies of distributions, it is also helpful to look at how categories or values are dispersed within the distribution. Again, the dispersion of values is especially helpful when one is comparing distributions from year to year or from group to group.

Variation Ratio

We can use a measure of dispersion to determine how typical the mode is in a distribution. Keep in mind that the mode simply tells you the most frequent category without any indication of how typical it might be. In some distributions there are two modes, and we speak of a bimodal distribution. The variation ratio (V) provides a useful adjunct to the mode and is an index of the amount of variation or the range of difference among the cases in a nominal distribution (Freeman, 1965, p. 40). In essence, the variation ratio is the proportion of nonmodal cases. The calculation is simple. In Table 2.6 we might want to determine how typical the modal category of property offenses is for males and how typical the modal category of status offenses is for females in this distribution.

In each case we add the nonmodal categories and divide them by the total:

Males V   = [(505 + 1382 + 1984 + 256)/6399] × 100 = 64.5%
Females V = [(97 + 437 + 415 + 116)/2470] × 100 = 43.1%

The smaller the V, the more typical is the mode, and therefore, the more satisfactory as an index for categories in the distribution. In the distribution in Table 2.6, the mode is a better indicator of type of offense for females than it is for males. The variation ratio is useful primarily in conjunction with the mode, and the two measures can provide a useful comparison for two groups when both groups are classified in the same categories. It is of little use when the distribution is bimodal.

Index of Qualitative Variation

Leonard (1976, pp. 85–91) provides a discussion of an index of qualitative variation (IQV) and an index of dispersion (D), both indices for nominal level data. The IQV index is the ratio of total observed differences in the nominal categories to the maximum possible differences (multiplied by 100 to put it on a standard scale), and D is a ratio of the variation that does exist between categories to the maximum variation that could exist.

We can examine the heterogeneity of the data in Table 2.8 using the index of qualitative variation. The computation for this procedure is contained in Chapter 6. We compare the observed differences in the fathers' political affiliation with the maximum possible differences that could occur (an even split between Labor and the Liberal/National Coalition) and obtain a ratio of .93. This is interpreted as a percentage (i.e., 93% of the possible variation that could exist, does exist). For the

Table 2.8

Political Party Affiliation of Fathers and Political Party Affiliation of
Students Entering the La Trobe University School of Social Work Program in
1979 (with two major political groupings only)

| Political Affiliation of Students | Political Affiliation of Fathers | | |
| | Liberal/National | | |
	Labor Party	Coalition Party	Total
Labor Party	16	6	22
Liberal/National Coalition	1	4	5
Total	17	10	27

SOURCE: Data obtained by Pilcher (1982).
NOTES: Number of variables: Two (father's PA, student's PA)
Level of measurement: Nominal dichotomous
Sample or population: Population
Statistical procedure: Cross-tabulation

offspring, the heterogeneity is not so great. Sixty percent of the possible
variation among the students that could exist, does exist. In other words,
the students are more homogeneous than their fathers in regard to
political affiliation.

Index of Dispersion

The Index of Dispersion is essentially the same type of measure as
the index of qualitative variation. The computation is less complicated,
but either measure yields the same index. See Chapter 6 for the calculation and an illustration of its use.

Interquartile Range

An index of variation for ordinal data (interquartile range) is provided by most standard statistical texts, but it is not usually discussed
as such. Leonard's text is an exception (1976, pp. 91–94). The interquartile range (Q) is derived from the family of fractiles, one of which
is the median (also the 50th percentile). The fractiles that most people
are familiar with are the percentile and the median. The use of percentiles requires that data are assigned values on a scale of 100. The
distribution can then be divided into percentiles (hundredths), deciles
(tenths), quintiles (fifths), or quartiles (fourths). The interquartile range
is the distance between the first quartile and the third quartile and covers
the middle 50% of the cases.

Table 2.9

Total Money Income of Families, by Race, United States, 1980

| | *White Families* | | *Black Families* | |
| | *(Numbers in Thousands)* | | | |
Total Money Income	*Frequency*	*Cumulative Frequency*	*Frequency*	*Cumulative Frequency*
Under $ 2,500	864	864	337	337
$ 2,500–$ 4,999	1,719	2,583	713	1,050
5,000– 7,499	2,814	5,397	845	1,895
7,500– 9,999	3,150	8,547	656	2,551
10,000– 12,499	3,725	12,272	574	3,125
12,500– 14,999	3,589	15,861	485	3,610
15,000– 17,499	3,840	19,701	434	4,044
17,500– 19,999	3,606	23,307	374	4,418
20,000– 22,499	4,003	27,310	373	4.791
22,500– 24,999	3,456	30,766	272	5,063
25,000– 27,499	3,519	34,285	240	5,303
27,500– 29,999	2,701	36,986	181	5,484
30,000– 32,499	2,776	39,762	195	5,679
32,500– 34,999	1,984	41,746	129	5,808
35,000– 37,499	1,949	43,695	123	5,931
37,500– 39,999	1,367	45,062	90	6,021
40,000– 44,999	2,332	47,394	118	6,139
45,000– 49,999	1,501	48,895	69	6,208
50,000– 59,999	1,843	50,738	72	6,280
60,000– 74,999	1,065	51,803	24	6,304
75,000 and over	908	52,711	13	6,317
Total	52,711		6,317	
Median	21,903		12,673	

SOURCE: From U.S. Bureau of the Census (1981)
NOTES: Number of variables: Two (race, money income)
Level of measurement: Families — nominal dichotomous; income — ordinal
Sample or population: Population
Statistical procedure: Distribution of raw data

   The Q index is sometimes used as a measure of inequality in income distribution data. Table 2.9 provides data on income distribution in the United States for 1980. If we compute the interquartile range for White and Black families, we find that the interquartile range for White families is $19,162 and the Q for Black families is $15,577. There is less variation in the incomes of Blacks than the incomes of Whites, accounted for in part by the fact that the incomes of Blacks cluster around the lower income ranges but they also cluster more tightly. The computation of this measure is demonstrated in Chapter 6.

The Standard Deviation, Average Deviation, and Variance

The simplest measure of dispersion for interval data is one we have already used, namely the range; but we also found that it was not very useful. The most common measure of dispersion for interval data is the standard deviation. It is an index of the spread or heterogeneity of the distribution. There are two other measures of variability that are of interest for interval levels of measurement: the average deviation and the variance. The average deviation is of interest primarily because it helps us see how the other two interval-level measures of dispersion are computed. Variance is of interest because it is the intermediary step to computing the standard deviation but it is also used in the computation of other statistical measures.

These three measures are computed as deviations from the mean of the distribution. The sample data from Table 2.5 are appropriate to demonstrate this computation (see Table 2.10 for computations).

The average deviation is seldom used primarily because the standard deviation is much more versatile and is used in other statistical procedures and mathematical conceptions, such as the normal curve. The variance does not have the intuitive interpretation of the other two measures. One can imagine an average deviation of 7.6 years or a standard deviation of 8.7 years as an index of dispersion, but a variance of 75.4 years in this distribution has no intuitive interpretation. However, the variance is an important statistical concept and forms one of the ingredients in a number of statistical formulas.

As you can see, the standard deviation is derived by computing the variation of each value from the mean, squaring that variation (the sum is the variance), and extracting the square root of that sum. In Table 2.11 we can compare the dispersion (spread, scatter, variability) of ages by gender.

The ages of males are more diverse than the ages of females, 8.3 years compared with 7.8 years. The mean tells us that the males tend to be slightly older, and the standard deviation tells us there is greater variability in their ages as well.

The mean and standard deviation are often used together in the analysis of data because it is important to have a measure of central tendency and a measure of dispersion to get a sense of the distribution.

Table 2.10

Age of a 10% Sample of Students Admitted to the University of Melbourne Social Work Program in 1984, Illustrating the Computation of the Average Deviation, the Variance and the Standard Deviation.

Ages	Deviation from the Mean[1]	Deviation from the Mean Squared	Computations
21	−8	64	To obtain the average
22	−7	49	deviation, we sum the
22	−7	49	deviations from the
22	−7	49	mean and divide by N.
22	−7	49	
31	2	4	76 ÷ 10 = 7.6
33	4	16	
33	4	16	To obtain the variance,
42	13	169	we square the devia-
46	<u>17</u>	<u>289</u>	tions and divide by N.
	76	754	754 ÷ 10 = 75.4

Average Deviation (AD) = 7.6 years
Variance (s^2) = 75.4 years
Standard Deviation (s) = 8.68 years
If these were population data, we would use σ^2 and σ for the variance and the standard deviation.

To obtain the standard deviation, we extract the square of the variance.

$$\sqrt{75.4} = 8.68$$

NOTES: Number of variables: One (age)
Level of measurement: Interval
Sample or population: Sample
Statistical procedures: Average deviation, standard deviation, and variance
[1]The mean is 29 (actually 29.4 but we have rounded it to make it simpler). Note that we have disregarded the sign in summing the deviations. If we did not disregard the signs, we would get a sum of zero. In calculating the average deviation we are concerned with absolute deviations.

In a study of teacher stress in schools, Feitler and Tokar (1986) compared perceived occupational stress at various school levels, using the mean and standard deviation (see Table 2.12). One could note from these data that the level of teacher stress is greater in high school than it is in middle or elementary schools, although the diversity in stress scores was similar for the middle and high school levels.

Table 2.11

Age and Gender of Students Admitted to the Melbourne University Social
Work Program in 1984, by Age Group

	Gender		
Age Groups	*Females*	*Males*	*Total*
19	2	0	2
20–24	39	8	47
25–29	16	2	18
30–34	12	4	16
35–39	6	2	8
40–44	3	3	6
45–49	4	0	4
50–54	1	0	1
Total	83	19	102
$\mu =$	27.42	29.84	27.87
$\sigma =$	7.82	8.26	7.92
range =	33	23	33

NOTES: The symbol for standard deviation of a population is the small Greek sigma (σ).
Number of variables: Two (gender and age)
Level of measurement: Gender: nominal dichotomous; age — ordinal (unequal units)
Sample or population: Population
Statistical procedures: Cross-tabulation, mean, standard deviation, and range

Table 2.12

Means and Standard Deviations of Perceived Occupational Stress of Teachers
by School Level, Showing Sample Size

	Perceived Occupational Stress of Teachers		
School Level	*Mean*	*Standard Deviation*	*Sample Size*
Elementary	2.90	.750	69
Middle	2.88	.891	33
High	3.08	.893	75

Adapted from Feitler & Tokar (1986, table 1, p. 262).
Number of variables: Two (occupational stress and school level)
Level of measurement: Occupational stress — interval; school level — nominal
Sample or population: Sample
Statistical procedures: Means and standard deviations

TESTS OF SIGNIFICANCE FOR ONE VARIABLE

Generalizations

In developing knowledge, it is inevitable that we generalize about relationships between variables or about the characteristics of a particular population. Thus we generalize that males are more likely than females to be involved in automobile theft, that nurses in psychiatric nursing situations experience "burnout" to a greater degree than do nurses in administrative situations, or that students electing to major in education are less scholastically endowed than those electing to major in the humanities or sciences.

There may or may not be adequate or sufficient observations to warrant such generalizations. Frequently it is not possible to obtain data on all episodes of interest (e.g., thefts, nursing situations, or the scholastic ability of tertiary-level students). In such instances, it is necessary to generalize from the available data. Clearly there are dangers in doing so, particularly when the generalization is used as a basis for developing policy or as a basis for allocating resources. How good are the generalizations we make from the limited data we have? What inferences can we make about a phenomenon that is based on the data obtained, and how much confidence can we have in making generalizations? These are the types of questions that may be answered by inferential statistics.

Inferential Statistics and Probability Sampling

Inferential statistics depend on probability sampling; that is, a sample drawn randomly from a population of units in which each unit has an equal chance of being selected. The reader unfamiliar with probability and nonprobability sampling should consult a research methodology text because it is essential that the researcher understand the necessity for probability sampling in making inferences from sample to the population. (For an example see Seaberg's chapter in Grinnell [1985].)

In a nonprobability sample, there is no way of knowing how representative the sample might be. In other words, one can have little confidence in generalizing from the sample to the larger population. With a probability sample, the representativeness of the data can be estimated with a known level of confidence (i.e., the level of significance of the data from the sample can be determined). Testing the significance of a single distribution requires the researcher to set up a hypothetical distribution, on the basis of known or logical estimation about the distribution. The significance level can then be tested between the actual (observed) distribution and the hypothetical distribution.

Tests of Significance

Our confidence in a generalization that is based on a sample can be confirmed or refuted by a test of significance. This test, computed on a sample to make inferences about the larger population from which it was drawn, can help us make a decision about the veracity of a generalization. An example may help the reader understand how and why this procedure is used.

About one-third of the students completing social and behavioral science degrees in Australia are males. Because most of the students admitted to social work programs are from the social and behavioral sciences, this information enables us to set up a hypothetical distribution (i.e., one would expect about one-third of the admissions into social work to be males). In 1984 only one-fifth of the students admitted to the University of Melbourne Social Work Program were males (Table 2.11). This is certainly a different result from that expected from our knowledge of the proportion of social and behavioral science students in tertiary education, but is the difference statistically significant?

Suppose we draw a 15% random sample from our 1984 admissions and examine the proportion of males admitted. The sample is drawn deliberately to demonstrate the use of a test of significance with data on one variable (see Table 2.13). Because we have the data on the population, it would not be necessary to draw a sample; we can make a generalization with confidence, at least for this particular population. Because we have the total population, we can also compare characteristics of our sample with the actual population.

What we find is that of the 15 in the sample, three are males. Incidentally that is almost exactly the proportion in the population of the 102 admissions (in this case we obtained a representative sample by gender). But only one-fifth of the students in the sample are males; we expected about one-third. Perhaps that is due only to chance. If it is a chance occurrence, we do not need to wonder too much about why this occurs. If it is not just a chance occurrence, we might want to question why fewer males are coming into the program than is expected. In other words, why would this be? Is this a trend or just a chance occurrence? Is it because females have better academic records and, therefore, are more likely to be admitted? Is there a gender bias by the selection

Table 2.13

Number of Students in a 15% Random Sample of Those Admitted to the
University of Melbourne Social Work Program in 1984, by Gender, Showing
Observed and Expected Frequencies.

	Observed	Expected
Males	3	5
Females	12	10
Total	15	15

$\chi^2 = 1.20$
$p. = .27$

NOTES: We determine probability ($p.$) by examining a Chi square probability table. In this case we had to interpolate because the table does not provide all the points on the probability curve. The table indicated that a χ^2 of 1.07 would have yielded a $p.$ of .30; a χ^2 of 1.64 would have yielded a $p.$ of .20.
Number of variables: One (gender)
Level of measurement: Nominal dichotomous
Sample or population: Sample
Statistical procedure: Test of significance

committee? Is social work more attractive to females than to males? Do males have more attractive career opportunities than females? It is for these reasons that we want to see whether or not this difference is due to chance alone, and we use the Chi Square Test of Goodness of Fit to make this determination.

Chi Square Test of Goodness of Fit (Nominal-Level Data)

The Chi Square Test of Goodness of Fit is an appropriate test to help us with this decision. When we compute the Chi Square Test of Goodness of Fit and consult the probability table, we find that the difference in our distribution in relation to our hypothetical distribution is not significant. The possibility of obtaining this distribution by chance is about 27 out of 100, not very good odds that something besides chance is operating. If we had obtained a probability of .05 (5 out of 100) or .01 (1 out of 100), we would have said that something besides chance is probably operating.

There are other measures that can be used in univariate analysis to test the probability of chance or, to put it another way, to test the significance of a distribution. As in the case of indices of central tendency and dispersion, tests of significance are often appropriate for specific levels of measurement. A goodness of fit test of significance for ordinal data is also available — the Kolmogorov-Smirnov Test.

Kolmogorov-Smirnov Test of Goodness of Fit (Ordinal-Level Data)

Sheila Collins (1984) examined the support of fathers of top-level female administrators, comparing social workers, nurses and teachers. We will examine these data in a later chapter, but we will look at the distribution of support for female social work administrators to help us decide whether or not to consider the various levels significant using the Kolmogorov-Smirnov Test (KS). We are making the assumption that our data are from a random sample (Table 2.14).

Let us assume that we know that in other professions fathers are generally classified in the three levels of support (low, moderate, and high) about equally. Our assumption is that one-third of the cases would fall into each of the categories if the fathers of social workers are like fathers of other professional women (in regard to career support). Thus we are testing our actual observations against a hypothetical distribution assuming that, out of 29 social workers, approximately 9 or 10 will be supported by their fathers in each of the three levels (statistically 9.66 in each category). The test helps us make a decision about the significance of the actual data. By virtue of the actual distributions, we know that social workers' fathers are clearly different in this respect from the fathers of other professional women (at least for fathers of nurses and educators). Is this difference significant or is it just a chance occurrence?

When we calculate the KS test for this distribution and consult a probability table we find that the difference between the hypothetical expectation and the actual data is not significant. We conclude that the difference between social workers' fathers and fathers of other professionals may be due to chance. Perhaps if we had a larger sample we could make a more definitive test. The KS test can be used with a small number of cases in instances where a random sample has been drawn from a population and the level of measurement is ordinal. (See Chapter 6 for the calculation of the KS test.)

The t Test and the z Test

The t Test and the z Test are well-known tests of significance that can be used in univariate situations. They are frequently used with two-variable or bivariate distributions and are discussed in the next chapter.

Table 2.14

Father's Support for Top-Level Female Administrators

Occupation	Low	Father's Support Level Moderate	High	Total
Social workers	7	9	13	29

Kolmogorov-Smirnov Test: $D = .12$, $p. = <.20$ (does not reach .20).

SOURCE: Taken from Collins (1984).
NOTES: Number of variables: One (father's level of support)
Level of measurement: Ordinal
Sample or population: Sample
Statistical procedures: Frequency distribution and test of significance

They are essentially the same type of index, with the z Test used for large samples and the t Test used for small samples. In spite of the distinction between "large" and "small" in many statistical books, this statement is not too helpful because the estimates of the distinction between large and small samples runs from 30 to 100 in various texts.

GRAPHIC PRESENTATIONS

Often in statistical analysis it is appropriate and helpful to provide a visual picture of the distribution. Frequency polygons and histograms are particularly useful in presenting such data, and when comparing two populations or samples on the same variable, they often demonstrate the differences or similarities much better than does a frequency distribution. For instance, if we take the data from Table 2.3, and add another group of students admitted in 1985, we can produce a useful comparison of these students by age groups for the two years 1984 and 1985.

In Figure 2.1 we can see that the two groups of students are not dissimilar in patterns of age. In both years the 19 to 24-year-old students predominate, but there is a difference in the proportion in their late twenties.

A histogram is also a useful visual aid for describing a frequency distribution. Figure 2.2 demonstrates this with the data we presented earlier on type of offenses committed by youngsters referred to the probation department.

The histogram shows clearly both the volume of each type of offense and the relative distribution from offense to offense and also the com-

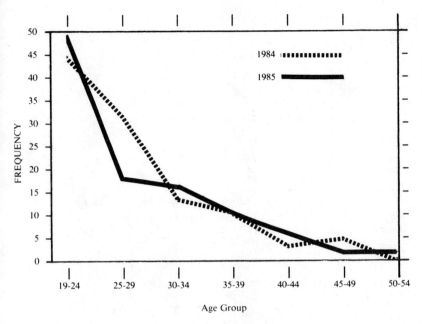

Figure 2.1

Number of students admitted to the Melbourne University Social Work
Programs in 1984 and 1985, by age group (random sample of population).

parative volume and relative distribution between males and females.
There are elaborate illustrations and discussions of graphic presentations in some of the standard statistical texts in the social and behavioral
sciences (e.g., Leonard, 1976; Loether & McTavish, 1980; Turney &
Robb, 1973).

SUMMARY

Most of the statistical procedures and indices in this chapter are
simple and straightforward. This should not detract from their use
because they are often the most appropriate statistics to use in describing distributions and comparing different sets of data.

Smith and Holland (1982, Table 10), for instance, use the mean, the
standard deviation and the range in their study of institutional resident
management practices. They provide the reader with indices that make

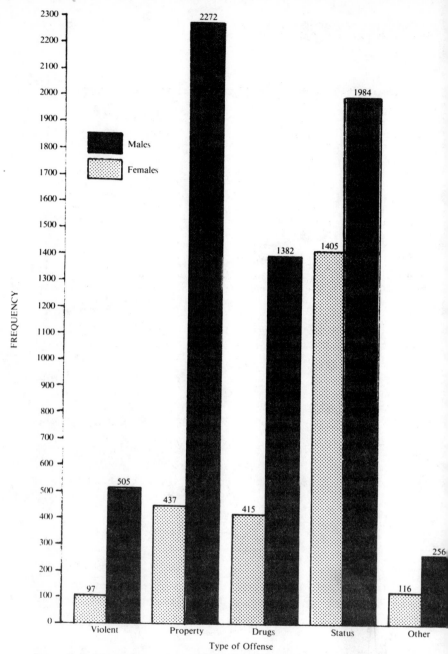

Source: Derived from data presented by Pope and Feyerherm in "Gender Bias in Juvenile Court Distributions," Journal of Social Service Research: 6, Nos. 1/2, 1982

Figure 2.2
Number of youngsters referred to the probation department by type of offense and gender (Pope & Feyerherm, 1982).

Table 2.15

Distribution of Scores on Resident Management Practices Scale[1]

Institution	No. Wards	Mean	Standard Deviation	Range
I	8	42.75	8.75	28–55
II	7	39.57	7.32	31–53
III	7	25.71	5.25	19–36
Total	22	36.32	10.27	19–55

SOURCE: Smith & Holland (1982).
NOTES: Number of variables: Two (scores on RMP and type institution)
Level of measurement: Institution – nominal; number of wards – interval
Sample or population: Population
Statistical procedures: Cross-tabulation, mean, standard deviation, and range
[1]High score indicates highly institutionally-oriented practices as opposed to individually-oriented practices.

it possible to discuss the scores obtained on management practices in terms of central tendency and dispersion (see Table 2.15). The range of scores in institution III was truncated compared with the other two (19 to 36, compared with 28 to 55 and 31 to 53), and this homogeneity was reflected in the lower standard deviation and the lower mean score.

In her study of sexual differences in job satisfaction with social work administrators, Haynes (1983) used ratios as an index of these differences, relating gender to pay levels of the administrators. In general the data show (Table 2.16) that in the two higher pay levels, the males outnumber females 2½ to 1 and 3 to 1.

Table 2.16

Number and Ratios of Male and Female Social Work Administrators, by Pay Levels

Pay Level	Total	Males	Females	Ratio(Male:Female)
16	202	128	74	1.73:1
17	318	194	124	1.56:1
18	125	89	36	2.47:1
19	133	101	32	3.15:1
Total	788	512	266	

SOURCE: Haynes (1983).
NOTES: Number of variables: Two (gender and pay level)
Level of measurement: Gender – nominal dichotomous; pay level – interval (categories are equal)
Sample or population: Population
Statistical procedures: Cross-tabulation and use of ratios

Table 2.17

Distribution Indices, Measures of Central Tendency and Dispersion, and
Tests of Significance for Univariate Distributions

Statistical Technique	Level of Measurement		
	Nominal	Ordinal	Interval
Categorical descriptions	Proportions Percentages Ratios	Proportions Percentages	Percentages
Measures of central tendency	Mode	Mode Median	Mode Median Mean
Measures of dispersion	Index of Qualitative Variation[1] Index of Dispersion[2] Variation ratio[3]	Interquartile range	Range Average deviation Variance Standard deviation Coefficient of variability
Tests of significance	Chi Square Test of Goodness of Fit[5]	Kolmogorov-Smirnov Test	z Test[4] t Test[6]

[1]Mueller, Schuessler & Costner, 1970; Leonard, 1976.
[2]Leonard, 1976; Loethar & McTavish, 1980; Hammond & Householder, 1962.
[3]Freeman, 1965, p. 40ff.
[4]For large samples.
[5]For random samples; not for population data.
[6]For small samples.

Note that Haynes used ratios with a nominal-level variable — gender; she could also have used percentages, but the ratios provide a simple index that can be grasped immediately. Smith and Holland (1982) used interval data and were able to use the mean and standard deviations as indices of central tendency and dispersion. By now, the reader is familiar with the notion that the level of measurement sets limits on what statistical procedures can be used.

Table 2.17 summarizes the common procedures and indices for univariate distributions for each level of measurement. The reader must be cautioned that using this chart without further study or reference to a thorough discussion that explains the derivation and rationale for the technique and the advantages and disadvantages and assumptions behind the indices is foolish at best and could lead to claims about the data that are erroneous and misleading. Where there are several alternative measures, it is obvious that additional information and knowledge are needed. All the chart can do is to point you in a particular direction with the expectation that fine tuning will be necessary if all of the advantages of the measures and techniques are to be taken. For instance the mode, median, or mean can be used with interval data as a measure of central tendency. The shape of the distribution is crucial in determining which index to use; for example, the instability of the mode can result in major fluctuations from one distribution to another, the sensitivity of the mean to extreme values makes it less useful in skewed distributions than the median, and the median is unstable when there are large gaps between values in the distribution.

Chapter 3

THE BIVARIATE DISTRIBUTION: NOMINAL DATA

MEASURES OF ASSOCIATION AND TESTS OF SIGNIFICANCE

Population or Sample

As noted in the introductory chapter, the researcher must be clear whether or not the subjects of a study are a population or a sample. If a population, descriptive statistics are of primary interest, although the researcher may want to determine the probability of obtaining the same results by chance. If a sample, both inferential and descriptive statistics will be of equal interest. With bivariate relationships, a sample will require the use of a measure of the strength of relationship and a test of significance.

Relationship Between Tests of Significance and Association

Although there is some relationship between the two indices (a test of significance and a measure of association), there is no direct correspondence between them. You can have a statistically significant relationship with a low level of association in the sample, and you can have a strong relationship in the sample that is not statistically significant. Statistical significance is closely related to the size of the sample. With a very small sample, a low level of significance is not unusual even when there is a strong relationship between two variables, and with a large sample it is not unusual to have a high level of significance even when the association is marginal in strength. This will be illustrated from time to time in the examples that follow.

THE IMPORTANCE OF NORMED OR STANDARDIZED INDICES

In selecting an index of the degree of association, a major consideration is whether or not the measure is standardized or normed. In other words we want to know if the measure yields an index on a common scale so that we can use it for different size tables. This is particularly important if we have several contingency tables with disparate numbers of categories, such as 2 × 2, 2 × 3, 3 × 3, 3 × 4, and so on. Some measures are standardized on a 2 × 2 table but not on larger tables; others are standardized on square tables only (where the number of rows equals the number of columns or r = c). Some of the more useful measures are standardized on all sizes of tables.

Usually, but not always, we expect an index of association to yield 1.00 (unity) if it is a perfect association, and that it will yield .00 if there is no association. If that is so, on a nominal scale, an association is perfect if all the cases in a 2 × 2 table fall in two diagonal cells. Ordinarily cases are distributed in all four cells such that the coefficient will have an index at some point between .00 and 1.00, depending on how closely two variables are related.

VARIABLE COMBINATIONS AND DICHOTOMOUS VARIABLES

In any given study, the researcher may be dealing with various levels of measurement. A given bivariate distribution may have any combination of levels of measurement. In this chapter we will be concerned only with nominal/nominal combinations. In some instances it is important to distinguish between nominal-level variables that are dichotomous (i.e., those that have two categories, such as gender) and those that have more than two categories. Therefore we will use the term *dichotomous* to indicate a specific type of nominal-level variable with only two categories. Ordinal categories can be dichotomous as well, but the usual 2 × 2 distribution has two dichotomous nominal variables.

WHEN BOTH VARIABLES ARE NOMINAL

In reviewing optional measures in this section, we will first discuss the measures of association that can be used with various sets of data and then discuss the tests of significance that can be used with each of the measures of association.

In the helping and educational professions, researchers almost invariably use nominal-level data in at least part of the analysis. Table 3.1 illustrates this in listing the characteristics of the subjects (nurses and physiotherapists) in a study of an educational program on attitudes toward death and dying.

Note the predominance of nominal-level variables. In this instance, age could be considered a nominal, ordinal, or even an interval variable (because the categories are equal in size and are dichotomous). Intensity of religious beliefs could be considered an ordinal variable (although it is a bit difficult to image what poor or fair intensity means in this context). All other variables are clearly nominal variables.

Delta Measures, PRE Measures, and the Uncertainty Coefficient

There are a number of statistical techniques for determining strength of association between two nominal variables. These include two families of measures widely discussed in the statistical literature, Delta and Proportionate Reduction of Error (PRE) measures. Another measure, the Uncertainty Coefficient (UC), will be discussed briefly.

Delta (the upper case Greek letter Δ) is the symbol for *difference* — difference between observed and expected frequencies in computing Chi square (see Table 7.4 Chapter 7). Expected frequencies are based on the null hypothesis that two variables are independent. We make use of the row and column totals to estimate the number of cases that would fall in each cell if the two variables were indeed independent. We will elaborate on expected and observed frequencies and the null hypothesis later in the chapter.

PRE measures are computed to determine the proportion of reduction in error in predicting where cases will fall in the categories of one variable when categories of the other variable are known.

Loether and McTavish (1980) and Leonard (1976) provide informative discussions of the PRE measures, and any basic statistics book will provide a discussion of Chi square computation and some of the measures of association derived from the Chi square computation, though

Table 3.1

Characteristics of Nursing and Physiotherapy Students in a Study of Attitudes Toward Death and Dying

Characteristics	Experimental Group (n = 33)		Control Group (n = 22)	
	No.	%	No.	%
Age				
20–25	32	97	20	90.9
26–30	1	3	2	9.1
Gender				
Female	33	100	21	95.4
Male			1	4.6
Marital Status				
Single	32	97	20	90.9
Married	1	3	2	9.1
Religion				
Catholic	11	33.3	9	40.9
Protestant	18	54.5	12	54.5
Other	4	12.2	1	4.6
Intensity of religious beliefs				
Poor	2	6.1	3	13.6
Fair	4	12.1	1	4.6
Average	20	60.6	11	50.0
Strong	7	21.2	7	31.8
Attended a funeral				
No	5	15.2	4	18.2
Yes	28	84.8	18	81.8
Death of an immediate family member				
No	10	33.3	7	31.8
Yes	23	69.7	15	68.2

SOURCE: Adapted from Caty & Tamlyn (1984, table 3, p. 51).
NOTES: Number of variables: Seven sets of two-variable distributions
Level of measurement: Nominal (some dichotomous), ordinal, and possibly interval
Directional or nondirectional: Nondirectional
Sample or population: Population
Statistical procedure: Cross-tabulations with number of cases and percentages

not all will refer to them as delta measures. Thus delta measures and PRE measures are two distinctly different types of association measures for contingency tables.

Uncertainty Coefficient

The SPSS programs (including SPSS-PC) include an additional measure for two nominal variables, called the Uncertainty Coefficient (UC). It is neither a delta measure nor a PRE measure but comes from information theory (Nie et al., 1975, pp. 226–277). It has the virtue of having both a symmetric and asymmetric version and in this respect differs from those discussed below: C, T, Φ, and V.

SYMMETRIC (NONDIRECTIONAL) RELATIONSHIPS

Given the limitations of other measures, the two most useful indices for symmetric analysis are Cramer's V and the uncertainty coefficient. Both are provided in the SPSS-PC package, although Φ is used instead of V in the analysis of 2 × 2 tables. Phi and V yield identical results with 2 × 2 contingency tables.

Delta Measures: Φ, T, V, C, and C~

Two measures frequently encountered in social and behavioral research and literature are Pearson's contingency coefficient (C) and Cramer's V. These two measures are derived from Chi square (χ^2) and consequently are called delta measures. C and V are used when no distinction is made between independent and dependent variables (i.e., with symmetric relationships). C has two limitations which will be mentioned below. There are two other delta measures for the symmetric situation with two nominal variables, and each of these has limitations too: Φ and Tschuprow's T.

The Φ coefficient has both a delta version and a PRE version and is a measure of the concentration of cases in the diagonal cells. The Φ coefficient is limited to but appropriate for 2 × 2 tables. Tschuprow's T is standardized on tables with equal numbers of rows and columns (r = c), and on square tables it is identical to Cramer's V. Because other measures are more versatile, T is primarily of historical interest. The Φ coefficient, Cramer's V, Tschuprow's T, and the contingency coefficient

Table 3.2

Number of Offenders Detained by the Court, by Gender

Detention	Gender			
	Females	Males	Total	
Yes	1,040	2,444	3,484	
No	763	2,238	3,001	
Total	1,803	4,682	6,485	

$\chi^2 = 15.73$ C = .05   V = .05 Φ = .05   T = .05
$p.$ = .001

SOURCE: Pope & Feyerherm (1982).
NOTES: Number of variables: Two
Level of measurement: Nominal dichotomous/nominal
Directional/nondirectional: Nondirectional
Sample or population: Sample
Statistical procedures: Degree of association and test of significance

will all yield identical coefficients with a 2 × 2 (dichotomous) table, although the index for C is not standardized on a unity scale.

An example may be instructive. In Table 3.2 the question of gender bias is examined in the propensity of courts to detain offenders. Thus we have two dichotomous variables in a 2 × 2 table. The three measures, V, Φ, and T, all provide the same coefficient, .05, indicating a very weak relationship between the two variables. C also yields an index of .05, but it does not have an upper limit of 1.00. If C were standardized (C~), it would yield an index of .07. Note from the table that the χ^2 is substantial and yields a probability of .001. This points up the fallacy of using a test of significance to suggest or imply a close relationship between two variables, a practice that occurs all too frequently in the literature.

What the level of significance of .001 tells us is that we can be confident in generalizing from the sample data about the total population of offenders from which the sample was drawn. We can also be confident that this is not just a chance relationship — but it is a weak one. It should be noted once more that it is not difficult to obtain a high level of significance with a large sample even with a negligible association between the variables.

Our analysis of the data should not stop there, however. As Pope and Feyerherm (1982) remind us, a higher proportion of females than males are likely to be held in detention (58% compared with 52%), even though males are charged with more serious offenses. When additional

Table 3.3

Number of Students Admitted to the La Trobe University Social Work
Program in 1979, by Gender and Occupation of Father

	Father's Occupation			
	ManagerialProfes-			
	sional and Middle-		*Blue*	
Gender	*management*	*Clerical*	*Collar*	*Total*
Male	5	0	5	10
Female	12	11	5	28
Total	17	11	10	38

$\chi^2 = 6.91$ $p. = .05$ C = .39   C~ = .57   V = .43

SOURCE: Pilcher (1982).
NOTES: Number of variables: Two
Level of measurement: Nominal dichotomous/nominal
Directional or nondirectional: Nondirectional
Sample or population: Population
Statistical procedures: Degree of association and test of significance

variables are taken into account — age, ethnicity, and whether or not a
formal petition was filed in the case — the relationship between gender
and detention is much stronger ($V = .14$, $p. = .001$) but still modest.

Let us take another example. In a study completed in 1966, Gockel
(1966) dubbed social work as the silk-stocking, blue-collar profession
because many of the females in social work came from upper or upper
middle-class families and many of the males came from blue-collar
backgrounds. Is this also true of nurses and elementary and secondary
educators? In 1966, it may have been.

In Australia, some twelve years later, this phenomenon was also
found to be evident for social work students, though not as strong as in
the United States (Pilcher, A., 1982). Table 3.3 provides data to test the
silk-stocking, blue-collar hypothesis with newly admitted students at
La Trobe University. The correlation between gender and father's occupation is substantial ($V = .43$), supporting the silk-stocking, blue-collar hypothesis.

In analyzing these data we cannot use Φ or T because neither are
standardized on this size table. Note that the C coefficient is less than
V on this table, but C is not standardized on a unity scale. The upper
limit for C on a table of this size would be .685 (see Leonard, 1976,
p. 283, for a table of upper limits for various size tables when using C).
If we divide the coefficient by the upper limit, we can standardize C on

the unity scale. Leonard expresses caution (1976, p. 284) in using a standardized C (C~) and I have found that it almost invariably exaggerates the strength of the relationship when compared with Cramer's V.

Several measures of association have unusual features or require some cautionary notation. Pearson's C is such a measure. It has been one of the most frequently used measures of association for nominal/nominal distributions. It can be applied to any size table ($n \times n$), but the fact that it is not standardized on a unity scale creates problems of interpretation and comparability. Thus a perfect association on a 2×2 table would be .707, not 1.00 (unity), and on a 3×3 table a perfect association would be .816. C can be standardized by dividing it by its upper limit, although one rarely sees this in the literature (for an exception see Pilcher, Ramirez & Swihart, 1968). Social science statistics books have noted this fact recently (see Leonard, 1976; Blalock, 1979; and later editions). Leonard (1976, p. 281ff) uses C with a bar over it to designate the standardized index and provides a table of the upper limits of C . I have designated it as C~.

The use of C~ has an advantage over the use of C when different size tables are analyzed in the same study, but even with C~ the index appears to be inflated, compared with Cramer's V. Pearson's C is not a preferred index of the strength of association for these reasons, but its frequent use in the literature requires that it be understood.

PRE Measure: Yule's Q

One additional measure of potential use to the helping professions when using dichotomous variables is Yule's Q. While there are problems in using Yule's Q, it does provide a useful measure for certain situations encountered when examining symmetric relationships. This measure requires a brief discussion of the necessary and sufficient condition in analyzing a 2×2 contingency table. The other measures discussed in this section assume a perfect correlation to require both a necessary and sufficient condition. Yule's Q will yield a perfect correlation (unity) if it meets either the necessary or sufficient condition. An example may help the reader understand how Yule's Q differs from other measures of association and what we mean by the necessary and sufficient condition.

If a strong parental attachment to children always results in a decision not to place a child in foster care, and if children without strong parental attachments are always placed in foster care, this would meet

Table 3.4

Relationship Between Worker's Assessment of Attachment Between Children
and Primary Caretakers and Placement Decision Made by Case Planning
Committee Illustrating the Necessary and Sufficient Condition
(hypothetical data)

| Placement Decision | *Worker's Assessment of Attachment* | | |
	Little or No Attachment	*Strong Attachment*	*Total*
Placement necessary or home release	0(*a*)	13(*b*)	13
Other placement: foster care and other	14(*c*)	0(*d*)	14
Total	14	13	27

Yule's Q = 1.00
Cramer's V = .999 or 1.00

NOTES: Number of variables: Two
Level of measurement: Nominal dichotomous
Directional or nondirectional: Nondirectional
Sample or population: Population
Statistical procedure: Degree of association

the necessary and sufficient conditions for a perfect association. Table
3.4 demonstrates the necessary and sufficient condition.

Note that I have followed the convention of designating each cell in
order as *a*, *b*, *c*, and *d*. This is a convenience for discussing the table as
well as being useful in creating formulas. In Table 3.4 all of the values
in the distribution fall in the diagonal cells *b* and *c* and illustrate a
perfect association between the two variables.

If, on the other hand, worker's assessment of a weak attachment
always resulted in placement, but assessment of a strong attachment
might or might not result in placement, this would be the necessary (but
not sufficient) condition (see Table 3.5).

In other words, the assessment of strong attachment is necessary for
a decision not to place, but not sufficient for that decision. Yule's Q
would yield an index of 1.00 with this distribution, indicating that it
meets the necessary condition perfectly. The distribution has a zero in
cell *a*.

Table 3.5

Relationship Between Worker's Assessment of Attachment Between Children
and Primary Caretakers and Placement Decision Made by Case Planning
Committee Illustrating the Necessary Condition (hypothetical data)

| Placement Decision | Worker's Assessment of Attachment | | |
	Little or no Attachment	Strong Attachment	Total
Placement not necessary or home release	0(a)	8(b)	8
Other placement: foster care and other	13(c)	6(d)	19
Total	13	14	27

Yule's Q = 1.00
Cramer's V = .63

NOTES: Number of variables: Two
Level of measurement: Nominal dichotomous
Directional or nondirectional: Nondirectional
Sample or population: Population
Statistical procedure: Degree of association

The sufficient (but not necessary) condition assumes a zero value in the other diagonal cell d; with this distribution a strong attachment is sufficient to prompt the decision of home release (or no placement) whereas little or no attachment is associated with either home release or placement. Table 3.6 presents data meeting this criterion.

The advantage of this measure for the helping professions is that approximating the necessary or sufficient condition can be used as a criteria of favorable outcome and, if Q approximates that criteria, would yield a high correlation. With the Φ coefficient or Cramer's V, it would not yield a high correlation unless it met both the necessary and sufficient condition (see Loether & McTavish, 1980, p. 202ff).

Yule's Q is an infrequently used measure in social and behavioral research but has potential for many applications when one wants to test the notion that a given factor is either a necessary or sufficient condition. One might use it to determine what factors are necessary or sufficient for an ex-patient to remain outside the mental hospital after discharge, for determining what factors are important for an ex-inmate

Table 3.6

Relationship Between Worker's Assessment of Attachment Between Children
and Primary Caretakers and Placement Decision Made by Case Planning
Committee Illustrating the Sufficient Condition (hypothetical data)

| Placement Decision | Worker's Assessment of Attachment | | |
	Little or No Attachment	Strong Attachment	Total
Placement not necessary or home release	5(a)	8(b)	13
Other placement: foster care and other	14(c)	0(d)	14
Total	19	8	27

Yule's Q = 1.00
Cramer's V = .67

NOTES: Number of variables: Two
Level of measurement: Nominal dichotomous
Directional or nondirectional: Nondirectional
Sample or population: Population
Statistical procedure: Degree of association

to remain out of prison after parole, or for determining the effects of a
school program to reduce truancy.

A study by Smith and Marcus (1984) made use of Yule's Q, but did
not identify it as such and, unfortunately, did not indicate that it makes
use of a less restrictive version of association. In fact the index was
presented without comment (see Table 3.7). It is important to designate
it as Yule's Q because the symbol Q is also used for other statistical
measures.

Using their data, I confirmed that it was indeed Yule's Q, but no
rationale was given for using this particular measure. The distribution
yielded a correlation of .73 (Q = .73). My calculation of Chi square was
slightly lower than the figure they obtained, 5.55 ($p.$ = .02) when not
corrected for continuity. Corrected for continuity, Chi square was 3.95
($p.$ = .05). Fisher's Exact Test yields a probability of .02. Again, when
small populations or samples are used, it is important to indicate
whether or not the correction for continuity was used in computing Chi
square. The use of the correction for continuity will be discussed in
more detail in Chapter 7. When populations or samples are small,

Table 3.7

Use of Volunteers, by Agency Type (1980)

Agency Type	None Reported	Some Volunteers Reported	Total
Established agencies	9	3	12
Proactive agencies	6	13	19
Total	15	16	31

$\chi^2 = 3.95$, 1 df, $p. < .05$ Yule's Q = .73   V = .36

SOURCE: Smith & Marcus (Summer, 1984, p. 30).
NOTES: Number of variables: Two
Level of measurement: Nominal dichotomous
Directional or nondirectional: Nondirectional
Sample or population: Population
Statistical procedures: Degree of association and test of significance (for chance occurrence)

Fisher's Exact Test is also feasible as a test of significance when both variables are dichotomous.

The distribution in Table 3.7 yields a Cramer's V of .36, using the restrictive version of association, compared with the nonrestrictive coefficient of .73. Cell *b* in the table approaches zero, illustrating that it is necessary but not sufficient for an agency to be proactive to make use of volunteers. That is the tendency, at least, and it would require a zero in cell *b* to make a flat statement to that effect.

Let us examine another study which made use of Yule's Q to deter-mine — you guessed it — whether or not a social worker's assessment of a strong attachment between children and primary caretakers was a necessary condition for the child to be retained in, or returned to his or her own home (Stewart, 1982). These data are presented in Table 3.8.

A Yule's Q computed on the distribution in Table 3.8 yields a high correlation (.85), as one would expect, because it approximates the necessary condition: cell *a* is nearly zero. The other measures, with a more restrictive criteria for a perfect association, requiring both the necessary and sufficient condition, would yield a coefficient consider-ably lower than the index above. Cramer's V, for instance, would be .42 for this distribution. Note again the capriciousness of C. Unstandard-ized, it cannot be compared with the other measures nor could it be compared with tables of other sizes. Standardized, it exaggerates the degree of the relationship.

Table 3.8

Relationship Between Worker's Assessment of Attachment Between Children and Primary Caretakers and Placement Decision Made by Case Planning Committee (this is not hypothetical data)

Placement Decision	Worker's Assessment of Attachment		Total
	Little or No Attachment	Strong Attachment	
Placement not necessary or home release	1(a)	12(b)	13
Other placement: foster care and other	7(c)	7(d)	14
Total	8	19	27

Yule's Q = .85   V = .42   C = .51   C~ = .72 χ^2 = 9.47
p. = .02 (Fisher's Exact Test)

SOURCE: Stewart (1982).
NOTES: Number of variables: Two
Level of measurement: Nominal dichotomous
Directional or nondirectional: Nondirectional
Sample or population: Population
Statistical procedures: Degree of association and test of significance (for chance occurrence)

In Table 3.8, if the analysis required the more restrictive version of association, then Cramer's V would be appropriate; if the analysis required the less restrictive version of *perfect association*, then Yule's Q would be appropriate, and this should be carefully noted in discussion and presentation of findings. For discussion of the vagaries of Yule's Q, see Mueller, Schuessler, and Costner (1970, p. 290ff).

ASYMMETRIC (DIRECTIONAL) MEASURES: NOMINAL/NOMINAL DISTRIBUTIONS

Lambda, Tau$_y$, and the Uncertainty Coefficient

Two PRE measures of particular interest when there is an independent and a dependent variable (an asymmetric relationship) are Guttman's lambda (λ, coefficient of reproducibility) and Goodman and Kruskal's tau$_y$ (τ). The "$_y$" is a symbol of the dependent variable. Lambda and τ_y are PRE measures. A third index of association has already been mentioned, the Uncertainty Coefficient (UC), which will become much more widely used because it is in the repertoire of the SPSS, SPSS-X, and SPSS-PC programs. The asymmetric version of the UC is the proportion of uncertainty in the dependent variable reduced by information from the independent variable. Nie et al. (1975) suggest that the approaches of λ and the uncertainty coefficient are similar. Unlike λ, however, and like τ, the UC considers the entire distribution, not just the modal value. The concept of uncertainty comes from information theory (Nie et al., 1975, p. 226).

The SPSS programs provide an asymmetric and symmetric version of λ and the Uncertainty Coefficient. Unfortunately τ_y is not computed by the SPSS packages. All of these asymmetric measures (λ, τ, and the UC) are standardized and suitable for any size table. The researcher should read about any difficulties and peculiarities involved in each of these three measures to determine which one is most suitable. In particular, λ requires further study (see, for instance, Blalock, 1981, pp. 310–311; Leonard, 1976, p. 293ff; Loether & McTavish, 1980, p. 224). It should be noted again that although λ and τ_y are both PRE measures, they do not entail the same kind of prediction. Lambda is a predictor of the modal value in the categories of a second variable when the distribution of the first variable is known, whereas Goodman and Kruskal's τ_y is a predictor of the distribution of values in all categories of a second variable when the distribution of the first variable is known.

It is important for the researcher to read about these measures in several texts because any one text may not include all of the nuances of a measure that might be considered. The fact that λ breaks down in certain instances and yields a correlation of .00 when there is actually some correlation is discussed in several texts (Blalock, 1981, pp. 310–311; Leonard, 1976, p. 293ff; Loether & McTavish, 1980, p. 224), but not all.

Both λ and τ_y can be computed on the distribution in Table 3.9, adapted from a study by Marshall (1982, p. 21).

To what extent can we predict the parole board's decision from the parole officer's recommendation? We can see from Table 3.9 that in most instances the board's decision is to parole when that is the recommendation of the parole officer and that when the parole officer recommends that parole not be given, that recommendation is usually followed. Both indices indicate a strong relationship ($\lambda = .59$; $\tau = .62$) between the two variables. Lambda predicts the modal value in the response of the parole board from the parole officer's recommendation,

Table 3.9

Parole Officer's Recommendation and Parole Board Decision in Cases
Considered for Parole

Parole Board Decision	Parole Officer's Recommendation			
	Positive	Neutral	Negative	Total
Yes	299	19	9	327
No	43	51	219	313
Total	342	70	228	640

$\lambda = .59$ $\tau = .62$

SOURCE: Abstracted from Marshall (1982, table 6, p. 21).
NOTES: Marshall had three additional categories in the independent variable, "negative but needs supervision," "negative but community needs protection," and "no report available." These categories were excluded for purposes of this presentation.
Number of variables: Two
Level of measurement: Nominal dichotomous/nominal
Directional or nondirectional: Directional
Sample or population: Population
Statistical procedure: Degree of association

and τ predicts the responses in all categories in the dependent variable from the values of the independent category, parole officer's recommendation, as does the uncertainty coefficient.

Another example of data suitable for use of τ_y, λ, or UC is presented in Table 3.10. It has often been suggested, and frequently observed, that the political party of parents determines the political affiliation of their sons and daughters. At La Trobe University in 1979, newly admitted social work students provided data on this question.

Two of the three measures of association shown yield almost identical indices, but one of the three, λ, yields an unusual index. This particular distribution illustrates one of the difficulties with λ. Because there is a concentration of cases in one row, λ breaks down and yields a zero correlation when in fact there is a correlation; $\tau = .18$; and UC = .19. I have included Cramer's V here to illustrate that when you are analyzing an asymmetric relationship, you are asking a more rigorous question than with a symmetric relationship. You are predicting a directional relationship which says that X brings about Y. That is a more rigorous prediction than simply predicting that X is associated with Y. In fact, if you have a calculator handy, you can quickly demonstrate that

Table 3.10

Political Party Affiliation of Fathers and Political Party Affiliation of
Students Entering the La Trobe University School of Social Work Program
in 1979 (with two major political groupings only)

| Political Affilia-
of Students | Political Affiliation of Fathers | | |
	Labor Party	Liberal/National* Coalition Party	Total
Labor Party	16	6	22
Liberal/National Coalition	1	4	5
Total	17	10	27

$\lambda = .00$ $\tau = .18$ $V = .42$
UC asymmetric = .19 (with student dependent)
Fisher's Exact Test $p. = .05$

SOURCE: Pilcher (1982).
NOTES: Number of variables: Two
Level of measurement: Nominal dichotomous
Directional or nondirectional: Directional
Sample or population: Population
Statistical procedure: Degree of association and test of significance (for chance occurrence)
*The National Party was formerly called the Country Party.

if you square V, you will obtain τ ($V^2 = \tau$). That is frequently, but not
always, the case.

What can we say about this distribution? We can say that there is
fairly modest confirmation of the hypothesis that the political party
affiliation of father determines the political party affiliation of offspring. Note that this is not a sample, so we are not estimating the level
of confidence in generalizing to a population; we have a population,
and we can generalize about this particular population of fifty-four
Australians.

A noted social statistician, Herbert Blalock, argues that there is a
place for significance tests when dealing with populations (1981, pp.
241–243). The use of such tests with populations serves a somewhat
different and theoretical purpose. Blalock poses a hypothetical skeptic
who persistently raises the question of whether or not the relationship
between two variables is just a chance occurrence (see also Henkel,
1976, pp. 85–86).

In the example above, for instance, the skeptic might say that the
relationship between father's and offspring's political affiliation may

be simply chance processes. When a second variable is introduced (father's political affiliation) to explain the variability in offspring's political affiliation, the skeptic can pose an alternative hypothesis with some spurious variable, suggesting, for instance, that offspring's political affiliation could be predicted equally as well by dividing this population into subpopulations on the basis of the third letter in their given names (with the early part of the alphabet in one group and the latter part of the alphabet in the other). If such a random process yields an association as high as that between father's and offspring's political affiliation, the skeptic can then argue that his explanation is as plausible as yours. Blalock suggests that if the skeptic's explanation is simpler (even if not more logical) than the researcher's, the association cannot be taken too seriously (Blalock, 1981, p. 242).

What random process can we use to make this test? Blalock suggests that we can (and should) use a test of significance to rule out the simple *chance process* alternative. A test of significance provides an alternative hypothesis, and Blalock argues that it is appropriate, therefore, to use a test of significance to put the finding on trial: could it be a chance occurrence? The astute researcher will assume that Blalock's omnipresent skeptic is standing just behind, peering over the shoulder.

To test the ubiquitous skeptic's suggestion that this is a chance occurrence in the population, we have computed the probability for this distribution using Fisher's Exact Test. The result suggests that the probability of obtaining this distribution by chance would be about 5 in 100. The odds are not bad, and we conclude that it is worth paying attention to the results. Actually when Ann Pilcher looked at the political preference of fathers and offspring for 11 of the 13 schools of social work in Australia in 1976, 1977, and 1979, she obtained similar results (1982).

However, finding a significant and close relationship between these two variables does not rule out the possibility that other independent variables may be operating that predict and explain the variability in both father's and offspring's political affiliation more accurately as a predictor and more logically as an explanation than parental influence or persuasion. One could imagine, for instance, that the occupation of offspring may play a significant role in political preference — arising from the similarity in parental and offspring occupations — and may account for the close association. It is even more likely that a number of influences, in various combinations, may provide the best prediction and explanation.

When a measure of association and a test of significance are used in conjunction, and appropriately applied, they can provide a good basis for making decisions about the relationship between variables and the feasibility of making generalizations. This is particularly important when using a test of significance with a sample. The literature is rife with examples of authors presenting a test of significance as if it signified a close relationship, without actually computing a measure of association. Even if you have favorable odds that the sample is representative of the population, it does not mean that the variables being analyzed are closely associated.

As an illustration, Antony Williams (1985) obtained data on occupational classification (using the Broom and Jones schema) of patients seen by psychiatrists in private practice. His aim was to examine the characteristics of such patients so that he could compare them with patients seen by psychologists. One facet of the study was to look at the differences in social class (as measured by occupational classification) between *psychotherapy* and *general psychiatry* patients.

Patients classified as being in psychotherapy were seen for one hour of conversation with one or more sessions weekly; patients classified as being seen in general psychiatry were seen for supportive discussions coupled with medication — usually with less than fifteen-minute sessions. His method of selecting respondents was a rather loose attempt at stratified sampling, and whether or not he ended up with a probability sample is questionable.

At any rate he found that the possibility of obtaining the distribution by chance was .003, although it is not clear what test of significance was used; I found it to be .01 using Chi square. In either case it should not be dismissed as a chance occurrence. And in either case we do not know from the report of the study how closely the two variables are associated. The data (see Table 3.11) could have been analyzed with Goodman and Kruskal's τ_y if the distribution is conceptualized as asymmetrical or Cramer's V if no distinction is made between dependent and independent variables. Had he used these measures he would have found that using the Broom and Jones occupational categories as a predictor of type of treatment yielded a modest asymmetric correlation ($\tau = .09$), and as a symmetric association it would have also yielded a modest correlation coefficient ($V = .30$). Note that the strengths of the association for symmetric and asymmetric measures are on the same scale but they are indices with different interpretations. The coefficient for τ is based on a more rigorous prediction than the coefficient for V.

Table 3.11

Occupations of Groups of People Attending Psychotherapy and General
Psychiatry

Occupational Group	Psychotherapy	General Psychiatry	Total
Upper professional	43	13	56
Lower professional	46	9	55
Managerial	13	7	20
Clerical	23	12	35
Crafts people	5	10	15
Not stated	15	17	32
Total	145	68	213

$\chi^2 = 16.56$; $df. = 4$; $p. = .01$
$\tau_y = .09$ with "not stated" category deleted.
$V = .30$ with "not stated" category deleted.

SOURCE: Adapted from Williams (1985, table 3, p. 255).
NOTES: The df, $p.$, and two measures of association were not given in the table as it appears in the source article.
The "not stated" cases were removed from the distribution before the statistical analysis was carried out. Williams notes that the "not stated" category consisted predominantly of tertiary-level students, probably destined for the upper three occupational groups.
Number of variables: Two
Level of measurement: Nominal, one dichotomous
Directional or nondirectional: Directional or nondirectional
Sample or population: Population or sample (see text)
Statistical procedure: Degree of association and test of significance (for chance occurrence)

Therefore the index of .09 would not be considered weaker than the index of .30; the two indices range over a different segment of the scale from .00 to 1.00.

The point of presenting the data from Table 3.11 is that the level of confidence or the probability figure cannot be taken as an indicator of a strong relationship; it is necessary to actually calculate a measure of association if you want to know how closely two variables coincide. Note once again with this distribution that $V^2 = \tau$.

TESTS OF SIGNIFICANCE AND PROBABILITY TESTS FOR NOMINAL VARIABLES

Populations

If you have a population, an index of the strength of association may be all that is required to make a decision about the relationship between two nominal variables. We alluded above to the contention about this in the sociological literature, but I believe Blalock has made a good case for computing a test of significance with a population (Blalock, 1981, pp. 241–243; see Henkel for a more elaborate discussion, 1976, p. 85). Let us consider another example drawn from Table 3.8.

The relationship between workers' assessments of parental attachment and the subsequent placement decision may have been a chance occurrence. To test this we might arbitrarily assign each case by a flip of a coin and then look at the placement decision for the cases that were "heads" and the cases that were "tails." If this produced as high a correlation as the one we obtained from the actual data, we would then suspect that the distribution might be a chance occurrence.

Or if we divided the children into two groups by eye color: blue or brown (although eye color could be an indicator of ethnicity or some other potentially important variable) and found that the results yielded as high a correlation as with the actual data, then our suspicions are again aroused about the chance occurrence of our distribution. A test of significance does the same thing; it tests the notion that the distribution is a chance occurrence. In Table 3.8, for instance, Fisher's Exact Test produces a probability of .02.

The probability of obtaining this distribution by chance is 2 out of 100, which leaves us with a sense that the relationship is not an accidental one, although there may be mediating variables that we have not included which would provide greater illumination about the relationship. This is a different use of a probability test than we encounter with a sample.

In Table 3.10, using Fisher's Exact Test, we find that the probability is .05, indicating that we can have some confidence in our alternative hypothesis that the political affiliation of father is associated with the political affiliation of student ($V = .42$). and that parental affiliation is predictive of offspring affiliation ($\tau = .18$)

Samples and Tests of Significance

If you have drawn a random sample of cases from a population, you need to make a decision about the level of confidence you have in generalizing to the population from which the sample was drawn. This requires a test of significance. Tests of significance are based on the assumption that data have been obtained from a probability sample such that cases or units are selected randomly. Selecting cases randomly, however, does not ensure an exact representative sample. If we take several samples from a population, we find that there is some variability in the results. For purposes of illustration, assume that we have 50 students at the first grade level in an elementary school. These ages in months are as follows:

72	78	64	69	71	73	70	74	65	67
67	73	71	72	66	68	75	77	72	76
76	72	77	71	74	65	68	75	73	71
70	68	70	72	69	75	78	65	69	77
68	70	66	71	76	70	69	64	70	68

We draw a series of 10% samples from a receptacle containing the names and ages of each of the 50 children on slips of paper. We record the mean age in months after each sample is drawn and place the slips back in the receptacle and draw the next sample. This is called sampling with replacement. If we did not replace the slips in the receptacle, it would be sampling without replacement. That would create a problem because each time you draw a sample there are fewer units in the receptacle and the probability of any slip being drawn is different. Sampling with replacement ensures that each unit has an equal chance of being drawn. Sampling with replacement also means that you may draw the same case twice in one sample. This does not present a problem — the case is simply counted twice, and the logical and theoretical purpose of the sample is not compromised.

Using these data, I drew 10 random samples with the results shown in Table 3.12.

The variation in the means of the 10 samples ranged from 69.8 to 72.5 months, the former varying from the population by a little over one month and the latter varying from the population mean by about 1.5 months. Most of the other samples varied less than a week or 10 days (.06 to .36 of a month) from the mean of the population. The point is that it cannot be assumed that a random sample is exactly representative of the population.

If you drew 200 or 300 samples and plotted the mean age for each sample on a graph, you would see a bell-shaped curve formed by the results. Most samples would have means extremely close to the population mean and very few would fall in the tails of the bell-shaped curve. Because repeated samples result in a bell-shaped curve, a normal distribution, it is possible to compute the probability of obtaining a

Table 3.12

Mean and Standard Deviation of Ten Random Samples Drawn from the
Sample Population

Number of Sample		Ages of Cases Drawn								Mean Age and Standard Deviation of Sample Drawn	
										μ	σ
1	77	71	69	70	70	70	76	72	68	69	71.20	3.01
2	69	70	71	65	76	76	73	71	77	77	72.50	4.01
3	65	68	76	66	73	71	70	71	76	76	71.20	4.08
4	73	68	75	66	66	68	73	64	75	70	69.80	3.99
5	68	74	78	72	73	69	66	70	71	69	71.00	3.43
6	76	75	77	72	68	67	72	73	67	65	71.20	4.21
7	77	74	70	71	78	72	78	70	70	71	71.30	3.38
8	67	72	70	74	69	73	71	76	64	77	71.30	4.00
9	76	66	66	78	74	73	67	72	68	77	71.70	4.64
10	72	72	71	68	73	72	70	71	70	68	70.70	1.70
Mean and standard deviation of all 50 cases										70.94	3.83

particular distribution. If the cases selected are not randomly selected, then a normal distribution cannot be assumed, and a test of significance which assumes random selection is meaningless. It is beyond the scope of this introductory text to discuss the details of the normal distributions and sampling distributions. The topic is adequately discussed in any of the major statistical texts written by psychologists, sociologists, and educators.

Chi Square Tests and Hypothetical Testing

One test of significance for the delta measures (V, T, C, C~, and Φ) and the uncertainty coefficient is made by entering a Chi square table (see Appendix B, Table C) with the χ^2 obtained from the sample distribution in the appropriate table row (determined by the degrees of freedom).

The term *degree of freedom* refers to the number of values free to vary in a given set of data (see Chapter 7 for an elaboration of degrees of freedom). For our purposes here, it is a guide to the set of figures in a probability table. Each size contingency table has a given probability curve, and the number of categories in a contingency table provides the information you need to compute the degrees of freedom: the product of the number of row categories minus one, times the number of column categories minus one or $(r - 1)(k - 1)$. The letter k in this simple formula stands for columns, a convention in statistics. The figures in a probability table are discrete points on a curve for a particular size contingency table.

The logic of our decision is usually couched in the context of hypothesis testing. Our working hypothesis on political affiliation, for instance, was that political affiliation of parents is associated with political affiliation of offspring (Table 3.10). However, we do not test that hypothesis. Instead we test the null hypothesis that there is no relationship between the political affiliations of offspring and parent. The reason for this is that it is possible to prove that two variables are not related but it is not possible to prove that two variables are related — there may be extraneous or fugitive variables related to the variables of concern that account for the apparent relationship. In other words, we can never be certain that we have included the relevant variables in a hypothetical equation. We test the null hypothesis, and we refer to our working hypothesis as the alternative hypothesis. If we reject the null hypothesis, we can then accept, with qualifications, the alternative hypothesis.

In posing a null hypothesis of no relationship, we are saying that political affiliations of parent and offspring are independent, they are unrelated. To test this hypothesis, we make use of the abstract or heuristic notion of expected frequencies. If the two variables are independent, what would we expect to find in each cell of Table 3.10? Using the marginals and the total number of cases, we can compute the expected frequency in each cell (see Chapter 7 for a more thorough explanation). We would expect to find 14 cases in cell a, 8 cases in cell b, 3 cases in cell c and 2 cases in cell d. You can work this out logically or accept the rule of thumb that the expected frequency in any cell can be obtained by dividing the product of the two marginals for that cell by the total number of cases in the distribution.

If we did find that observed and expected frequencies were the same, we would conclude that there was no relationship between the two variables. If the difference between expected and observed frequencies is large, we conclude that there is some relationship. How large does that difference have to be to conclude that the difference is statistically significant?

The calculation of the difference results in an index, Chi square. This index is then examined in relation to the Chi square distribution of probability. The convention in social science research is to accept a probability of .05 as being significant. Conventions can be questioned, and there may be instances when a different level of probability should be used as the critical point in determining significance. Using this convention, however, if the probability is .05, .04, .03, .02, .01, .001, and so on, we reject the null hypothesis; if it is .06, .07, .10, .20, or lower, we accept the null hypothesis and conclude that the two variables are independent (see Cowger, 1984; Crane, 1976; Fitz-Gibbon & Morris, 1978, p. 37).

When we reject the null hypothesis, we usually accept the alternative hypothesis. Rejecting the null hypothesis leaves the possibility that there is a consequential relationship between the two variables, but it is only a possibility. The reason for this, as we have noted, is that other variables, not included in the equation, may actually account for the apparent relationship.

In Table 3.2, discussed earlier in the chapter, suppose we had a working hypothesis that there would be an association between gender and the use of detention by the court (i.e., gender is associated with the use of detention). We then test the null hypothesis that there was no association between the two variables. Our test yields a probability of .001. Consequently we reject the null hypothesis which leaves the possibility that our alternative hypothesis is viable. However, the association is a weak one ($V = .05$).

Assumptions of Chi Square

Chi square is an appropriate measure if the distribution meets the assumptions of the test. These include the stipulation that the data are derived from a truly random sample, providing there is a sufficient number of cases (usually considered to be at least 30), that expected frequencies meet certain criteria (for criteria, see Chapter 7), and that observations are independent. The last stipulation means that if we make two observations on the same variable for the same case at two different points in time, we cannot use Chi square as a test of independence of the two observations. Neither can we do so if we are comparing matched individuals.

Chi square is a complex measure and requires careful study before it can be adopted as a test of significance. Chi square is one of the most misused statistics in the social science literature — either being used when underlying assumptions are clearly not met or being used as if it were a measure of the degree of association between two variables (see Duggan & Dean, 1968). Often it is used when the data are not generated from a random sample or when there are too few cases. When there are few cases, the expected frequencies are likely to be small and a correction for continuity is advised (see Blalock, 1981, p. 290ff). This correction is seldom carried out in studies reported in the literature (see Chapter 7 for a discussion of the correction for continuity), although the increased use of computer programs for analysis, to the extent that the correction is built into the program, will ensure that it is carried out.

Fisher's Exact Test

If there are fewer than 30 cases or Chi square is not advisable for other reasons, Fisher's Exact Test may be used to determine significance if both nominal level variables are dichotomous. When using Chi square, a table of associated probabilities is required to determine the level of significance. With Fisher's Exact Test (P), no such table is required because the formula itself produces the exact probability. It can be used in tables with more than 30 cases as well, but with large numbers of cases the computation by hand becomes difficult. Calculators with a factorial key and most computers can be programmed or used directly in calculating Fisher's Exact Test. Siegel provides a table for estimating level of significance for this test if there are not more than 30 cases and the right-hand marginals are not more than 15 (Siegel, 1956, p. 96ff). Some of the calculators with a factorial key can compute P with as many as 69 cases, and this capacity will undoubtedly increase as calculators become more powerful and programs more sophisticated.

P can also be used with PRE measures on any distribution of two dichotomous variables. If the researcher is mathematically astute, Pierce (1969, chap. 8) has demonstrated how it can be extended beyond the 2×2 table and can be written in computer language.

Other Tests of Significance: t and z

For the PRE measures discussed above, λ and τ_y, Chi square, or P can be used if the data meet the requirements of these two measures. Both Harshbarger (1977, p. 481) and Jacobson (1976, p. 450ff) provide a formula for testing the significance of λ using a z table, but Harshbarger cautions that sample size should be at least 50 for this test. There do not appear to be unique tests of significance designed specifically for Goodman and Kruskal's τ_y or the Uncertainty Coefficient. In the 2×2 situation, Fisher's Exact Test may be used, or if the distribution meets the requirements, Chi square may be used for these two measures. If the distribution does not meet the assumptions of Chi square but no other measure is available, the discussion of results should make it clear which assumptions have not been met.

A formula for converting Yule's Q coefficients to z scores is described in Jacobson (1976, p. 173ff) and Leonard (1976, p. 286). This enables the researcher to determine the level of significance for Q, given a sample distribution, if Fisher's Exact Test is not feasible.

With a classical experimental design, it may be possible to use the t statistic to determine whether or not significant change has occurred in a sample distribution or to determine whether or not the observed differences in an experimental and control group are statistically significant. It was noted earlier that if we make observations on an individual (or group) at two different points in time, we cannot use Chi square as a test of significance. We speak of this as a related sample because the observations in the first instance are made with the same population in the second instance, after the introduction of the independent variable, and the first observations are *ipso facto* related to the second, which confounds the evaluation of the significance of differences.

McNemar Test

A test of significance for related (dependent) samples, has been developed by McNemar. The McNemar Test can be used in a pretest/posttest situation with dichotomous nominal data. In a fairly extensive search of recent literature, I was not able locate a set of data in the professional education, nursing, or social work journals that would provide an illustration of this test. I found articles that used the test, but unless the individual values for each subject are given in a study, you do not have a basis for computing the McNemar Test. I also found instances where the McNemar Test could have been used but again without the necessary data to provide an illustration. Caty and Tamlyn (1984), for instance, in their study of changes in attitudes about death and dying, could have used the McNemar Test. Because we do not have actual data, we must resort to a hypothetical illustration.

Table 3.13

Hypothetical Change in Smoking Behavior Before and After a Seminar on
Substance Abuse

Status After Seminar	Status Before Seminar		Total
	Smoker	Nonsmoker	
Nonsmoker	10	19	29
Smoker	6	1	7
Total	16	20	36

$df = 1$ $M^2 = 5.82$ $p. = .02$ Yule's Q = .84

NOTES: Number of variables: Two
Level of measurement: Nominal dichotomous
Directional or nondirectional: Nondirectional (could be considered directional)
Sample or population: Hypothetical sample
Statistical procedure: Contingency table with McNemar Test of Significance

Let us assume that we have data on a random sample of hospital
nurses and social workers enrolled in a seminar on substance abuse in
a large metropolitan hospital. We take a random sample at the beginning
of the seminar and determine how many in the seminar are smokers and
how many are nonsmokers. At the end of the seminar, 15 weeks later,
we again determine whether or not the same individuals are smokers.
Assume that we have the results indicated in Table 3.13.

Some of the nonsmokers took up the practice during or immediately
after the seminar; some of the smokers gave up the practice during or
immediately after the seminar; and in fact, there was more change in
those designated as smokers at the beginning of the seminar than those
designated as nonsmokers. What level of confidence can we have that
this change was significant, and can we, with confidence, generalize to
the population of nurses and social workers in the hospital? With the
McNemar test we make use of the Chi square table.

Our calculation yields an M^2 of 5.82 and we consult the Chi square
table in the appendix to determine that the level of confidence is .02, a
promising if optimistic result. Consequently we can have considerable
confidence in the finding, although we cannot conclude that the seminar
itself (or alone) contributed to the behavioral change. We do not know
what other variables might have been operating. Consult Chapter 7 for
the calculation and for elaboration on the McNemar Test.

SUMMARY

There are other tests of significance for nominal/nominal variables that might be discussed for the significance of changes for "before and after" designs for related and independent samples. Leonard discusses several of these: the Wald-Wolfowitz and the Runs Test for independent samples and the Sign Test for related samples (Leonard, 1976, pp. 213–224). See also Siegel (1956, p. 68ff) and Blalock (1981, p. 236ff). The reader may wish to examine these tests if "before and after" designs are of interest.

In general, I have included only those tests and measures that I believe to be of primary interest to practitioners and to students engaged in research or anticipating the commencement of a research project. The criteria for selecting these measures have been discussed above and provide the reader with additional references on the use of measures of association and tests of significance, but the researcher should always read about the individual measures in two or more texts before adopting them for a given set of data. The reason for this has been alluded to earlier: sometimes the texts do not call attention to all of the pitfalls or idiosyncracies of a particular measure. In addition, the assumptions behind the measures need to be studied carefully, and these are not always discussed in every text.

Table 3.14 outlines the commonly used measures together with some of the new ones that are potentially useful with nominal data. The table indicates whether or not the association measures are symmetrical or asymmetrical and provides information about associated tests of significance where available.

The reader should keep in mind that, in any given study, a number of variables—some nominal, some ordinal, some interval—might be involved so that various combinations of variable types might be examined and analyzed; therefore, in any given study a researcher might use several measures of association, each corresponding to a specific pair of variables being described or examined. Because different measures of association may have different tests of significance attached to them, a variety of tests of significance might also be used. The next chapter discusses measures used with various variable combinations.

Table 3.14

Measures of Association and Tests of Significance When Both Variables
are Nominal

Both Variables Dichotomous (2 × 2)	One Variable Dichotomous, One Not Dichotomous (2 × n)	Neither Variable Dichotomous (n × n)
Delta Measures		
C* <> χ^2_2 P	C* <> χ^2_2	C* <> χ^2_2
C~ <> χ^2_2 P	C~ <> χ^2_2	C~ <> χ^2
Φ <> χ^2_2 P	Φ <> χ^2_2	
T** <> χ^2_2 P		T** <> χ^2_2
V <> χ^2 P	V <> χ^2	V <> χ^2_2
PRE Measures		
Q~ <> z P		
Φ^2 <> χ^2 P		
λ <> > z P	λ <> > z	λ <> > z
τ > χ^2_2 P	τ > χ^2_2	τ > χ^2_2
UC <> > χ^2 P	UC <> > χ^2	UC <> > χ^2

Explanatory symbols:

* Not standardized on unity scale
** Standardized on $r = c$ tables only
~ Standardized on 2 × 2 tables only
<> Symmetric (nondirectional)
> Asymmetric (directional)

Symbols for measures of association and tests of significance used in this chapter:

C	Pearson's contingency coefficient
C~	Standardized contingency coefficient
Φ	Phi coefficient
T	Tschuprow's T
V	Cramer's V
UC	Uncertainty Coefficient
P	Fisher's Exact Test
Q	Yule's Q
Φ^2	Phi squared or mean square contingency
λ	Lambda (Guttman's coefficient of predictability)
τ	Goodman and Kruskal's Tau
χ^2	Chi square
z	z Test

NOTES: Each symbol for a measure of association is followed by an indication of whether it is symmetric (<>) or asymmetric (>), and then by one or two appropriate tests of significance. In some instances, a measure has both a symmetric and asymmetric version.

Several texts use charts to show measures of association and tests of significance by level of measurement: Andrews , Klein, Davidson, O'Malley, & Rogers, 1981; Blalock, 1981; Harshbarger 1977; Leonard, 1976; Loether & McTavish 1980; Siegel, 1956.

Chapter 4

THE BIVARIATE DISTRIBUTION: VARIOUS COMBINATIONS – NOMINAL, ORDINAL, AND INTERVAL DATA

In any given study, the researcher may be dealing with various levels of measurement combinations. Greene (1983), in her study of death anxiety and ageism, compiled sets of data, each set of which could have been analyzed with a different measure of association: Pearson's correlation (r), Cramer's V, and Spearman's rho (ρ). She also used different tests of significance, the Analysis of Variance with F values and the Chi Square Test for Independence. She could have used an additional test of significance, the t Test, for the ranked data. In other words, she had a mixture of interval, ordinal, and nominal data.

The various possible combinations of variables are given here, with notations on where examples of each combination, except one, may be found in this book:

1st Variable/2nd Variable	Example
nominal/nominal	Table 2.6, Chapter 2; Table 3.2, Chapter 3
nominal/ordinal	Tables 4.1 & 4.2, this Chapter
nominal/interval	Tables 4.4 & 4.5, this Chapter
ordinal/ordinal	Tables 4.7–4.10, this Chapter
ordinal/interval	None
interval/interval	Table 5.3, Chapter 5

As we noted earlier, in some instances it is important to distinguish between nominal variables that are dichotomous (i.e., those that have two categories, such as gender), and those that have more than two categories. Ordinal categories can be dichotomous as well, but the usual 2 × 2 distribution has two dichotomous nominal variables. We have already discussed the nominal/nominal combinations, and interval/interval combinations will be discussed in the next chapter. The remaining combinations are discussed in this chapter.

NOMINAL/ORDINAL MEASURES OF ASSOCIATION AND TESTS OF SIGNIFICANCE

Theta, Mann-Whitney U Test, and Kruskal-Wallis H Test

Nominal variables are frequently examined in combination with ordinal variables, and there is one measure of particular interest and importance for this combination. In fact, Freeman, in devising theta (Θ), the coefficient of differentiation, nominated it as the only suitable measure for nominal/ordinal data (Freeman, 1965). Leege and Francis (1974) also designate it as the only measure for this combination of variables. Jacobson (1976, p. 462ff) argues that the correlation ratio can also be applied to distributions that are nominal/ordinal combinations. Because the correlation ratio is ordinarily used with nominal/interval variables, we will discuss it in that context later in this chapter.

Although it is seldom seen in the literature, θ is a very useful measure. Either researchers rarely develop this combination, which seems unlikely, or they have used measures that assume nominal/nominal or ordinal/ordinal levels of measurement when in fact they had a nominal/ordinal combination. Leege and Francis demonstrate that neither λ or Cramer's V will distinguish differences in rank order in certain distributions, whereas θ will do so (Leege & Francis, 1974, p. 292), bearing out the adage that level of measurement is a major consideration in selecting a measure of association if sensitivity of measure is important.

Theta may be interpreted in terms of comparisons of the rankings of individuals in different nominal categories (Freeman, 1965, p. 113). Its magnitude signifies the extent to which order can be predicted on the basis of the category of the nominal variable (Leege & Francis, 1974, p. 294). Jacobson (1976, p. 472) notes that θ is actually a modification

Table 4.1

Number and Percentage (Rounded) of Clinical Social Workers by
Gender and Age

Gender	35 & Under No.	%	36–45 No.	%	46–55 No.	%	56 & Over No.	%	Total No.	%
Female workers	57	(71)	91	(58)	130	(69)	88	(81)	366	(69)
Male workers	23	(29)	66	(42)	58	(31)	20	(19)	167	(31)
Total	80	(100)	157	(100)	188	(100)	108	(100)	533	(100)

$\chi^2 = 16.87$ $(p. = .001)$ V = .18 θ = .14   U = 2.75 $(p. = .003)$

SOURCE: Raw data from Jayaratne & Ivey (1983, table 1).
NOTES: Indices were not included in the table as it appears in the source article.
Number of variables: Two
Level of measurement: Ordinal and nominal dichotomous
Symmetric or asymmetric: Asymmetric
Sample or population: Sample
Statistical procedures: Degree of association and test of significance

of Somer's d, to be discussed below. An example of a distribution suitable for the use of θ can be seen in Table 4.1.

The data in Table 4.1 were taken from a study presented by Jayaratne and Ivey (1983) in which they computed a Chi square statistic on the relationship between gender and age. Their goal apparently was simply to test the significance of the distribution. Our goal extends beyond a test of significance. We want to answer the question of whether or not there is a consistent ordered pattern at various age levels in the composition of the profession by gender. In answering this question, we can also determine the level of significance.

Jayaratne and Ivey did not compute a measure of association for the distribution. They did present a χ^2 of 16.87. The derived probability from Chi square answers the question of whether or not the sample data are significant (i.e., can one have confidence that the difference in age between males and females is not due to chance). They found that it was significant ($p. = .001$); nevertheless the relationship is not a strong one. Had they computed Cramer's V on the distribution, it would have been .18 and the calculation of θ would have yielded a somewhat lower coefficient, .14. Cramer's V does not take into consideration the order of the variable (age). It is a more rigorous exercise to do so, and it is consistent that the θ coefficient is lower than Cramer's V.

It seems clear in this case that age is an ordinal variable because the intervals are not measured in standard units. We can see why the coefficient of differentiation (θ) is relatively weak if we look at the percentages. There are more women in the older age group and fewer in the 36 to 45 group than one would expect (if we assume a consistent increasing or decreasing trend by age group), but in the youngest age group and the 46 to 55 category, women comprise the proportion that one would expect from the percentages computed for the row totals. For these 533 social workers we can see that in only 14% of the comparisons made by gender are there systematic and ordered differences in age, not an impressive statistic. Note that we are not making a distinction between dependent and independent variables.

Because Jayaratne and Ivey (1983) drew a systematic sample (a probability sample if there was no bias in the arrangement of cases), we are interested in the confidence we can have in generalizing to the population of national association members who are in clinical social work.

Depending on the number of categories in the nominal variable, one of two tests of significance can be used with θ: the Mann-Whitney U test for $2 \times n$ tables and the Kruskal-Wallis H test for $n \times n$ tables (Harshbarger, 1977, p. 488; Leege & Francis, 1974, p. 324ff). In Table 4.1, the Mann-Whitney U test would have been an appropriate test of significance in conjunction with θ. Both θ and the calculation of U and H are easily programmed.

In Table 4.1, a Chi square was computed by Jayaratne and Ivey, and reference to the Chi square table results in a probability of .001 (see Appendix B, Table C). Had the authors used θ and the Mann-Whitney U test, they would have obtained a probability of .003. To summarize, there are two important facts about this table: first, one can be confident in imputing the findings from the sample to the population and second, age and gender in this population are not closely associated (θ = .14). Substantively, the older clinical social workers were more likely to be female, and the clinical social workers in their late thirties and early forties, while still predominantly female, were more nearly balanced by gender.

Sheila Collins (1984) conducted a study on the career supports and barriers for female professionals in education, social work, and nursing. The study examined, among other relationships, the support given by

Table 4.2
Fathers' Support for Top-Level Administrators

| | Fathers' Support Level | | | | | | | |
| | Low | | Moderate | | High | | Total | |
Occupation	No.	%	No.	%	No.	%	No.	%
Social work	7	(24.1)	9	(31.0)	13	(44.8)	29	(100.0)
Nursing	21	(47.7)	10	(22.7)	13	(29.5)	44	(100.0)
Education	5	(20.8)	13	(54.2)	6	(25.0)	24	(100.0)
Total	33	(34.0)	32	(33.0)	32	(33.0)	97	(100.0)

$H = 119$ $p. = .001$ $\theta = .16$

SOURCE: Collins (1984).
NOTES: Number of variables: Two (Indices not in original table)
Level of measurement: Ordinal and nominal
Symmetric or asymmetric: Asymmetric
Sample or population: Sample
Statistical procedures: Degree of association and test of significance

fathers to their daughters in pursuing their careers. Table 4.2 presents these data and compares the three professions by level of career support from fathers.

By inspection, the table shows that only about one-third of the women received a high level of support in their careers from their fathers, but female social workers received more support than female nurses or educators. This can readily be seen by examining the percentages. Note that in this table we are trying to predict the order of support from the nominal occupational classifications. This rudimentary type of analysis is essential, and when completed, it can be put into perspective by determining how much of the order can be predicted by knowing the classification. If you know the occupation of a female administrator, how well does this help you in predicting the level of support from her father? The answer is, not too much: the θ coefficient is modest ($\theta = .16$). However, the finding should not be ignored and one can be confident of the finding ($p. = .001$).

Note that the test of significance used with this distribution was the Kruskal-Wallis H Test, which is appropriate for nominal ordinal distributions with more than two nominal categories. The Mann-Whitney U Test could not have been used with this distribution because it is limited to the nominal/ordinal situation with a dichotomous nominal variable.

Table 4.3
Health Concerns Related to Age

Age Group	Physical	Mental	Life-style	None	Total (Nos.)
	Health Concerns (Percentages)				
29 and under	17.36	8.21	31.05	43.39	2,535
30–39	19.72	13.71	24.43	42.15	1,846
40–49	23.73	12.92	19.50	43.85	805
50–59	33.84	13.41	16.16	36.59	328
60–69	43.85	8.33	9.90	38.02	192
70–79	51.70	7.48	10.88	29.93	147
80 and above	58.06	3.23	—	38.71	31

$p. = .0001$ (Chi square test of significance)
Contingency coefficient (C) = .225 (see text)

[The data below are presented after percentages were converted to raw data and the table rotated]

Health Concerns Related to Age

Health Concerns	29 & under	30–39	40–49	50–59	60–69	70–79	80 and above	Total
				Age Group				
Physical	440	364	191	111	84	76	18	1,284
Mental	208	253	104	44	16	11	1	637
Life-style	787	451	157	53	19	16	—	1,483
None	1,100	778	353	120	73	44	12	2,480
Total	2,535	1,846	805	328	192	147	31	5,884

$\theta = .16$

SOURCE: MacRae & Johnson (1986, table 7).
NOTES: Number of variables: Two
Level of measurement: Ordinal and nominal
Symmetric or asymmetric: Asymmetric
Sample or population: Population
Statistical procedures: Degree of association and test of significance (see text)

   Isabel MacRae and Barbara Johnson (1986) presented data on the relationship between health concerns and age in Canada in which employees of a large business firm completed a questionnaire identifying health priorities (see Table 4.3).

They used the contingency coefficient (C) and Chi square to analyze their data. It would have been more appropriate to analyze the data by use of θ as a measure of association. The reader may recall that the contingency coefficient tends to exaggerate the degree of association and assumes a nominal/nominal combination. Note in Table 4.3 that the contingency coefficient is .225; if C were standardized, the coefficient would be .25 (the upper limit of a 4 × 7 table would be .888, thus C~ = .225/.888 or .25).

Some would argue that the Chi square, as a test of significance, is inappropriate here because the data are derived from a population. Henkel (1976) notes that at least three different arguments have been advanced as meaningful interpretations when tests of significance are used with populations. One can assume that the data provide a "random sample" from some hypothetical universe composed of other populations like those at hand. One can also assume that the source of randomness in the data is due to random measurement error, thus testing to see whether or not the distribution could be explained by random measurement error, including errors in observation. The third argument advanced, the one mounted by Blalock (1981), is based on the assumption that the data might have been generated by some unspecified random process.

Had we desired to test whether or not the findings might be due to chance, the Kruskal-Wallis H test, along with theta, would have been a more appropriate method of analysis. Because the data are provided in percentages (Table 4.3), the actual calculation of θ had to be made after converting the percentages to cardinal numbers to obtain the raw data (see lower half of table). Using the raw data, θ turns out to be .16, not a strong correlation. From examination of the percentages, it is clear that physical health concerns could be readily predicted from age, but mental health concerns could not, nor could the absence of health concerns. Life-style concerns also show a clear trend by age.

Theta is a useful measure that has often been overlooked, and it is not included in the SPSS packages. Predicting order from nominal categories is a frequent type of distribution used by the helping professions, and in such cases θ should be the preferred measure.

NOMINAL/INTERVAL MEASURES OF ASSOCIATION AND TESTS OF SIGNIFICANCE

Eta and the Correlation Ratio; the F Test

There are only two measures of association specifically designed for nominal/interval data — eta (η) and its derivative, the correlation ratio (η^2). Pearson's r can be used with this combination if the nominal variable is dichotomous, because any dichotomous variable has the mathematical qualities of an interval variable (see Freeman, 1965, p. 120; Leege & Francis, 1974, p. 294; Mueller, Schuessler, & Costner, 1970; Nie et al., 1975, p. 373ff).

The asymmetric measure η is usually applied to the combination of an interval-level dependent variable and a nominal-level independent variable, although the prediction can also run the other way with the nominal-level variable dependent. If η is squared, it then has a PRE interpretation (i.e., it is an index of the proportion of variance in the dependent variable which is eliminated by taking the independent variable into account). Eta squared is called the correlation ratio. With a dichotomous-level nominal variable, the prediction line is linear, but η squared reflects linearity and curvilinearity equally well when the nominal variable has more than two categories. This is a useful property of η. As we will see in the next chapter, Pearson's correlation coefficient has the limiting assumption of linearity and requires transformation of data (e.g., logarithmic or exponential curves) if assumptions other than linearity are made.

When a scattergram or tabular presentation of data with nominal/interval variables suggests a nonlinear relationship, η or the correlation ratio is particularly useful. The use of η is preferable to reducing the interval data to nominal categories and using τ_y or Cramer's V. There is no symmetric form of η.

The correlation ratio and η are not used as frequently as they might be, and it is difficult to find an article in the human services literature that has made use of it, although a cursory review of recent articles from social work, education, and nursing journals suggests that it could have been used to advantage in several studies. Close (1983, p. 17) used η to advantage in a study of denial of equal access to child welfare services, comparing White, Black, and Hispanic groups (see Table 4.4).

To the question of whether or not there is equal access of Hispanics, Blacks, and Whites to services, one could conclude from Table 4.4 that

Table 4.4

Mean Number and Percentage of Contacts by Staff with Children and
Principle Child-caring Persons, by Racial Groups

Racial Groups	Contacts with the Children		Contacts With PCCPs[1]		Contacts with Children and PCCPs[1]		All Contacts with Client System	
	$\overline{X}$ No.	N	$\overline{X}$ No.	N	$\overline{X}$ No.	N	$\overline{X}$ No.	N
White	1.045	700	3.679	511	1.751	565	7.247	425
Black	.666	296	1.776	210	.862	227	2.857	153
Hispanic	1.099	80	1.494	65	1.162	72	3.336	54
Total	.937	1,076	2.990	786	1.469	864	5.849	632

Statistics $(df = 2)$:

F =	2.54	18.33	11.71	24.25
p. =	.08	.0001	.0001	.0001
η =	.064	.212	.163	.268
η^2 =	.004	.045	.027	.072

SOURCE: Slightly modified from Close (Winter, 1983, table 1, p. 17).
NOTES: The correlation ratio was not given in the table as it appears in the source article.
Number of variables: Four two-variable matrices
Level of measurement: Nominal and interval
Symmetric or asymmetric: Symmetric
Sample or population: Sample
Statistical procedures: Degree of association and test of significance
[1]PCCP = Principle Child-caring Person

there is a differential access to services, although the relationship is not
a strong one. The relationship between the number of staff contacts with
the client system (right-hand column) was marginally associated with
race (.27); only about 7% of the variance in number of contacts could
be predicted from race. Nevertheless the direction of the relationship is
clearly that Whites are favored over Hispanics, and Hispanics are
favored over Blacks. The test of significance suggests that one can be
confident in making this judgment about the population from which the
sample was obtained. Note that the F statistic and probability are given
for each relationship.

The F statistic has no apparent and obvious meaning in and of itself
in this instance, but it enables one to determine the significance of the
data by resorting to an F table (Appendix B, Table D). All except one
of the associations is significant at the .0001 level (1 in 10,000); the
relationship between racial group and contacts with children is slightly

Table 4.5

Ideological Orientation and Change in Per Capita Energy Consumption, 1950
to 1974, Nine Nations

Ideological Orientation	Change in per Capita Energy Consumption
Situational	
El Salvador	2.44
Haiti	.82
Iraq	5.43
Syria	5.02
Traditional	
Afghanistan	15.75
Ethiopia	14.50
Jordon	4.99
Saudi Arabia	4.95
Thailand	12.64

$\eta = .69$
Correlation ratio$(\eta^2) = .48$
$F = 8.33$ $p. = .05$

SOURCE: Author's data, drawing from categorical data on ideological orientation provided by Adelman and Morris (1971).
NOTES: Number of variables: Two
Level of measurement: Nominal and interval
Symmetric or asymmetric: Symmetric
Sample or population: Population
Statistical procedures: Degree of association and test of significance (for chance occurrence)

less (.08) than the conventional level arbitrarily determined to be significant (.05). (See Crane, 1976; Henkel, 1976, pp. 83–87; Leibowitz, 1968; Orme & Combs-Orme, 1986, for discussions of this arbitrary determination).

In another study by the author (unpublished) η and the correlation ratio were applied to energy consumption data compiled by the author combined with nominal variables used by Adelman and Morris (1971) to examine the relationship between ideology and energy consumption in selected countries. Energy consumption per capita is often used as an indicator of economic development.

In Table 4.5 these data are set forth as examples of distribution suitable for η and the correlation ratio. The nine nations are divided into two ideological orientations: situational and traditional, a nominal variable. The change in per capita energy consumption is an interval variable.

In applying η to this distribution, one can say that the association between the two variables is quite strong (.69). One can also say that nearly half (48%) of the variation in energy consumption can be predicted from knowing the ideological orientation of the nation. In other words, it is apparent that change in energy consumption per capita (economic development) is strongly related to ideological orientation. That is not the same thing as saying that ideological orientation directly brings about economic development.

What about a test of significance? Keep in mind that these were not data drawn from a sample. This is a population. In such instances one may want to answer the skeptic who suggests that this is a chance correlation that could be explained by some presumed nonpertinent variable, such as proportion of left-handed people in the nation. In such instances it is useful to provide the probability figure obtained from the F table to counter such arguments.

The F statistic for the distribution in Table 4.5 is 8.33. The probability, determined by consulting an F table (Appendix B, Table D), is .05 (i.e., the odds of obtaining this distribution by chance is 1 in 20 or 5 in 100). Therefore, one can have some confidence that, given the data and the size of population, this is not a chance distribution.

Nevertheless, one should examine the data closely and not just accept the indices as representing all one needs to know. It can be noted, for instance, that two of the traditional nations have a slightly lower change in energy consumption than two of the nations in the situational category. In order to determine whether or not ideological orientation is closely related to per capita energy consumption, additional cases are needed. Note the two different uses of the test of significance in these two sets of data (Tables 4.4 and 4.5).

Whether a population or sample, the appropriate test of significance for η or the correlation ratio is based on the analysis of variance, the F test statistic. Leege and Francis describe the calculation of F from the correlation ratio (1974, p. 328ff). This is easily programmed for calculator or computer, as is the η measure itself. The SPSS, SPSS-X, and SPSS/PC repertoire of measures of association include η. See Table 4.6 for a summary of nominal combinations.

Table 4.6

Measures of Association and Tests of Significance When One Variable is
Nominal and the Other Is Either Ordinal or Interval

Correlation Measure	Interpretation	Ties	Symmetry	Size of Table	Test of Significance
Nominal/Ordinal: If Nominal Variable Has Two Categories:					
θ	Predicts order from nominal classification	Takes into account	>	$2 \times n$	Mann-Whitney U Test
Nominal/Ordinal: If Nominal Variable Has More Than Two Categories:					
θ	Predicts order from nominal classification	Takes into account	>	$n \times n$	Kruskal-Wallis H Test

Correlation Measure	Attributes/ Interpretation	Size of Table	Test of Significance
Nominal/Interval:			
η	Reflects linear relationship	$2 \times n$	F Test
η	Reflects linear and curvilinear relationship	$n \times n$	F Test
η^2 is PRE interpretation $2 \times n$ or $n \times n$ tables (correlation ratio)			F Test
Pearson's correlation coefficient (r)			F Test

Theta is also called Freeman's coefficient of differentiation (see Freeman, 1965; Harshbarger, 1977; or Leege & Francis, 1974).

WHEN BOTH VARIABLES ARE ORDINAL

Ranked Data: Spearman's Rho

There are five common measures of association for ordinal-level relationships in which no distinction is made between dependent and independent variables (symmetric relationships). The best known to most people in social and behavioral science is Spearman's rho (ρ). The

Greek symbol for rho is ρ. Some writers designate it as either r prime (r') or r with a subscript s standing for Spearman (r_s). Spearman's ρ is the commonly used measure when individual cases are ranked on two attributes, preferences, or responses, or when two individuals (or groups) are ranked on the same attributes, preferences, or responses. Spearman's ρ is a product-moment correlation (like Pearson's correlation coefficient) for ranked data. It also has a PRE interpretation (ρ^2) which is seldom, if ever, used.

Spearman's ρ loses its effectiveness as a measure of association as the number of tied ranks increases. The existence of a few ties is not problematic, but a substantial number of ties will exaggerate the magnitude of ρ. In such instances a correction can be applied (see Siegel, 1965, pp. 202–210), or the data can be cast into ordinal categories and one of the other ordinal/ordinal measures substituted (see also Nie et al., 1975, for note on corrections for ties with Spearman's ρ). The SPSS/PC package does not include ρ.

Rho (r_s or ρ) is a symmetric measure and r_s^2 or ρ^2 is the PRE interpretation of it. Rho provides an index of the direction of the association and will yield a positive coefficient if ranks are similar on two variables and a negative coefficient if ranks are reversed.

Berlin and Jones (1983) made use of Spearman's ρ in their study of terminated AFDC (Aid for Families of Dependent Children) recipients in determining the relationship between employment status after termination and several other variables. Challis and Shepherd (1983) used ρ to determine the similarity between psychologists and social workers in assessing mentally handicapped patients.

McGrath (1986) studied family functioning in families where the husband or the wife had suffered a myocardial infarction. The husbands and wives rated their level of functioning after the heart attack in various areas of functioning (see Table 4.7). McGrath was interested in determining whether couples reported similar perspectives on their functioning. Table 4.7 provides the data on one couple.

The table reveals a fairly high correlation ($\rho = .55$) between spouses in ranking the relative levels of family functioning. Because this was a population, not a sample, the concern is that posed by the skeptic: could this have been a chance occurrence? Given the number of areas ranked and the fact that there are only two closely related subjects, the similarity in ranking is not a particularly unusual event as revealed by the probability figure, $p. = .15$ (i.e., the possibility of this distribution being a chance occurrence cannot be ruled out).

Table 4.7

Comparison of Family Functioning Level by areas of Functioning for
Husbands and Wives after Heart Attack

Area of Functioning	Rank Order of Level of Functioning Husband	Wife
Family relationships	8	8
Individual behavior	4.5	7
Care of children	4.5	3.5
Social activities	7	5.5
Economic conditions	3	2
Home and household	1	5.5
Health conditions	2	1
Use of community resources	6	3.5

$\rho = .55$ $t = 1.60$ $p. = .15$ (approximately)

SOURCE: Data from McGrath (1986, table E.20, p. 368).
NOTES: Number of variables: Two
Level of measurement: Ordinal/ordinal
Symmetric or asymmetric: Symmetric
Sample or population: Population
Statistical procedures: Degree of association and test of significance (for chance occurrence)

Dunster (1978) wanted to determine whether or not Australian mayors, town clerks (municipal administrators), and social workers viewed the functions of social work in different ways. She found that they did. Table 4.8 presents data on items ranked by three different municipal officials. The use of Spearman's ρ enables us to determine how closely the three municipal functionaries ranked the importance of various social work activities.

Mayors and town clerks were more similar in views with each other about the priority of functions than they were with social workers. There were actually 17 items on the scale. Only seven have been included here to avoid some of the ties. With fewer items to rank, it becomes more difficult to obtain a significant probability index. Actually, when Dunster included all items, the distributions were significant. With the small number of cases included here, only one of the relationships proved to be statistically significant, that between the town clerks and mayors ($p. = .04$).

In her study of attitudes about age and death anxiety, Roberta Greene (1983) obtained data from two groups of social workers, one group practicing with a geriatric caseload and the other group with a nongeriatric caseload. Greene examined their preferences in working with

Table 4.8

Priority of Social Work Functions as Ranked by Mayors, Social Workers, and Town Clerks in Municipal Councils

| | | Average Rank by | |
Social Work Functions	Mayors	Social Workers	Town Clerks
Collecting and providing information	3.5	1	1.5
Identifying and assessing needs	1	2	3
Developing programs	5	3	5.5
Administering welfare section	2	4	1.5
Acting as linkage agent	6	5	7
Encouraging and assisting community groups	7	6	5.5
Monitoring services/evaluating programs	3.5	7	4

Mayors and social workers	$\rho = .47$	$t = 1.19$	$p. = .25$[1]
Mayors and town clerks	$\rho = .79$	$t = 2.88$	$p. = .04$[1]
Social workers and town clerks	$\rho = .52$	$t = 1.36$	$p. = .23$[1]

SOURCE: Dunster (1978, p. 126).
NOTES: Number of variables: Two
Level of measurement: Ordinal/ordinal
Symmetric or asymmetric: Symmetric
Sample or population: Population
Statistical procedures: Degree of association and test of significance (for chance occurrence)
[1] Approximate: interpolated from the t table.

six client populations: frail elderly, middle-aged widows, cancer patients, young married couples, disturbed children, and adolescent offenders. The two samples (drawn randomly from national association membership) differed considerably in their preferences for working with the various groups (see Table 4.9). Although she presented the data in a form for computing Spearman's ρ, she did not cite the index nor the significance level of the distribution.

Both groups of social workers ranked middle-aged widows as second preference and ranked adolescent offenders as a low (but not identical) preference. Otherwise their preferences were considerably different. The Spearman ρ coefficient on this distribution is .09, not a close correlation between rankings; on the other hand note that it is not a negative correlation. The t value for this distribution was too small to show up on the probability table. In summary, the two groups did differ appreciably on preference for practice with some client populations, but the distribution is not statistically significant. It should be noted that the rankings given in Table 4.9 are aggregate rankings for approxi-

Table 4.9

Preferential Ranking of Six Client Populations by Two Groups
of Social Workers

Rank		Social Workers in Aging (geriatric caseload)	Social Workers in Nonaging (nongeriatric caseload)
Most preferable	1	Frail elderly	Young married couples
	2	Middle-aged widows	Middle-aged widows
	3	Cancer patients	Disturbed children
	4	Young married couples	Frail elderly
	5	Disturbed children	Adolescent offenders
Least preferable	6	Adolescent offenders	Cancer patients

$\rho = .09$; $p.$ = not significant.

SOURCE: Adapted from Green (1983, pp. 55-69).
NOTES: Number of variables: Two
Level of measurement: Ordinal/ordinal
Symmetric or asymmetric: Asymmetric
Sample or population: Sample
Statistical procedures: Degree of association and test of significance (for chance occurrence)

mately 200 workers with a geriatric caseload and 200 workers with a
nongeriatric caseload.

Symmetric Ordinal Categories: Gamma, Kendall's Tau$_a$ and Tau$_b$

When data on two ordinal variables are grouped and given in categorical order (as contrasted to ranks), we want to determine whether or
not the relative positions of categories on two scales go together: will
knowing the order of categories on one variable help us predict the order
of the categories on the other variable? There are several measures
available for this type of analysis: Kendall's τ_a, Kendall's τ_b, Stuart's
τ_c (based on Kendall's work), and gamma (γ). These are all measures
of association for symmetric relationships. There is also a symmetric
version of Somer's d, but because it is the only symmetric measure for
ordinal/ordinal data, it will be discussed separately. Kendall's τ_a and τ_b,
Stuart's τ_c, and γ are based on the notion of concordance, discordance,
and ties of pairs (i.e., pairs of observations). Pairs that are ranked in the
same order on two variables are considered concordant pairs; pairs that
are ranked in the opposite order on both variables are considered to be
discordant pairs. It is also possible to determine the ties that occur with
the first variable but not on the second; ties that occur with the second
variable but not on the first; and finally, ties on both variables. The

computation of an index is a ratio of these elements, and the rationale for them can be found in a number of texts (see Blalock, 1981, p. 433ff; Leege & Francis, 1974, p. 298ff; Leonard, 1976, p. 298ff; Loether & McTavish, 1980, p. 227).

There are some idiosyncracies with these measures that must be mentioned. Kendall's τ_a is not standardized if there are ties and is useful and appropriate only when no ties exist. τ_b takes ties into account, is standardized and suitable for square tables ($r = c$). τ_c makes an adjustment for ties and is appropriate for all size tables, but Blalock (1981, p. 441) and Loether and McTavish (1980, p. 236) note difficulties in interpreting it. Therefore I have not included it in the discussions that follow.

Gamma (γ — sometimes given in upper case, Γ) does not take ties into account but is appropriate for all size tables; it can reach 1.00 even if the table is not square (Leonard, 1976, p. 305; Loether & McTavish, 1980, p. 238; Mueller, Schuessler & Costner, 1970, p. 286). Although versatile in terms of the size of tables, it has a less restrictive version of perfect association than do the other ordinal measures and requires careful study if it is to be adopted. Yule's Q, with a similar restrictive version of perfect association discussed in the last chapter, is a special case of γ, applied to dichotomous data. An extensive discussion of these measures can be found in Loether and McTavish (1980, p. 227ff) and in Blalock (1981, pp. 439–443). As will be demonstrated below, γ can attain the upper limit of 1.00 (or −1.00) even when cases do not fall exclusively in the diagonal cells (i.e., when the ordered categories do not correspond exactly).

McGrath (1986), in her study of factors related to adjustment after a heart attack, examined a number of variables related to family functioning. One variable was number of days in the hospital. Table 4.10 provides these data.

If we consider this to be a symmetric relationship (i.e., no distinction is made between dependent and independent variables), γ is an appropriate index of the degree of relationship. There was a moderately substantial correlation between levels of individual adjustment after the heart attack and number of days in the hospital ($\gamma = .21$): the longer the hospitalization, the poorer the adjustment of the patient. With only 13 cases we cannot have too much confidence in this finding — it may be a chance occurrence ($p. = .38$). Actually McGrath considered it to be an asymmetric relationship and used Somer's d as an index. Note in Table 4.10 that some cases do not fall in the diagonal cells. With most

Table 4.10

Relationship Between Days in Hospital and Individual Behavior and
Adjustment After the Heart Attack

Level of Individual Behavior and Adjustment	*Number of Days in Hospital*			
	1–10	*11–20*	*21 +*	*Total*
Most	3	0	1	4
In Between	2	2	0	4
Least	4	1	0	5
Total	9	3	1	13

$\gamma = .21$ $z = .32$ $p. = .38$

Asymmetric d = .15 $z = .23$ $p. = .41$

SOURCE: McGrath (1975, p. 363).
NOTES: Number of variables: Two
Level of measurement: Ordinal/ordinal
Symmetric or asymmetric: Symmetric
Sample or population: Population
Statistical procedures: Degree of association and test of significance (for chance occurrence)

measures we would expect a correlation of 1.00 (or –1.00) only if all cases fall in the diagonal. This is not the case with γ. To illustrate this idiosyncrasy, some hypothetical distributions will be used to demonstrate the less restrictive features of γ (see Figure 4.1).

Without changing the row totals in Figure 4.1, the cases have been shifted to represent several different distributions in order to examine γ as an index of association. With two cases falling outside the diagonal (i.e., outside cells c, e, and g), the index is 1 ($\gamma = 1.00$). With three cases outside the diagonal, the index drops to .96; and with four cases outside the diagonal, it drops to .91. Note that Somer's d, the asymmetric version, is consistently lower than γ, as we would expect. Cramer's V, an inappropriate measure for the data, has a lower index than either γ or Somer's d because cases are distributed outside the diagonal. This is no longer the case when seven cases fall outside the diagonal. V does not take order into account and loses its effectiveness with ordered data as the distribution becomes more diffuse. This illustration should alert the reader to some of the vagaries of γ, particularly at the upper levels of association and the inappropriate use of V with ordered data.

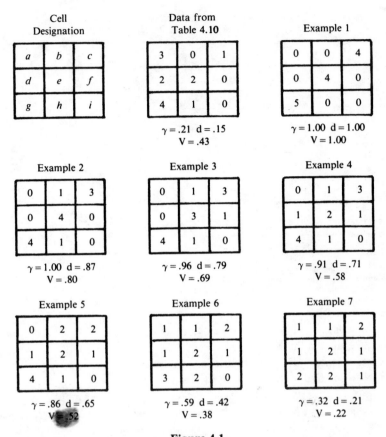

Figure 4.1
Illustration of variations in the gamma index with different distributions.

Asymmetric Ordinal Categories: Somer's d

When we wish to distinguish between dependent and independent variables, we use the asymmetric version of Somer's d for ordinal/ordinal combinations. It takes into account the number of tied pairs on the dependent variable and is a versatile index. It can be used on any size table. Somer's d has a PRE interpretation. When using this measure, it is important to identify the dependent and independent variables because a different coefficient is likely to result, depending on which

Table 4.11

Number of Children in Family by Degree of Poverty

Degree of Poverty	Number of Children in Family				Total	
	Two or Less		Three or More			
	No.	%	No.	%	No.	%
Very poor	17	7.5	26	36.6	43	14.5
Poor	26	11.6	25	35.2	51	17.2
Near poor	182	80.9	20	28.2	202	68.3
Total	225	100.0	71	100.0	296	100.0

Asymmetric d = −.41   z = −2.77   p. = .003

SOURCE: Study by Sue Picot; unpublished.
NOTES: Number of variables: Two
Level of measurement: Ordinal/ordinal
Symmetric or asymmetric: Asymmetric
Sample or population: Population
Statistical procedures: Degree of association and test of significance (for chance occurrence)

variable is considered dependent. In fact, Loether and McTavish (1980, p. 236) suggest that τ_b can be expressed as the square root of the product of two Somer's d's computed each way. Note that the SPSS packages include an asymmetric version of Somer's d.

Table 4.11 presents data suitable for use of ordinal measures when ordinal variables are grouped and given in categorical order. Because we are considering it to be an asymmetrical relationship, γ is not used here. You may have noticed in Table 4.10, and in Figure 4.1, that γ was higher than Somer's d. This is another example of the fact that prediction from one variable to the other is more difficult than just predicting that two variables will be closely associated. In other words, the asymmetric measure is more stringent than symmetric measures. Asymmetric Somer's d is a measure of how well we can predict the degree of poverty if we know the number of children in the family.

In Table 4.11 it is clear that the two variables are closely related, and by knowing the number of children in the family, we can predict with some accuracy the degree of poverty likely to exist in the family, and we can be confident in accepting the relationship as a real one (p. =

.003). As reflected in Table 4.11, 7.5% of families with one or two children were very poor, but 36% of families with three or more children were very poor. More of the larger families also fell in the poor category than the small families. The large families were less likely than the small families to fall in the near poor category.

All of the ordinal/ordinal measures discussed have negative and positive versions; that is, they can range from a negative 1.00 through zero, if there is no association, to a positive 1.00 (−1.00 to 1.00) if the association is perfect. Only Somer's d has both a symmetric and asymmetric version and, given its versatility, is certainly the preferred measure for ordered categories. Spearman's ρ is the preferred measure for straightforward ranking, unless there are a substantial number of tied ranks.

Tests of Significance: t Test and z Test

The test of significance for ρ is either z or t. Leonard provides a formula for computing t from ρ (Leonard, 1976, p. 313). Some electronic calculator programs provide z for ρ. The test of significance for the other ordinal/ordinal measures is z, and again, Leonard provides calculations that can easily be programed for calculator or computer.

ORDINAL/INTERVAL MEASURE OF ASSOCIATION AND TEST OF SIGNIFICANCE

Jaspen's M and the F Test

What if we want to determine the association between an ordinal variable and an interval variable? Jaspen's M (coefficient of multiserial correlation) is an appropriate measure if the relationship is linear. M is described by Freeman (1965, p. 131ff) and Leege and Francis (1974, p. 303ff). It is a special version of Pearson's r. One could use it, for instance, with scaled attitude (ordinal) data and an interval scale variable. However, it is rarely used. I could find no example of it in the recent literature in social work, education, or nursing.

A test of significance can be obtained for distributions using Jaspen's M, if the data are from a random sample, by use of the F value and F tables (Leege & Francis, 1974, p. 338ff). Because it is rarely used, I will simply draw attention to Jaspen's M.

The F statistic, however, is frequently used as a test of significance in distributions with an interval variable. As we have seen, it can be used with η, the correlation ratio, and M. It is also used with Pearson's r and the statistics applied to distributions where interval/interval level variables are analyzed.

The F statistic is a ratio derived from the Analysis of Variance (ANOVA) procedure. It is a complex test but is easily programmed for computation. The Analysis of Variance carries an assumption that the data are derived from a random sample. It is described in most of the statistical texts in social and behavioral science cited in this book and is included in the Sage monograph series on quantitative applications in the social sciences (Iversen & Norpoth, 1976).

The Analysis of Variance involves a computation of the sums of squares between and within categories of the nominal or ordinal variables, and it is the ratio of these two sums, taking the degrees of freedom into account, that yields F. It is a test of differences in central tendencies that is based on a comparison of variances. Consulting an F table provides a probability figure. It is a powerful tool for analyzing data, including controlled experiments, but one should not use it in testing the significance of a sample without studying it thoroughly. (See Andrews, Morgan & Sonquist, 1969, chap. 1, 2, & 6; Blalock, 1981, chap. 16; Iverson & Norpoth, 1976; Leonard, 1976, chap. 11; Loether & McTavish, 1980, chap. 15, for a thorough discussion of this important measure; but keep in mind that it is a test of significance, not a measure of association).

The Analysis of Variance, ANOVA, can be used with one independent variable or in the multivariate situation. The independent variables can be nominal or ordinal with the dependent variable at the interval-level of measurement. It is called a one-way analysis of variance if only one independent variable is involved.

Wodarski (1986) used the F Test in testing the differences between experimental and control groups in a study of the effects of traditional and social learning techniques on drinking patterns of adolescents.

In this section of the chapter we have discussed various ordinal combinations and the measures of association and tests of significance appropriate for this type of data. See Table 4.12 for a summary of the ordinal measures.

Table 4.12

Measures of Association and Tests of Significance When One Variable Is
Ordinal and the Other Is Either Ordinal or Interval

Ordinal/Ordinal Ranked Data

Measure of Association	Interpretation	Symmetry	Ties	Size of Table	Test of Significance
			Interpretation, Symmetry, Ties, Size of Table, and Associated Tests of Significance		
rho	Difference between 2 ranks	<>	Problematic[1]	$2 \times n$	z or t
rho^2	PRE interpretation	<>	Problematic[1]	$2 \times n$	z or t

Ordinal/Ordinal Ordered Categories

Tau_a	PRE among all	<>	Cannot have ties	$n \times n$	z
Tau_b	PRE[2]	<>	Can have ties on one variable; not on both	$r = c$	z
Tau_c	PRE[2]	<>	Can have ties	$n \times n$	z
Gamma (γ)[3]	PRE[4]	<>	Excludes or ignores ties	$n \times n$	z
Somer's d	PRE among predicted pairs	<> and >	Takes account of ties	$n \times n$	z

Ordinal/Interval Relationships

Correlation Measure	Test of Significance
Jaspen's M (Coefficient of multiserial correlation)	F Test

[1]Can be corrected for ties (Siegel, 1956, pp. 202ff, 206–210).
[2]Ties on both variables considered to be trivial (Loether & McTavish, 1980, p. 235).
[3]Has a less restricted version of perfect association.
[4]Though Loether and McTavish suggest that interpretation as PRE measure is difficult (1980, p. 236).

STATISTICAL PROCEDURES IN
SINGLE-SUBJECT DESIGNS

In recent years there have been increasing use and interest in single-case research in education, social work, psychology, and psychiatry

(Nelson, 1984) and more recently in combining data across several studies using this technique (Nurius, 1984). Incorporating such designs in the everyday practice of social work settings has been emphasized in the professional social work research journals (Schilling et al., 1988) and recent research methodology texts (Grinnell, 1985; Schuerman, 1983a).

The use of computers in single-subject research has also been prominent in recent literature (Benbenishty & Ben-Zaken, 1988; Clark, 1988; Finn, 1988) as a way of providing a more economical means of analyzing both visual and statistical data (Bronson & Blythe, 1987).

Single-subject designs are ordinarily bivariate with a dependent (outcome) variable and an independent (intervention) variable. These variables could be nominal, ordinal, or interval. For this reason statistical procedures in single-subject research are discussed in this chapter.

The emphasis in the last few years in the social work literature on single-subject experiments has given rise to discussions about the use of statistics in evaluating outcomes of intervention with single cases (e.g., individuals, groups, units) for the individual practitioner. At this point the matter is in much dispute, with some writers arguing that visual inspection of carefully constructed graphic representations is more appropriate than statistical tests of significance (Baer, 1977a; Paronson & Baer in Kratochwill, 1978) but other writers recommend the use of statistics wherever possible (Bloom & Fischer, 1982).

Gingerich (in Rosenblatt & Waldfogel, 1983) distinguishes between applied and experimental significance. Similarly, Gambrill (1983) distinguishes between experimental criteria of change, reflected in tests of significance, and practice criteria, reflected in evaluation of whether or not changes have made a difference to clients themselves and to significant others (see also Gold, 1969, p. 44; Hudson, 1982; Hudson, Thyer & Storks, 1985). Gambrill also notes that statistical significance is not necessarily correlated with clinical significance: You can have a statistically significant change with no change of import or consequence to the client (or group), and you can have a change that is important to the client which is not statistically significant (Gambrill, 1983, p. 340). While this is certainly true, it can also be argued that clinical expectations can be built into the statistical test (White, in Keogh, 1984, p. 88).

Most investigators would recommend the use of charts (line graphs) and pragmatic (clinical, practical) criteria in evaluating change resulting from intervention, but Paronson and Baer see charting as the primary source on which decisions are based in the single-subject experiment (in Kratochwill, 1978). White (in Keogh, 1984) points out some of the pitfalls in drawing conclusions from charted data without careful analysis. He illustrates, by use of line charts, instances in which graphs, supplemented by statistical analysis, clarified findings that would have otherwise been misinterpreted (see also Kazdin, 1979). Statistical tests may temper findings that would otherwise be exaggerated or underestimated.

For examples of charting see the study by Wong, Woolsley, & Gallegas (1986) in a study of treatment of chronic psychiatric patients and the study by Thomas and his associates (1986) on the use of therapy with spouses of alcoholics. Pinkston, Howe, & Blackman (1986) used charting to good effect in their study of managing urinary incontinence in the elderly (see also, Edleson, 1985).

Various authors suggest additional procedures that are over and above charting and pragmatic considerations. These include first difference transformations and moving average transformations (Bloom & Fischer, 1982), the two-standard deviation method (Bloom & Block, 1977a, 1977b; Gottman & Leiblum, 1974; Jayaratne, 1978), randomization tests (Edgington, 1975a; 1975b), and the Philip method (Philip, 1969). The t Test and Analysis of Variance and Time Series Analysis are also suggested by Jayaratne (1978).

Some of the problems arising from the use of statistical procedures with the single-subject experiment revolve around assumptions inherent in the use of those procedures: independence of observations, as in the binomial distribution (Hudson, 1977; Loftus & Levy, 1977), data originating from a random sample, and the related assumption that the baseline data are normally distributed (Hudson, 1977; Jayaratne, 1978). Various devices are suggested for handling the problem of auto-correlation (Hudson, 1977; Jayaratne, 1978; and others). Serious questions are raised about sampling problems by Baer (1977a, 1977b).

It is not always clear in the single-subject experiment whether baseline data are a sample, and if so, whether or not the data are random. For investigators wishing to use statistical tests, assuming a random sample, this is a difficult case to make (see Schuerman, 1983a, pp. 56–58).

It would be remiss not to chart data generated from single-subject experiments and slipshod not to study the charts carefully. Nevertheless visual inspection of line graphs is not foolproof (see De Prospero & Cohen, 1979), and statistical procedures may be useful in augmenting them, as noted by White (in Keogh, 1984) and Kazdin (1979). Baer provides an extensive discussion of the analysis and presentation of graphic data (in Kratochwill, 1978) as does Gingerich (in Rosenblatt & Waldfogel, 1983).

For a combined use of charting and statistical analysis, see Rani Benbenishty's study of task-centered intervention with families (1988), Sharon Berlin's study of relapse-prevention (1985), and Marsh and Shibano's article on clinical time-series data (1984).

Students interested in this problem should consult the citations given in these paragraphs and keep up with the most recent literature in this area. Unlike most of the statistical problems and procedures discussed in this chapter, tests of significance for single-subject data have had relatively little exploration. It is not possible in this chapter to do justice to the questions raised nor to suggest specific measures for analysis of the single-subject study. In the summary charts, I have not included the statistical procedures discussed under single-subject designs except in those instances when they apply as well to other study designs.

Chapter 5

BIVARIATE AND MULTIVARIATE DISTRIBUTIONS WITH INTERVAL- AND NOMINAL-LEVEL DATA

We turn now to indices for the interval level of measurement, first for two-variable situations, then for distributions involving three or more variables. Interval data permit greater statistical precision than is possible with ordinal and nominal data and enable us to ask more definitive questions about the relationship between two variables. Unless both variables are interval scales, it is difficult to do any more than describe how closely categories of one variable correspond with categories of another or how well one can predict values of one variable from another.

INTERVAL/INTERVAL MEASURES OF ASSOCIATION AND DERIVATIVE INDICES (TWO VARIABLES)

Pearson's Correlation Coefficient and Regression Analysis

Central to any discussion of correlation with interval data is Pearson's r. We have discussed PRE measures earlier, and Pearson's correlation coefficient r, is just such a measure, one that is well known and used widely in social science research. Less well known are some of the statistical indices related to the correlation coefficient that provide additional and, generally, more useful indices: coefficients of determination, and regression coefficients. The term *coefficient* refers to a

Table 5.1

Relationship Between Independent Variable X and Dependent Variable Y
for Subjects A to M.

Cases/ Subjects	Dependent Variable X	Dependent Variable Y	Prediction Error
A	0.6	0.8	− .92
B	0.8	1.2	− .86
C	1.2	3.6	.84
D	1.2	2.2	− .56
E	1.8	4.0	.21
F	2.6	7.0	1.82
G	2.6	5.0	− .18
H	2.8	5.4	− .12
I	3.0	6.0	.13
J	3.8	7.6	.35
K	4.0	8.6	1.00
L	5.0	8.8	.53
M	5.4	8.8	−1.22

$r = .95$ $r^2 = .91$ $\alpha = .68$ $\beta = 1.73$ $F = 106.52$ $p. = .0001$

Regression equation for two variables: $Y = \alpha + \beta X$. The equation for this distribution is $Y = .68 + 1.73X$. Using this equation, if $X = 1$, $Y = 2.41$; if $X = 4$, $Y = 7.60$. This establishes two points to enable us to draw the regression line on a graph.
Number of variables: Two
Level of measurement: Interval
Symmetric or asymmetric: Asymmetric
Sample or population: Hypothetical data
Statistical procedures: Degree of association, coefficients of determination, regression coefficient, and test of significance

number that serves as a measure of some property or characteristic and in this book it is used as a synonym of index.

In examining the relationship between two interval-level variables, we are interested in the degree of association (the correlation coefficient), whether the association is positive or negative, the amount of variance in the dependent variable that can be attributed to the independent variable (the coefficient of determination), and the amount of change in the dependent variable that can be attributed to each unit of change in the independent variable (the regression coefficient or the beta weight). Fortunately these four abstract statistical attributes can be visually examined by use of a table and a scattergram.

Tables 5.1 and 5.2 present hypothetical data showing the relationship between an independent (X) and a dependent (Y) variable, and these data

Table 5.2

Relationship Between Independent Variable X and Dependent Variable Y
for Subjects N to Z

Cases/ Subjects	Independent Variable X	Dependent Variable Y	Prediction Error
N	2.0	1.8	−.63
O	2.1	2.2	−.27
P	2.3	3.4	.85
Q	2.9	3.4	.62
R	3.2	2.6	−.30
S	3.9	3.0	−.17
T	4.1	3.2	−.05
U	4.9	3.6	.04
V	5.0	3.8	.20
W	5.6	3.2	−.63
X	5.9	4.0	.05
Y	6.2	4.0	−.07
Z	6.6	4.6	.38

$r = .82$ $r^2 = .68$ $\alpha = 1.65$ $\beta = .39$ $F = 23.02$ $p. = .0006$

NOTES: The regression equation for two variables: $Y = \alpha + \beta X$. The equation for this distribution is $Y = 1.65 + .39X$. Using this equation, if $X = 1$, $Y = 2.04$; if $X = 6$, $Y = 3.99$. This establishes two points to enable us to draw the regression line on a graph.
Number of variables: Bivariate
Level of measurement: Interval
Symmetric or asymmetric: Asymmetric
Sample or population: Hypothetical data
Statistical procedures: Degree of association, coefficients of determination, regression coefficient and test of significance

are presented in scattergrams (Figures 5.1 and 5.2). The tables and scattergrams will be used to illustrate these four statistical abstractions.

Two additional concepts must be introduced to complete the picture: the method of least squares and a functional form (or equation) that reflects the prediction relationship between the two variables.

An examination of the data in the tables should provide the reader with some basic information about the relationship between the dependent and independent variables. Tables 5.1 and 5.2 show a close and positive relationship between the two variables. It is possible, by studying the data carefully, that you can see that one distribution (Table 5.1) has a stronger correlation than the other (Table 5.2), and this is reflected in the correlation coefficients (.95 compared with .82). By careful examination you can also see that the change in the dependent variable

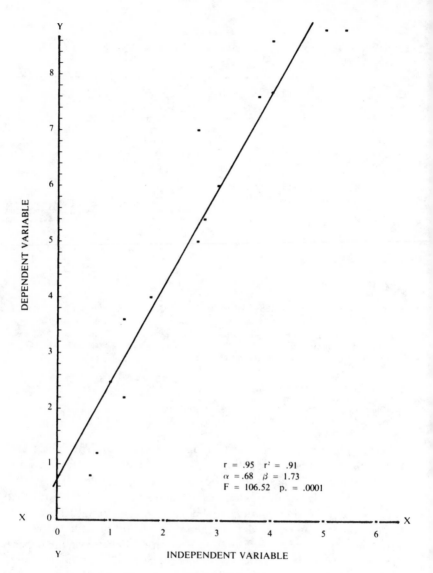

Figure 5.1
Relationship between independent variable *X* and dependent variable *Y*
for subjects A to M.

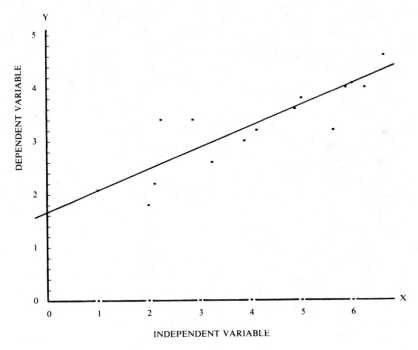

NOTE: $r = .82$, $r^2 = .68$, $\alpha = 1.65$, $\beta = .39$, $F = 23.02$, and $p. = .0006$.

Figure 5.2
Relationship between independent variable X and dependent variable Y
for subjects N to Z.

in Table 5.1 is greater for each unit of change in the independent variable than it is in Table 5.2.

If you study the data in Table 5.1 carefully, you can see that for each subject the value of Y is roughly twice that of X. The regression equation reflects this: beta (β) approaches 2.00 (actually 1.73). If, for each unit of change in X there was a unit change in Y, β would be 1.00 and would be represented by a 45° angle on the graph. This is much easier to grasp, however, with a visual picture in the form of a scattergram.

Scattergrams and the Method of Least Squares

To obtain a visual picture of these relationships, we need a scattergram (Figures 5.1 and 5.2). A scattergram provides two axes with the independent variable on the horizontal scale and the dependent variable on the vertical scale; each dot represents the values of the two variables for each particular case or subject. For example, subject A falls at .6 on the horizontal scale and at .8 on the vertical scale Figure 5.1.

The scattergram in Figure 5.1 shows clearly that there is a close association between the two variables. By inspection we could draw a straight line to graphically represent the relationship. If N is small, this is not difficult. If N is large, data are dispersed, or there are extreme values, it becomes problematic. However, there is a mathematical way of determining the best fitting line, called the method of least squares.

The method of least squares allows us to establish the line of best fit, as we have done in Figures 5.1 and 5.2. This line can be represented by an equation with the form $Y = \alpha + \beta X$. Each distribution will have a line of best fit that enables one to predict (with less error than any other line) the values of Y, given the values of X (Blalock, 1981, p. 381ff). The derivation of the two unknowns in the equation, α and β, will be discussed below, and their use in the prediction equation will be explained.

Both from the table and the scattergram, one can see that the correlation is strong, almost perfect, and is positive (i.e., high values of one variable correspond with high values of the other variable). This provides us with two attributes of the relationship: strength and direction. You should note that Pearson's r is a symmetrical index; if we reverse the dependent and independent variables, we would get the same value of r.

Coefficient of Determination

By squaring the correlation coefficient, we obtain the coefficient of determination (r^2) which is an index of the amount of variance in one variable that can be predicted from variation in the other (Blalock, 1981, p. 405ff; Edwards, 1967, p. 110; Johnson, 1977, p. 109; Leege & Francis, 1974, p. 310ff; Leonard, 1976, p. 324ff; Loether & McTavish, 1974, p. 26ff; Nie et al., 1975, p. 279). The regression equation has been used to fix a regression line on the graph. The slope of this line is important because it shows the magnitude of the change in Y for a unit change in X. An index can be calculated to represent this magnitude. It is called a beta coefficient. In other words, β is an index of the slope and indicates by how many units Y changes for one unit change in X. These β coefficients are an index of a directional or asymmetric prediction. Alpha is the point where the regression line crosses (or intercepts) the vertical axis (i.e., the value of Y when X is zero); it is also known as the "intercept" and in the SPSS/PC printout is listed as the *constant*.

Now let us look at the other distribution (Table 5.2 and Figure 5.2) which is similar in direction to the preceding table and figure (being positive) and in having a strong association, but with a different functional form and a different slope. By careful examination of the table we can see that the dependent variable Y increases about one-half unit (somewhat less) for each unit increase in the independent variable X for each subject. The relationship between the two variables will be quite different from that used in our prior illustration, although r is still strong. This is illustrated in Figure 5.2.

Figure 5.2 has a shallow regression line compared with the steep line in Figure 5.1. For each unit of change in X, Y is increased less than half a unit (.39). The impact of X in this example is not nearly as great as the impact of X in the previous one. It turns out that regression coefficients (betas) are more useful than either the coefficient of determination or the correlation coefficient, if you want to measure the effects (or impact) on the dependent variable from the independent variable.

Note that we have considered the regression line to be linear (i.e., a straight line). We shall discuss some transformations later in the chapter that can be made if the scattergram suggests that the best fitting line might not be linear.

It would be unusual to find the distribution given in Tables 5.1 and 5.2 and Figures 5.1 and 5.2. They are unusual in that the associations are nearly perfect and that one can predict the value of Y from X with little error, although there is some error as can be seen from both the tables (right-hand column) and the figures (the distance of each case from the regression line). There is always variation in Y that X fails to account for; this could be due to measurement or observation error or to variables other than X that are influencing Y. If all points were exactly on the regression line, we could predict values of Y, given values of X, with no error. The correlation coefficient, r, is an index of how closely these points fall on the regression line as well as an index of the strength of the association between the two variables.

To review briefly, Pearson's r provides us with an index of the strength of association, and the direction of the association and by squaring that index, we can determine the coefficient of determination (i.e., the amount of variance in one variable that can be predicted from another). The nature of the association and the impact of an independent variable on a dependent variable are determined by an additional step, regression analysis, which makes use of a prediction formula or equation. These regression equations (functional forms) enable us to predict the numerical value of a dependent variable (with some error) from the numerical value of an independent one. Blalock suggests that this is the most elegant and simplest way to express a relationship between two variables (Blalock, 1981, p. 383). Perhaps the use of an example is the best way to illustrate the regression equation.

Distinction Between the Correlation Coefficient, the Coefficient of Determination, and the Regression Coefficient

A clear distinction should be made between the correlation coefficient, the coefficient of determination, and the regression coefficient (β). The correlation coefficient, r, is an index of the degree of covariation (the extent to which two variables vary together (i.e., the strength of their relationship); the coefficient of determination, r^2, tells you how much of the variation in the dependent variable can be attributed to the independent variable; and the regression coefficient tells you the degree of impact of one variable on another (Johnson, 1977, p. 110); that is, an index of how many units Y tends to change when X is changed by one unit.

Let us look at some actual data and ask several questions about the relationship between two variables. In this instance, the researcher is interested in a possible link between increases in amount paid to employees, as a proportion of national income, and the proportion of the national income received by the highest income earners the following year. In other words, if salaries and wages increase overall in a nation in a given year, who benefits?

We know these two factors vary year by year. Level of compensation of employees is one part of the national income referred to by economists as *factor shares*. Other factor shares would be income from rent, income from interest, and income from dividends.

We would expect the highest income groups to benefit from an increased level of national income from rent, interest, and dividends, but we would expect them to have somewhat lower incomes if there is more paid out in salaries and wages (which is a good part of *compensation of employees*). The two sets of data come from two different sources. We will consider compensation of employees to be the independent variable and the share of the top 10% of income earners (top decile) as the dependent variable. Because factors like these take some

Table 5.3

Compensation of Employees as Proportion of National Income and the Share
of the National Income Received by the Top Decile in the Following Year,
United Kingdom, 1953 to 1967.

Year	Compensation of Employees (%) (X)	Year	Share of Top Decile (%) (Y)
1953	70.0	1954	30.6
1954	70.6	1955	30.2
1955	72.5	1956	29.8
1956	72.8	1957	29.6
1957	72.5	1958	29.4
1958	72.1	1959	29.4
1959	71.9	1960	28.6
1960	72.6	1961	27.2
1961	73.3	1962	28.2
1962	73.9	1963	28.0
1963	72.8	1964	29.8
1964	73.2	1965	27.6
1965	74.4	1966	28.0
1966	75.4	1967	26.4

(linear assumption)

$r = -.79$ $r^2 = .63$ $\alpha = 80.3$ $\beta = -.71$ $F = 20.2$ $p. = .0007$

SOURCE: Pilcher (1981).
The regression equation for two variables is $Y = \alpha + \beta X$. The equation for this distribution: $Y = 80.3 - .71X$. Using this equation, if $X = 70$, $Y = 30.69$; if $X = 75$, $Y = 27.15$. This establishes two points to enable us to fix the regression line on a graph.
Number of variables: Bivariate
Level of measurement: Interval
Symmetric or asymmetric: Asymmetric
Sample or population: Population
Statistical procedures: Degree of association, coefficients of determination, regression coefficient, and test of significance

time to have an impact, we lag the dependent variable by one year. Table 5.3 presents the data.

Analysis of a Set of Data

What can we learn from a regression analysis? Is the association between the two variables positive or negative? How strong is the association? What is the nature or form of the association? How much of the variation in the share of the top decile can be attributed to (or at least predicted from) the independent variable? What is the impact of the independent variable on the dependent variable? These are some of the questions we can ask about the relationship between two interval variables.

Table 5.3 demonstrates a strong but negative association ($r = -.79$). As compensation of employees increase as a proportion of national income, the share of the top decile drops. We can predict about 63% of the variation in the top decile share from the independent variable, compensation of employees ($r^2 = .63$), a substantial proportion of the variation in the dependent variable. You can see that the slope is fairly steep ($\beta = -.71$), indicating a considerable change in the top decile's share a year after the total compensation of employees (primarily wages and salaries) fluctuates.

Insofar as one independent variable has an impact on the dependent variable, one unit of change in compensation of employees brings about 71/100's of a unit change in top decile shares. However, there is considerable error in the prediction. Note particularly the year 1960 but several other years as well (see Figure 5.3). In addition, note the extreme values in the independent variable in 1966 and in 1953 and 1954. A few extreme values when N is small can produce a strong correlation where the correlation is weak among the remaining cases. If the three extreme cases were deleted from this distribution, the correlation coefficient drops to $-.46$; the coefficient of determination drops to .21; and β becomes $-.58$.

Note also that, with the exception of 1963, there is a considerable amount of clustering in contiguous years, and in fact, if one looks at 1955 through 1959, there is a positive correlation between the two variables! Again, with the exception of 1963, the other cluster (1960 through 1965) shows the same pattern. Often it is important to examine such clusters closely, as well as any deviant cases, so as to better understand the relationship and perhaps to provide a means of identifying mediating variables.

F Value as a Test of Probability

If the data from Table 5.3 (Figure 5.3) were from a random sample, we could ask an additional question about the association: how confident can we be that these data represent the population from which they are drawn? It is not a sample; therefore, we can ignore a test of significance or we can anticipate the skeptic by determining the likeli-

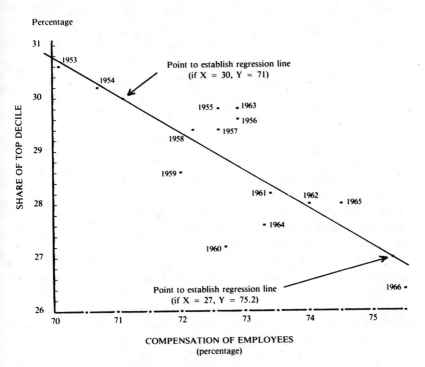

NOTE: $r = -.79$, $r^2 = .63$, $\alpha = 80.3$, $\beta = .71$, $F = 20.2$, and $p. = .0007$. The regression equation for two variables is $Y = \alpha + \beta X$. The equation for this distribution is $Y = 80.3 - .71X$. Using this equation, if $X = .71$, $Y = .30$; if $X = 75.2$, $Y = 27$. These two points enable us to fix the regression line accurately on the graph.

Figure 5.3
Compensation of employees as a proportion of the national income and
the share of the top decile of national income in the following year,
United Kingdom, 1953–1966 (linear assumption).

hood of obtaining this distribution by chance. We can compute an F
value with only two ingredients, r and N. In this case F turns out to be
20.2, and by reference to an F table, we can determine probability. (See
Table D in Appendix B, but note that it does not go beyond the .01 level.)
Actually, the SPSS/PC program provides a *p*. of .0007 on the basis of
the F Test, and our inclination is to dismiss the skeptic.

This cursory analysis of the data set for 14 years provides an illustration of the complexity of relationships between variables and the

danger of drawing conclusions prematurely. Blalock observes that a single summarizing measure, no matter how superior it may be to other measures, can often be misleading (Blalock, 1981, p. 403). There is no statistical substitute for understanding the variables and the phenomenon you are dealing with and studying the empirical data carefully. Clearly one needs more data before drawing firm conclusions about the relationship between compensation of employees and share of the top decile.

Importance of Scattergrams with Interval/Interval Data

Of particular importance in analyzing interval data is the construction of a scattergram. Scattergrams are constructed by hand or by computer on routine SPSS programs. A scattergram will enable the researcher to grasp the configuration of a relationship and determine whether or not a relationship between the two variables is actually linear. If it is not linear, there are several options available. Figure 5.4 illustrates three alternative data curves, incorporating transformation of one or both variables to a logarithmic scale.

If the X values are on a logarithmic scale and the Y values are on a linear scale, it is called an *exponential curve*. If the Y values are on a linear scale and the X variable is on a logarithmic scale, it is a *logarithmic curve*. If both X and Y values are on a logarithmic scale, it is called a *power curve*.

The formulas for these curves are given in Edwards (1967, p. 85ff). Curves using these transformations can be plotted on semilogarithmic or logarithmic paper. Use logarithmic paper for the power curve, plotting X and Y values as logarithms. Use semilogarithmic paper with X values on the linear scale and Y values on the logarithmic scale for exponential curves; and with Y values on the linear scale and X values on the logarithmic scale for logarithmic curves.

Computers and some electronic calculators can make this transformation for you (see the SPSS manuals). Some of the electronic calculators can be programmed and have a key for transforming linear data to logarithmic data. If two variables are involved and one variable can be logically reduced to a nominal scale, the correlation ratio can be used for nonlinear relationships (see Chapter 4).

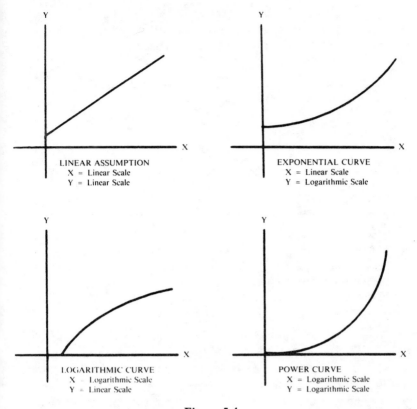

Figure 5.4
Curvilinear alternatives to linear assumptions derived from transforming one
or both variables to logarithmic scales.

TESTS OF SIGNIFICANCE

As noted, if the interval data are derived from a sample instead of a
population, the test of significance will also be of concern. The F
statistic is used to test the significance of the r, r^2, and regression
coefficients, as well as η, the correlation ratio, and Jaspen's M. We
discussed the F statistic in Chapter 4. The derivation is described in the
standard statistical texts and is easily programmed on computers and
calculators (see Chapter 9).

Table 5.4
State Anxiety (Spielberger's S.T.A.I. Scale) Before and After Counselling Patients With Retinitis Pigmentosa

Subject	Pretest Score	Posttest Score
A	35	23
B	33	27
C	29	24
D	31	21
E	34	29
F	37	40
G	35	27
H	33	26
I	28	27

SOURCE: Merry (1986).
Number of variables: Bivariate
Level of measurement: Interval/interval
Symmetric or asymmetric: Asymmetric
Sample or population: Sample
Probability test: Generalization to population

The t Test

Sometimes we want to test for significance without regard to a measure of association. This can be done by use of the t Test with either related or unrelated samples. It can be used, for instance, in the pretest, posttest situation. For example, Gordon Merry (1986), used the t Test in evaluating a change in anxiety level after counseling. The data are presented in Table 5.4.

He also used the t Test statistic to evaluate the statistical significance of the difference between his experimental and control groups. For this he used the unrelated samples (independent samples) version of the t Test. The data for that test are presented in Table 5.5.

In the first instance, with a pretest, posttest analysis, the result is a t of 3.75, which is significant at the .01 level (one-tailed test) with eight degrees of freedom. In other words, the possibility of obtaining this distribution by chance is about 1 out of 100. The difference in this instance is worth paying attention to.

In the posttest of the experimental and control groups, t was only 1.11, which is not statistically significant at the .10 level (one-tailed test) with sixteen degrees of freedom. In other words, the difference is probably not worth paying attention to except that the small number of

Table 5.5

A Comparison of State Anxiety (Spielberger's S.T.A.I. Scale) Levels for
Patients in Experimental and Control Groups, After Counseling

Group I (Experimental)	Group II (Control)
23	24
27	36
24	22
21	24
29	28
40	28
27	58
26	25
27	42

SOURCE: Merry (1986).
Number of variables: Bivariate
Level of measurement: Interval/interval
Symmetric or asymmetric: Asymmetric
Sample or population: Sample
Probability test: Generalization to population

cases may account, in part, for the lack of significance. This suggests
that a larger sample should have been used (See Wodarski, 1986, for
use of the F statistic in testing the difference between experimental and
control groups).

It is important to note that in Merry's study, the data arise from a
random sample. A one-tailed test was used because there is an independent and dependent variable involved (see Chapter 7 for a discussion
of one-tailed and two-tailed tests). In consulting the probability tables,
it is necessary to identify the degree of freedom in the distribution. The
degree of freedom is important because it determines which probability
curve will be used. The researcher does not usually examine the probability curve but only the points on the curve that correspond to the
various levels of significance. The tables for both Chi square and the t
Test can be found in most statistical texts and are given in Appendix B
of this book.

The t Test can also be used with a comparative *ex post facto* design
(without a pretest observation and without randomization) in comparing
the attributes between groups. Sister Nuala Dolan (1987) conducted a
study of nurses in general psychiatric and administrative roles to deter-

Table 5.6

Comparison Between Groups on Job Satisfaction and Burnout Ratings in
Various Nursing Situations

Groups	Mean Difference	Standard Error	df	t value
Comparison Between Groups on Job Satisfaction Ratings:				
General versus administrative	1.92	0.39	52	4.86[1]
Psychiatric versus administrative	1.29	0.29	53	4.53[1]
General versus psychiatric	0.63	0.37	57	1.71(ns)
Comparison Between Groups on Maslach Burnout Ratings:				
General versus administrative	1.58	0.35	52	4.40[1]
Psychiatric versus administrative	1.02	0.28	53	3.65[1]
General versus psychiatric	0.57	0.37	57	1.60(ns)

SOURCE: Adapted from Dolan (1987, table 1 & 2, p. 7).
NOTES: ns = not significant.
Table A in Appendix B suggests that a t value of 1.71 with df 57 reaches the .10 level and that the t
value of 1.60 with df 57 nearly does so (two-tailed test).
Number of variables: Bivariate
Level of measurement: Nominal, one dichotomous
Symmetric or asymmetric: Asymmetric
Sample or population: Population
Statistical procedure: Degree of association and test of significance (for chance occurrence)
[1]$p. = .0001$

Table 5.7

Correlation Coefficients and Related Statistical Procedures in Relationships
with Interval Variables

Correlation Measure	Tests of Significance
Interval/Nominal Relationships[1]	
Pearson's correlation coefficient (r)	F Test
Interval/Interval Measures and Derivative Indices and Procedures	
Regression equation	
Scattergram	
Pearson's correlation coefficient (r)	F Test
Coefficient of determination (r^2)	F Test
Regression coefficient (beta weights or slope)	F Test

[1]Where nominal value is dichotomous.

mine the level of job satisfaction and stress (see Table 5.6) in order to compare stress levels and satisfaction in different areas of nursing.

Note that in both job satisfaction and "burnout" ratings, the differences between general and psychiatric nurses was not found to be significant, but the differences between administrative nurses and both general and psychiatric nurses was found to be significantly different (see also the study of job satisfaction conducted by Parry & Smith, 1987, using correlational and regression analysis).

See Table 5.7 for a summary of the measures used with interval data in the bivariate situation.

ANALYSIS OF MULTIVARIATE DISTRIBUTIONS – WITH THREE OR MORE VARIABLES

With nominal/nominal tables we found that we could learn something of the relationship between two variables by using percentages, first by looking at the percentages in the row totals, then by examining the percentages in each category of the other variable. This should be a first step in analyzing nominal/nominal data. Loether and McTavish have an excellent chapter on cross classification of variables (1980, chap. 6) and Hirschi and Selvin provide a useful discussion on analyzing contingency tables (1967).

If the table contains more than two variables, it is also possible to partition the table to see which categories contribute the most to the Chi square. Blalock demonstrates how to do this in his chapter on contingency tables (1981, p. 297ff). While much can be learned from looking at the relationship between two variables, we often want to know how that relationship might be mediated by other variables. This involves examining three or more variables in the same table.

Multivariate analysis is not one statistical procedure but the application of various methods of dealing with simultaneous relationships among three or more variables (Dillon & Goldstein, 1984, p. 1–2; see also Schuerman, 1983a, p. 188ff.).

If there are several or a large number of possible independent variables that might jointly influence the dependent variable and one is interested in determining the relative effects or the absolute effects of these variables, then complex multivariate procedures are required. We will discuss only a few of the less complicated procedures and in the most simplified form. If the neophyte statistician wishes to use multi-

Table 5.8

Percentage of Male and Female Respondents Who Are Regular Users or
Nonusers of Computers

Respondents	Irregular or Nonusers		Regular Users		Total	
	Male	Female	Male	Female	(%)	(N)
Student	13	18	37	32	(100)	1,857
Parent	27	41	22	10	(100)	1,323
Teacher	23	27	22	28	(100)	385
Total	19	28	30	23	(100)	3,565

SOURCE: Hattie & Fitzgerald (1987, table 3, p. 10).
Number of variables: Multivariate (three variables)
Level of measurement: Nominal, two dichotomous
Symmetric or Asymmetric: Asymmetric
Sample or population: Sample
Statistical procedure: Cross-tabulations and percentages

variate analysis, as with other measures described in this chapter,
extensive study will be necessary (see chapter 7 in Johnson, 1977; or
chapters 19 and 20 in the second edition of the *SPSS Manual*, Nie et al.,
1975; and chapter 33 in the *SPSS-X User's Guide*, Nie, 1983. For a more
elaborate treatment, see Dillon & Goldstein, 1984; and Schuerman,
1983b).

Multivariate analysis does not necessarily involve regression analysis, although it is often associated with that procedure. Neither is it
limited to interval data, although it is most often used with interval data.
As we have illustrated, one can examine several variables in a contingency table using percentages to analyze relationships.

Multivariate Analysis with Nominal Data

Hattie and Fitzgerald (1987) used percentages to analyze a multivariate distribution in their study of the use of computers. This is a simple
illustration of the analysis of three variables in the same table, using
percentages to compare regular and irregular users of computers by
gender for students, parents, and teachers (see Table 5.8).

Table 5.8 can be re-organized to provide a separate 2 × 2 table for
each class of computer user: students, parents, and teachers. Cross-
tabulations of four variables can also be managed as illustrated in the
simulation study in child protective services in Table 5.9.

Table 5.9

Proportion of Child Protective Service Workers Recommending Court Action

| | | Nature of Injury | | | |
| | | Mild Injury | | Serious Injury | |
		No Previous Report	Previous Report	No Previous Report	Previous Report
Explanation consistent with injury	Positive parent reaction	.000	.132	.184	.395
	Negative parent reaction	.079	.289	.263	.553
Explanation not consistent with injury	Positive parent reaction	.105	.211	.289	.632
	Negative parent reaction	.211	.368	.658	.868

SOURCE: Craft, Epley, & Clarkson (1980, table 1).
Number of variables: Multivariate
Level of measurement: Nominal
Symmetric or asymmetric: Asymmetric
Sample or population: Population
Statistical procedures: Contingency table

Craft, Epley, and Clarkson (1980) examined the factors influencing legal disposition in child abuse investigations using such an analysis. In one table they examined four nominal-level variables to see what effect they had on recommendations for court action by protective workers: the seriousness of injury, the consistency of the explanation given for the injury, parental reaction, and whether or not a previous report had been made. These data are shown in Table 5.9.

The table shows clearly that the combination of a serious injury, a previous report, a negative parental reaction, and an explanation not consistent with the injury was likely to result in a recommendation for court action. Given four of these variables but a mild injury, the result was quite different. It is possible in this table to explore several inter-

Table 5.10

Comparison of Death Attitude Mean Scores at Each Time of Measurement, by
Experimental and Control Groups: Nursing and Physiotherapy Students

Measurement time	Experimental Group[1]				Control Group[2]			
	N	Range	$\bar{X}$	SD	N	Range	$\bar{X}$	SD
1	33	48–86	69.06	7.65[3]	22	65–104	76.27	9.10
2	29	51–83	67.79	8.23	18	67–86	75.94	6.00
3	31	48–87	63.06	9.37[3]	21	60–97	73.80	8.28

SOURCE: Caty & Tamlyn (1984, table 4, p. 51).
SD = standard deviation
Number of variables: Multivariate
Level of measurement: Interval
Symmetric or asymmetric: Asymmetric
Sample or population: Population
Statistical procedures: Mean, range, and standard deviation
[1]Nursing students
[2]Physiotherapy students
[3]$p. = .005$

esting combinations to see what factors played the most important part
in decision making. It should be noted that this was a simulated study
and decision making was hypothetical.

Use of Means and Standard Deviations with Three or More Interval Variables

Means and standard deviations can also be used to compare experimental and control groups. Caty and Tamlyn (1984) used these procedures to examine their data on the effects of education on third year
baccalaureate nursing students' attitudes toward death and dying (see
Table 5.10).

Their control group consisted of a group of third year physiotherapy
students. Only nursing students participated in the two-day death education seminar (the experimental group). The Winget, Yeaworth, and
Kapp Questionnaire was administered prior to, three months following,
and 14 months following the seminar. The lower the score, the more
open and flexible the attitude of the student. Note that the experimental
group in the pretest situation had a lower score than the control group.
This score declined at the fourteenth month posttest situation by six
points. The scores for the physiotherapy students also declined in the
same period but by only 2.47 points. Caty and Tamlyn explore other

Table 5.11

Pearson Correlations Between Questionnaire Variables: Level of Learning in Subject, Effectiveness of Professor, Quality of the Course, and Anticipated Letter Grade Among Undergraduates in Tertiary Institutions

	Variables			
Variables	1	2	3	4
1. Learn about subject matter	—	.86	.88	.18
2. Overall professor rating	—	—	.89	.28
3. Overall course rating	—	—	—	.33
4. Anticipated letter grade	—	—	—	—

SOURCE: Baird (Copyright 1987,The American Psychological Association. Adapted by permission of the author.).
NOTES: Number of variables: Multivariate (four variables)
Level of measurement: Interval (derived from ordinal scales)
Symmetric or asymmetric: Asymmetric
Sample or population: Population
Statistical procedures: Correlation analysis

factors, such as actual experience of a death in the family (many had experienced such a loss) and the experience of nursing dying patients (for the experimental group).

Multivariate Distributions with Interval Data

Multivariate distributions, data in which three or more attributes are of interest, may have any combination of levels of measurement but are most commonly applied to interval data. The balance of this chapter will discuss some basic procedures in use for interval/interval data involving three or more variables.

A typical analysis of data will present a Pearson correlation, often between several variables, as in the analysis by Baird (1987) in his study of perceived learning in relation to evaluation of instruction (Table 5.11). The validity of student evaluations was at issue in Baird's study. To what extent does a student's grade in a subject affect the student's evaluation of teacher effectiveness? Scaled responses were made by students on how much they had learned about the subject, the effectiveness of the professor, the quality of the course, and anticipated letter grade.

Table 5.11 presents the relationship between the four variables in the conventional fashion. The correlation between "how much they had learned" and the professor rating and course rating were high (.86 and .88, respectively) and the correlation between the professor rating and course rating were high (.89), but the correlations with anticipated letter grade with the other three variables were low (.18, .28, and .33).

In exploring a phenomenon to determine which independent variables are related to a given dependent variable, if we want to know the strength or degree of association, the focus will be on the correlation coefficient, R. Note that we capitalize R to signify a multivariate index. Once variables are found that seem to be important (i.e., the relationship is moderate or strong), we want to know more about the relationship between the apparently important variables. If we want to know how much of the variation in a dependent variable is due to a set of independent variables, the focus will be on the coefficient of determination (R^2). If, however, we want to know the nature of the relationship, the impact of one variable on another, and to be able to predict the value of one variable from the value of another (allowing for some error), the focus will be on the regression equation and, more specifically, on the regression coefficients or β weights.

When two or more of the important independent variables seem to be moderately or strongly associated, we will then want to know whether or not the effect of one is mediated through the other. In other words, given two independent variables and a dependent variable, we may want to control for the effects of one independent variable to determine how much of the variation in the dependent variable can be attributed to the second independent variable. We call the relationship between two variables a zero-order relationship; when we control for one independent variable, we call that a first-order relationship.

Partial Correlations

When we find a strong statistical relationship between two variables, we must always raise the question of spuriousness: Is it a veridical relationship or could it be explained by a third variable? A partial correlation analysis may help us unravel these relationships by identifying spurious relationships and locating variables that intervene between an independent and dependent variable.

Pascarella, Smart, Ethington, & Nettles (1987) used partial correlations in examining the influence of tertiary education on self-concept, comparing both academic self-concept and social self-concept between Black and White women and men (see Table 5.12).

Note that some variables stand out as having relatively high correlations when controlling for all other variables in the model (grade point

MULTIVARIATE DISTRIBUTIONS WITH INTERVAL-DATA   131

Table 5.12

Partial Correlations of Specific Collegiate Academic and Social Experiences with 1980 Self-Concept Measures[1]

Academic and Social Experiences	Academic Self-Concept				Social Self-Concept			
	White Men	Black Men	White Women	Black Women	White Men	Black Men	White Women	Black Women
Academic integration								
Cumulative undergraduate grade point average	.161[7]	.079	.160[7]	.263[6]	−.021	−.006[4]	.018[2,6]	.158[5]
Member of an academic honor society	.040	−.016	.035	.045	.046	−.045	−.005	−.028
Social leadership/involvement								
Knew professor or administrator personally	.053[7]	.036	.005	.029	.073[7]	.177[4,6]	.026	.081[4,6]
President of one or more student organization	.023	.041	.002	−.003	.050	.141[6]	.075[7]	.030
Served on university or departmental committee	−.018[3]	−.025	.048[3,7]	.066	.030[3]	.070	.098[3,7]	.076
Had a part in a play	−.029	.087	−.003	−.045	.010	.074	.046	.066
Won a varsity letter	.008	.102[6]	.004	.030	.047	.104[6]	.028	.051
Edited a school publication	−.014	.075	.000	−.003	−.009	.008	.033	−.020

SOURCE: Pascarella, Smart, Ethington & Nettles (Spring, 1987, table 7, p. 69).
NOTES: Number of variables: Multivariate (eleven variables)
Level of measurement: Interval and nominal
Symmetric or asymmetric: Asymmetric
Sample or population: Sample
Statistical procedures: Partial correlation and tests of significance
[1]Controlling for all other variables in the model, and all other specific types of academic integration and social leadership/involvement.
[2]Significant between White & Black Women
[3]Significant between White Men & Women
[4]Significant between Black Men & Women
[5]Significant between White & Black Women & Black Men & Women
[6]Partial correlation, $p. = .05$
[7]Partial correlation, $p. = .01$

average, particularly), although much more so for academic self-concept than for social self-concept. Not all of the correlations are significant, and the level of significance varies, depending upon the variables being examined.

The student desiring to use partial correlation analysis should read the SPSS manual, Chapter 19 (Nie et al., 1975), or the *SPSS-X User's Guide*, Chapter 32 (Nie, 1983). Chapter 7 in Johnson (1977) will be useful, as would Chapter 8 in Loether and McTavish (1980) or Chapter 19 in Blalock (1981). A more elaborate and complete discussion of multivariate analysis generally is provided in Dillon and Goldstein (1984) and Schuerman (1983b).

Multiple Regression with Interval Data

In social science or social work research it is seldom that we find relationships that involve only three, let alone two, variables. It may be that a number of independent variables are related to a dependent variable, and the problem is to determine the relative effects on the dependent variable of each of the independent variables. Partial correlation is a bivariate procedure that can be extended to include a number of independent variables in the form of multiple regression. Multiple regression allows us to find what constellation of variables seems to have the greatest effect on a dependent variable and to predict the value of that dependent variable given the values of the independent variables. It also provides the raw material to determine the impact that each independent variable has when the effects of the remaining independent variables are held constant.

From the multiple regression procedure we obtain a multiple correlation (multiple R), a multiple coefficient of determination (multiple R^2), and regression coefficients (β weights), just as we did for bivariate situations. The beta weights must be standardized to enable us to compare one relationship with another and, when standardized, are called standardized partial slopes as well as standardized β weights.

Marjoribanks (1987) used a multivariate analysis in examining social class categories and academic aspirations of adolescents, by gender. He used several indicators of family environment and parental influence. Summary data are presented in Table 5.13. Three variables stand out in the analysis: parental aspirations ($R^2 = .208$), parental concern for independence ($R^2 = .255$), and parent-child interactions ($R^2 = .215$). In all three instances, R^2 was significant at the .001 level.

Table 5.13

Standardized Mean Scores and Multiple Correlations Between Gender/Social
Class Categories and Measures of Family Environments and Adolescents'
Aspirations

| Aspirations, Inter-actions, Independ-ence, and Parental Support | Gender/Social Class Categories | | | | | | |
| | Female | | | Male | | | |
	Ser-vice $n=37$	Inter-mediate $n=111$	Work-ing $n=118$	Ser-vice $n=34$	Inter-mediate $n=96$	Work-ing $n=120$	Mul-tiple R
Parents' aspirations	49.4	47.3	49.5	53.9	49.3	51.4	.208[1]
Parent-child inter-actions	54.0	49.4	48.0	52.0	51.0	48.5	.215[1]
Parents' concern for independence	55.5	51.4	49.1	52.9	51.2	46.3	.255[1]
Perceived mother's support	49.9	49.2	49.1	52.9	51.2	46.3	.088
Perceived father's support	50.1	49.6	49.5	51.4	52.2	48.4	.144
Educational aspira-tions	49.6	49.3	49.2	53.2	50.8	50.2	.094
Realistic occupa-tional aspirations	49.8	49.1	49.2	52.1	51.5	47.8	.146

SOURCE: Marjoribanks (April, 1987, table 1, p. 48).
NOTES: R refers to the correlation between the six gender/social class groups considered as a set of dummy variables and each of the environment and aspiration measures.
Number of variables: Seven sets of three variables
Level of measurement: Interval and nominal
Symmetric or asymmetric: Asymmetric
Sample or population: Sample
Statistical procedures: Mean scores and multiple correlations
[1] Significant at the .001 level.

Path Analysis

The results of multiple regression can be represented by a path analysis that sets forth the relationship in a diagrammatic form and is often used to represent a model of independent variables and their effects on a dependent variable. To use this complex but definitive means of examining relationships between variables requires careful and intensive study. However, the effort required is well worth it if data are sufficiently precise to enable one to use these techniques. Again the SPSS 1970 manual, second edition (Nie et al., 1975), provides an excellent discussion and illustration of path analysis, as does Blalock

Table 5.14

Correlations Between Feelings of Helplessness and Pessimism and Nine
Other Variables

Variables	Variables								
	2	3	4	5	6	7	8	9	10
1. Helplessness-pessimism	−.01	−.20	−.26	−.19	−.01	−.08	−.03	−.18	.08
2. Employment importance		.16	.00	−.09	−.09	.17	.05	−.10	.07
3. Job guidance			.11	−.03	−.02	.10	.02	.07	.10
4. Internal attribution				.01	−.01	−.03	−.02	.14	−.01
5. School performance					.31	.07	−.17	.15	−.08
6. Year leave school						−.01	−.08	.02	.04
7. Father employed							.03	.24	.01
8. Work experience								−.04	.00
9. Social class									−.02
10. Sex of Subject									—

SOURCE: Feather (April, 1986, table 2, p. 39).
NOTES: These are termed zero-order correlations because they represent an index of the relationship between two variables without regard to the mediating effects of other variables.
Number of variables: Bivariate
Level of measurement: Interval
Symmetric or asymmetric: Asymmetric
Sample or population: Sample
Statistical procedures: Degree of association

in *Causal Inferences in Nonexperimental Research* (1964) and Johnson in *Social Statistics Without Tears* (1977).

Feather (1986) demonstrates the use of path analysis in her study of helplessness about potential unemployment among students in secondary schools. Feather wanted to determine how youngsters in the upper levels of secondary school would react to the threat of unemployment, and more specifically, how social class, gender, importance of work, extent of job guidance, internal attribution (extent unemployed blamed for unemployment), school performance, father's employment, year of leaving school, and work experience affect feelings of helplessness and pessimism about unemployment. More than 300 youngsters in year eleven in five high schools in Adelaide, Australia, completed questionnaires that provided data for this study. Table 5.14 shows the correlations between these variables.

Note in the table that job guidance, internal attribution, school performance, and social class are negatively and modestly correlated with helplessness and pessimism. Those who had high scores on helplessness-pessimism tended to be those who had little job guidance and low school performance; they also tended to be from the lower social class and were unlikely to blame unemployment on the unemployed. You will see that there are intercorrelations among the independent variables too (e.g., school performance and year of school leaving, school experience and work experience, school performance and social class, and father's employment and social class). These are zero-order correlations; that is, the correlations are between one independent variable and the dependent variable or between one independent variable and another without holding the correlations of the other variables constant.

Path analysis makes use of the beta weights or regression coefficients, providing an index of the impact on each independent variable when the effects of other independent variables are held constant. The path analysis diagram also shows the mediating effects of the various independent variables. Using these same variables, Feather (1986) provides a path analysis diagram of these data (see Figure 5.5). Because the regression coefficients are standardized, we can compare their magnitudes from variable to variable. When used in a path diagram, they are called path coefficients.

We note that social class has a stronger impact on certain variables than others, notably father's employment, school performance, and internal attribution, and these variables in turn have a major impact on helplessness and pessimism. On the other hand, direct effects of social class on helplessness and pessimism are weak. Low levels of guidance, though not strongly influenced by social class, show relatively strong effects on helplessness and pessimism.

Note that the causal assumption goes in one direction, from social class to the other six independent variables (but with social class prior or antecedent) and the six mediating variables are prior or antecedent to helplessness and pessimism in this model. Social class is not affected by other variables in the model, and it is, therefore, called an exogenous, as opposed to endogenous, variable. It is important to realize that these indices (path coefficients) represent independent effects of each variable in the model (see Poulin, 1985, and Van Tran, Wright, & Mindel, 1987, for additional examples of path analysis).

Three other indices could have been given for this set of data: a multiple R, a multiple R^2, and the coefficient of alienation. The R would be an index of the total correlation of all the independent variables acting together on the dependent variable, and the R^2 would provide the proportion of variation in the dependent variable that can be attributed

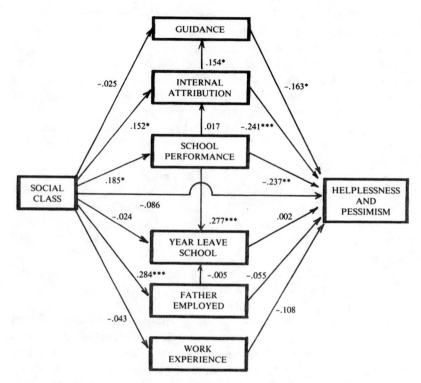

NOTE: An asterisk (*) indicates a *p.* of .05, ** indicates a *p.* of .01, and *** indicates a *p.* of .001.
SOURCE: From Feather (April, 1986, fig. 1, p. 41).

Figure 5.5
Path diagram linking social class and other variables to
helplessness-pessimism.

to the effects of these variables. The difference between R^2 and unity (1.00) would give us the amount of variation in the dependent variable not attributed to the independent variables in the model (called the coefficient of alienation), which is theoretically due either to the impact of variables not included in the model, or to measurement error, or both. Unfortunately these three indices are not provided by Feather.

The reader interested in using this intriguing and powerful method of analysis should consult, as a beginning, Johnson (1977) and the SPSS manual (Nie et al., 1975).

Table 5.15

Statistical Procedures for Multivariate Distributions

Correlation and Other Procedures	Test of Significance
Multiple R	F Test
Multiple R^2	F Test
Regression coefficient (beta weights or slope)	F Test
Partial correlations	F Test
Multivariate analysis	F Test
Path analysis	F Test

Probability figures can be computed for regression coefficients just as they can for correlation coefficients. Note in the path analysis figure that some coefficients have higher levels of significance than others.

If the interval data are derived from a sample instead of a population, or if the researcher wishes to counter the arguments of the skeptic, the test of significance will also be of concern.

Test of Significance

The F statistic is used to test the significance of the multiple R, the multiple R^2, and the path coefficients. The derivation is described in the standard statistical texts and is easily programmed on computers and calculators as noted earlier (see Chapter 9 for the formula).

Table 5.15 provides a listing of the multivariable interval/interval measures discussed above.

OTHER MULTIVARIATE PROCEDURES

There are other multivariate procedures, which require more explanation than is possible here; factor analysis, cluster analysis, and discriminant analysis are procedures that might be found useful in human service research (see Dillon & Goldstein, 1984, pp. 19–22 for other procedures commonly used).

Factor analysis can be used to sort out what is common among a set of complex variables, and the procedure can enable the researcher to develop a new set of variable constructs that reflect some attribute or characteristic which is common in the population under consideration (see Dillon & Goldstein, 1984, chap. 3; Nie et al., 1975, the SPSS manual, 2nd ed., chap. 24; Kim & Mueller, 1978a, 1978b).

Cluster analysis is useful in searching for sets of variables that reflect meaningful systematic differences; that is, homogeneity within the clusters and heterogeneity with other clusters in the set of data (see Dillon & Goldstein, 1984, chap. 5).

Discriminant analysis is used to differentiate between two or more groups of cases such that we can distinguish them along some dimension, such as political attitudes, propensity to commit property offenses, or the effects of chemical substances on individuals (see Dillon & Goldstein, chap. 10, or the SPSS manual, 2nd ed., Nie et al., 1975 for discussion and illustration). An application of the discriminant analysis procedure is illustrated in a recent study on child placement decisions (Schwab, Bruce, & McRoy, 1985; see also Cocozzelli's article, 1988). The SPSS/PC+ (Norusis, 1986) repertoire does not include discriminant analysis, cluster analysis, or factor analysis.

Because reference has been made specifically to the earlier SPSS manual, perhaps it is useful to point out that the SPSS-X manual (Nie, 1983) provides a less useful discussion than the older SPSS second edition for the novice wanting to understand the basics of statistical procedures, but the SPSS-X manual does provide the necessary information for data processing for these procedures.

SUMMARY

In these five chapters we have examined guiding principles in relation to a number of specific statistical measures with the aim of providing the student with a means of making preliminary decisions about useful and appropriate statistical procedures for various sets of data. References have been provided that will enable the researcher to examine in detail these potentially useful measures to see whether or not they meet the purposes of the research and whether or not the data at hand meet the requirements of the measure or procedure. The chapters are intended as a general guide, not a definitive one, in making decisions about useful and appropriate measures. The reader is cautioned, when pursuing a particular statistical procedure, to study carefully the material provided in relevant texts.

In the next four chapters, guidance on setting up data for analysis and the actual computations for the statistical procedures discussed in Chapters 1 through 5 are presented and discussed.

PART TWO

STATISTICAL COMPUTATIONS AND PREPARATION OF DATA FOR ANALYSIS

In the following chapters, computations and illustrations of various procedures are provided. Included in some of the formulas will be symbols that are used with computers. These symbols may not be as familiar to the reader as the conventional symbols, notably the division and multiplication symbols. In computer language the division symbol, $\div$ is represented by a slash, /, and the multiplication symbol, ×, is represented by an asterisk, *. Thus $12 \div 2$ is written 12/2 and 12×2 is written 12 * 2.

Some statistical texts use complicated mathematical symbols in the equations presented. I have avoided the more complex mathematical symbols while retaining the symbols that are essential for understanding the computations. There is no way of avoiding symbols, and the novice is required to make some effort to learn them in order to comprehend the presentation and the logic of the calculation.

In some instances indices have been included in a table that are not appropriate for that set of data. This is to illustrate what the consequences would be if an alternative measure were applied or to illustrate certain differences in the indices.

For more elaborate and technical aspects of these statistical procedures, citations have been provided for the reader.

Chapter 6

COMPUTATIONS AND ILLUSTRATIONS: UNIVARIATE DISTRIBUTIONS

In this chapter we examine statistical procedures in the one-variable situation: percentages, ratios, measures of central tendency, measures of dispersion, and tests of significance for one variable.

Tables 2.1 to 2.5 in Chapter 2 illustrated how raw data are compiled into arrays, percentage distributions, frequency distributions, grouped frequency distributions, and cumulative frequency distributions. The reader may wish to review these few pages before continuing with this chapter.

PERCENTAGES AND RATIOS

In Chapter 1 we examined source of referral of youngsters to the probation department. The raw data are presented here:

Referral Source		
Law enforcement agency	7,543	
School	966	categories
Parents	292	
Total	8,801	base number

Because we often wish to conceptualize such figures in relative terms of proportion, we compute percentages or ratios. We could simply make use of raw figures and state that 7,543 youngsters out of a total of 8,801 were referred by law enforcement agencies and 966 were referred by schools, but the categorical dimensions are more easily comprehended by percentages and ratios. Percentages and ratios also make it possible to compare one distribution with another, whereas statements about raw figures that "so many out of so many" fall in a particular category are not much help in comparing two or more distributions or in visualizing categories in proportional terms.

To determine the percentage of cases referred by the three categories, we simply divide each category by the base number and multiply by 100 to put it on a percentage scale. If we did not multiply by 100 we would have a decimal. A decimal expresses the number of units as a fraction of some power of 10. Decimals are useful in making computations, but it is customary to express proportions in percentages, for example:

Category			Base No.		Decimal				Percentage
Law enforcement	7,543	÷	8,801	=	.857	×	100	=	85.7%
School	966	÷	8,801	=	.110	×	100	=	11.0%
Parents	292	÷	8,801	=	.033	×	100	=	3.3%

We usually round such numbers and would express the proportion of referrals from law enforcement as 86%. Essentially we are using a scale of 100 and saying that out of every 100 cases, approximately 86 youngsters are referred by law enforcement agencies.

Similarly, ratios provide a simple way of conceptualizing the distribution and can be compared from one distribution to another. The ratio of one number to another is the first number divided by the second. The ratio of school referrals to parental referrals is 3.31 (966 ÷ 292) or about 3:1. The ratio of law enforcement referrals to school referrals is 7.81 (7,543 ÷ 966) or about 8:1. The ratio of law enforcement referrals to school and parental referrals is 5.99 [7,543 ÷ (292 + 966)] or 6:1.

When there are a large number of categories to be converted to percentages it is advisable to use an electronic calculator or computer. A calculator with memory capacity can be easily programmed to perform repeated calculations using the same base number and multiplying by 100 so that all that is required is to feed in the categorical values to obtain the percentages for each category.

MEASURES OF CENTRAL TENDENCY

Measures of central tendency were discussed in Chapter 2: the mode, median, and mean. It is quite easy to determine the mode and the median of a distribution: The mode is the category with the greatest frequency, and the median is simply the value of the midpoint in the distribution.

Determining the Median Value in a Distribution

If there are extreme scores or values in a distribution, the median can be a useful index of central tendency. Data can be assembled in a simple array, or they can be assembled in a frequency distribution. In either case, the midpoint of a distribution is called the median. Leonard defines it as the value "in a distribution that divides the observations in the middle"(1976, p. 67). It is also the 50th percentile in a set of ranked scores or values. In other words, half of the cases fall above that value and half of the cases fall below it (in a general sense).

In an array, if the number of cases is odd (if N is odd), the median will be the value of the middle case (distribution A, in Table 6.1). If N is even (distribution B), there will be no single middle case, and the number falling equally between the two adjacent cases in the middle of the distribution will have the theoretical property of dividing the scores or values into two equal groups. Thus the median is arbitrarily defined if N is even and, by convention, we take as the unique value of the median the arithmetic mean of the two middle cases.

Table 6.1

Hypothetical Data on Age of Recent Applicants at Two Nursing Homes (examples of determining median with raw data)

Distribution A	Distribution B
86	86
81	81
72 ← median	72
	← median
69	69 (69 + 72)/2 or 70.5[1]
57	57
	55

[1]If the two middle values happen to be the same, the median will be that value.

Table 6.2

Hypothetical Data on Number of Times Hospitalized, by Diagnostic Groups
A, B, & C (example of determining median in a frequency distribution)

No. Times Hospitalized	Diagnostic Groups		
	A	B	C
1	1	1	1
2	2	2	2
3	3	3	3
	← median		
4	1	0 ← median	0
			← median
5	5	1	0
6	0	5	1
7	0	0	5
Median =	3.5	4.0	4.5
N =	12	12	12

Determining the median when data are arranged in a frequency distribution is a bit confusing because the frequencies are read from the left-hand column. See Table 6.2. The median number of hospitalizations for Group A is 3.5, compared with 4.5 for group C and 4 for group B.

Determining the median with grouped data is a bit more complicated.

Determining the Median from Grouped Data

Occasionally data are obtained in grouped categories or compiled by class intervals as they appear in Table 6.3. In such instances a formula is useful in determining the median. One cannot be certain of obtaining the exact median because it must be interpolated. Follow the calculations in the table and note the definition of the symbols used in the formula.

From inspection, the reader will discover that the median in this table will be found in the second age group, 25–29. By use of the formula it is interpolated within that interval to be 28.9. The data are from an actual distribution of ages and grouped for purposes of this illustration. Therefore, we can compare the true median from raw data (28) with the computed median using grouped data (28.9), which is close to the true median. However, it does point up the fact that some precision is lost when data are grouped.

Table 6.3
Age of Students Admitted to a Social Work Program
(example of determining the median with grouped data)

The Data Class Interval	Frequency	Cumulative Frequency	The Computation Formula:
20–24	28	28	$Mdn. = L + \dfrac{N/2 - F}{f} * i$
25–29	41	69	
30–34	26	95	
35–39	12	107	$Mdn. = 25 + \dfrac{60 - 28}{41} * 5$
40–44	8	115	
45–49	3	118	$Mdn. = 25 + \dfrac{32}{41} * 5$
50–54	1	119	
55–59	1	120	$Mdn. = 25 + .78 * 5$
			$Mdn. = 25 + 3.90$
			$Mdn. = 28.90$

SYMBOLS:
$*$ = multiply and $/$ = divide
$Mdn.$ = median
N = number of cases
i = width of interval containing median
L = lower limit of interval containing median
F = cumulative frequency corresponding to lower limit
f = number of cases in interval containing median

This is essentially the same process used to determine other fractiles: percentiles, deciles, quintiles, and quartiles. Because the median is the 50th percentile, N is divided by 2 ($N/2$).

There is one situation in which the formula can be confusing, but if you follow the literal meaning of the symbols, you should not go wrong. Table 6.4 provides an example of a distribution in which the median is in the lowest class interval. Once more, follow the computation in the table. Note that the median is found in the class interval at the lower end of the age range, 20–24. The data in this table were grouped from raw data for purposes of illustration. The true median in this distribution was 24. The interpolated median is not far off.

If one is going to use the median as a measure of central tendency, it is better to have the raw data than to use grouped data if important or intricate comparisons are going to be made. In constructing a questionnaire or interview schedule, it sometimes seems convenient to use grouped categories but it means that precise medians (and means)

Table 6.4
Age of Students Admitted to a Social Work Program
(example of determining the median with grouped data)

The Data Class Interval	Frequency	Cumulative Frequency	The Computation Formula:
20–24	46	46	$Mdn. = L + \dfrac{N/2 - F}{f} * i$
25–29	16	62	
30–34	5	67	
35–39	6	73	$Mdn. = 20 + \dfrac{86/2 - F}{46} * i$
40–44	7	80	
45–49	2	82	
50–54	4	86	$Mdn. = 20 + \dfrac{43 - 0^1}{46} * i$
			$Mdn. = 20 + .93 * 5$
			$Mdn. = 24.67$

SYMBOLS:
* = multiply and / = divide
$Mdn.$ = median
N = number of cases
i = width of interval containing median
L = lower limit of interval containing median
F = cumulative frequency corresponding to lower limit
f = number of cases in interval containing median
[1] Number of cases less than 19 = 0; therefore $F = 0$.

cannot be computed. On the other hand if raw data are obtained, in this case the age at last birthday, medians (and means) can be computed, and the data can still be cast into class intervals for tabular and graphic presentations.

Calculating the Arithmetic Mean

The arithmetic mean, usually referred to as the *mean*, is designated by two different symbols as you may remember from Chapter 2. The mean of a population is designated by the lowercase Greek letter mu (μ) and the mean of a sample is designated by X-bar ($\overline{X}$). Do not confuse $\overline{X}$ with X. One of the conventions in statistics is to designate the values in a distribution as X. As we will see below, X is also used as a symbol for the midpoint in a range or class interval.

Each value in a distribution can be designated as a distinctive value if we want to do so: X_1, X_2, and so on. The subscript designates that value as a distinct value in the distribution. To indicate the summation

Table 6.5
Age of Students Admitted to the University of Melbourne
Social Work Program in 1984

23	26	21	22	21	25	34	34	21	45	25	21	26	23	34	23
26	33	20	42	20	20	25	27	26	34	22	27	27	24	47	23
29	21	25	21	22	21	36	26	22	21	21	21	22	32	22	45
19	32	20	34	27	22	22	44	21	21	43	37	22	22	52	26
33	31	43	39	23	23	38	31	46	20	20	39	21	34	40	25
37	22	21	27	29	22	37	38	31	22	23	21	22	31	24	33
24	22	40	19	21	33										

of all the values in a distribution, we use the uppercase Greek letter sigma (Σ). Thus if we want to indicate that we are summarizing all values, we write ΣX.

The total number of values in a distribution is symbolized by N. Now we have the symbols necessary for writing the formula for computing the mean:

$$\mu = \frac{\Sigma X}{N} \quad \text{or} \quad \bar{X} = \frac{\Sigma X}{N}.$$

Table 6.5 provides the raw data for computing a mean. I have listed the values (ages) in 16 columns. They could be listed in a single column or any number of columns.

If we sum the values (ΣX) in the distribution, we obtain a total of 2,843. There are 102 students and one value (age) for each student:

$$\mu = \frac{\Sigma X}{N} \quad \text{or} \quad \mu = \frac{2843}{102} = 27.87.$$

Note that because we have a population, we use the symbol μ.

Calculating the Mean from Grouped Data

We do not always have the raw data in the form of individual values for each case, although it is desirable, when possible, to obtain data in that form. The reason is that you can obtain more accurate indices, and you can also use more different statistical procedures for analyzing data when you have individual rather than grouped data.

Nevertheless, sometimes data are collected on the basis of a class interval (a grouped frequency distribution). To illustrate how we com-

Table 6.6

Age of Students Admitted to the University of Melbourne Social Work
Program in 1984, by Class Interval

Class Interval (age groups)	Frequency
15–19	2
20–24	47
25–29	18
30–34	16
35–39	8
40–44	6
45–49	4
50–54	1

pute a mean from grouped data, we have cast the data from Table 6.5
into class intervals in Table 6.6.

The formula for computing the mean from raw ungrouped data is
simple, and we only need one additional symbol to construct a formula
for computing the mean from grouped data. We need the midpoint of
the class interval. In some texts, X is the symbol assigned to the
midpoint, and f is the frequency in that class interval. In other texts m
is used to designate the midpoint, and f is the frequency in that class
interval.

Thus the formula can be written:

$$\mu = \frac{\Sigma fX}{N} \quad \text{or} \quad \mu = \frac{\Sigma fm}{N}.$$

In either case you are performing the same calculation.

The symbols fX or fm, written without a space between the two
letters, indicates that they are to be multiplied. In words rather than
symbols, we can say that the mean for grouped data can be computed
by summing the products of the midpoint of each class interval and the
frequency of values in that class interval and dividing by the total
number of values in the distribution. Table 6.7 is constructed to show
the calculation.

With the data from Table 6.7 we can calculate the mean, $2854/102 =
27.98$. To put it into the formula, it would look like this:

Table 6.7

Age of Students Admitted to the University of Melbourne Social Work
Program in 1984, by Class Interval, Showing the Tabulations for the
Calculation of the Mean for Grouped Data

Class Interval (age groups)	Frequency (f)	Midpoints (m)	Frequency X Midpoints (fm)
15–19	2	17	34
20–24	47	22	1,034
25–29	18	27	486
30–34	16	32	512
35–39	8	37	296
40–44	6	42	252
45–49	4	47	188
50–54	1	52	52
	N = 102		Σfm = 2,854

$$\mu = \frac{\Sigma fm}{N} \quad \text{or} \quad \mu = \frac{2854}{102} = 27.98.$$

Note that some accuracy was sacrificed in grouping the data. Using
the ungrouped data we obtained a mean of 27.87; using the grouped data
we obtained a mean of 27.98. Of course when we round it off, we obtain
the same mean (i.e., 28). Usually no greater accuracy is required, but
in some instances where increments of measurement are small, this
could make a difference in interpretation and decision.

There is a shorter method of computing the mean from grouped data.
In the age of computers and calculators, this method loses its appeal but
the reader may find it of interest. It involves guessing what the mean
will be and then computing from that point — it does not matter whether
or not the guess is close — it still works out.

The guessed mean (sometimes referred to as the coded mean), is
symbolized by μ' and it must be the midpoint of one of the class
intervals. Let us assume that we think the midpoint of the class interval
20–24 is likely to contain the mean. This time we will use a new symbol,
d, to designate deviation from the guessed mean and a new symbol, i,
to designate the width of our class interval.

Our formula now becomes:

$$\mu = \mu' + \frac{\Sigma fd}{N} * i.$$

Table 6.8

Age of Students Admitted to the University of Melbourne Social Work
Program in 1984, by Class Interval, Showing the Tabulations for the
Calculation of the Mean for Grouped Data Using the Guessed Mean

Class Interval (age groups)	Frequency (f)	Deviation from μ' (d)	Frequency X Deviation from (fd)
15–19	2	-1	-2
20–24[1]	47	0	0
25–29	18	1	18
30–34	16	2	32
35–39	8	3	24
40–44	6	4	24
45–49	4	5	20
50–54	1	6	6
	N = 102		Σfd = 122

[1]Guessed mean is in this interval, i.e., the midpoint of that interval is the guessed mean, 22.

Putting it into words becomes a bit more complicated. Using words
rather than symbols, we can say that the mean is the ratio of the sum of
the product of the frequency of each class interval and the deviation of
each value from the guessed mean in that class interval to the number
of cases, with the product of that ratio and the class interval added to
the guessed mean. As you can see, it is much easier to read the formula.

It is convenient to construct a table for calculation of the mean when
using the guessed mean method (Table 6.8).

Now we can calculate the mean, 22 + (122/102 * 5) = 27.98. Put into
the formula, it would look like this:

$$\mu = \mu' + \frac{\Sigma fd}{N} * i \quad \text{or} \quad 22 + \frac{122}{102} * 5 \quad \text{or} \quad 22 + (1.20 * 5)$$

$$\text{or} \quad 22 + 5.98 = 27.98; \ \mu = 27.98.$$

If we had selected a guessed mean in the interval 25–29, we would have
obtained the same answer.

Note again that some accuracy was sacrificed in grouping the data
but that we obtained the same figure as we did in using the other method
for grouped data. The advantage of the latter method is that our calcu-

lations are simpler. On the other hand, the formula is somewhat more complicated with the guessed mean method.

MEASURES OF DISPERSION

The calculation of the average deviation, the variance, and the standard deviation was illustrated in Chapter 2. The standard deviation is the most common measure of dispersion, and it is used with interval data. Less common measures of dispersion are the index of qualitative variation and the index of dispersion, both used with nominal data. We examined another index in Chapter 2, the Variation Ratio, and illustrated the computation so it will not be repeated here.

Index of Qualitative Variation

Measures of dispersion have been described as measuring variation, variability, diversity, scatter, heterogeneity, spread, and other synonyms. In looking at nominal (categorical, qualitative) variables, perhaps heterogeneity is the best word to use. What kind of an index can we use to put the heterogeneity of a nominal variable in perspective?

Let us examine the heterogeneity in Table 6.9 (from Chapter 2).

Mueller, Schuessler, and Costner (1970, 2nd ed.) focus on the number of differences in the categories of a variable as being the key factor in determining heterogeneity. How heterogeneous are the categories in the variables in Table 6.9? Are the fathers more heterogeneous than their student offspring? In regard to political party affiliation, 22 of the students are inclined to Labor, 5 to the Coalition party. What is the total number of differences in the categories of this variable? Each of the 22 Labor affiliates differ in political attributes from the 5 Coalition attributes, making a total of 110 differences (22 × 5) when each individual in one category is compared with each individual in the other category. This is hardly a meaningful index. How can we make a meaningful index of the differences and how can we find a way of standardizing the index so that it will be useful in comparing distributions?

One way of doing this is to obtain a ratio of the total observed differences and the maximum possible differences, given the total N and the number of categories. The total observed differences would be 110 as we noted. What are the maximum possible differences in this distribution? If all were Labor voters, the heterogeneity index should be zero. If the students were divided evenly between Labor and Coalition affil-

Table 6.9

Political Party Affiliation of Fathers and Political Party Affiliation of Students Entering the La Trobe University School of Social Work Program in 1979 (with two major political groupings only)

| Political Affiliation of Students | Political Affiliation of Fathers | | |
	Labor Party	Liberal/National Coalition Party	Total
Labor Party	16	6	22
Liberal/National Coalition	1	4	5
Total	17	10	27

SOURCE: Pilcher (1982).

iates, that would be the maximum heterogeneity and the index should be 1.00, although with an odd number of cases the maximum heterogeneity could not reach 1.00.

The maximum possible difference turns out to be an equal distribution between the categories. This can be verified by setting out the different possible combinations, given 27 cases:

$26 \times 1 = 26$ $22 \times 5 = 110$ $18 \times 9 = 162$ $14 \times 13 = 182$
$25 \times 2 = 50$ $21 \times 6 = 126$ $17 \times 10 = 170$ $13 \times 14 = 182$
$24 \times 3 = 72$ $20 \times 7 = 140$ $16 \times 11 = 176$
$23 \times 4 = 92$ $19 \times 8 = 152$ $15 \times 12 = 180$

Selecting the maximum possible difference, the ratio is:

$$\frac{\text{observed differences}}{\text{maximum possible differences}} \quad \text{or} \quad \frac{110}{182} = .60 \text{ or } 60\%.$$

Sixty percent of the possible variation that could exist does exist.

Now let us compare the variation in political affiliation of offspring with fathers. Seventeen of the fathers indicated an affiliation with Labor, ten for the Coalition:

$$\frac{\text{observed differences}}{\text{maximum possible differences}} \quad \text{or} \quad \frac{170}{182} = .93 \text{ or } 93\%.$$

In the case of fathers, 93% of the possible variation that could exist does exist. Thus the fathers are much more heterogeneous than their offspring in regard to the attribute of political affiliation. Another obvious way to describe it is to say that the student offspring are much more homogeneous than their fathers in regard to the attribute of political affiliation. In summary, we can devise our own formula for the index of qualitative variation (IQV):

$$\text{IQV} = \frac{\text{Total Observed Differences (OD)}}{\text{Maximum Possible Differences (MPD)}} \text{ or IQV} = \frac{\text{OD}}{\text{MPD}},$$

where

$$\text{OD} = \text{C1} * \text{C2} \quad \text{(category 1} \times \text{category 2)}$$
$$\text{MPD} = N/C_n \quad \text{(}N \text{ divided by number of categories).}$$

This computation can be extended to any number of categories. Our data on probation offers a good example. How do males and females differ in diversity of offenses as reflected in Table 6.10? With more than two categories in a variable, determining the maximum possible difference becomes a bit tedious and cumbersome, although the formula is the same. With five categories in the distribution in Table 6.10, we are required to perform the following calculations to compute the total observed differences for males,

$(505 \times 2{,}272) + (505 \times 1{,}382) + (505 \times 1{,}984) + (505 \times 256) +$
$(2{,}272 \times 1{,}382) + (2{,}272 \times 1{,}984) + (2{,}272 \times 256) + (1{,}382 \times 1{,}984) +$
$(1{,}382 \times 256) + (1{,}984 \times 256) = 14{,}809{,}238.$

In order to determine the observed differences, we take the number of cases in each category in the column and multiply it by the number of cases in every other category.

The work involved can be reduced by using percentages but even then the calculation is cumbersome.

The calculation for the maximum possible differences is no less cumbersome, but first we divide the total number of observations (N) by the number of categories (types of offenses). If there were an equal number of males in each of the five offense categories (the maximum possible heterogeneity), there would be approximately 1,280 in each category. We proceed to make the same calculations as above, except

Table 6.10

Number and Percentage of Youngsters Referred to the Probation Department
by Type of Offense, by Gender

| | Gender | | | | | |
| | Males | | Females | | Total | |
Type of Offense	No.	%	No.	%	No.	%
Violent	505	7.9	97	3.9	602	6.8
Property	2,272	35.5	437	17.7	2,709	30.5
Drugs	1,382	21.6	415	16.8	1,797	20.3
Status	1,984	31.0	1,405	56.9	3,389	38.2
Other	256	4.0	116	4.7	372	4.2
Total	6,399	100.0	2,470	100.0	8,869	100.0

SOURCE: Derived from data presented by Pope & Feyerherm (1982).

that we are using hypothetical data, assuming 1,279.8 cases in each
category (6,399/5 = 1,279.8):

$(1,279.8 \times 1,279.8) + (1,279.8 \times 1,279.8) + (1\ 279.8 \times 1\ 279.8) +$
$(1,279.8 \times 1,279.8) + (1,279.8 \times 1,279.8) + (1,279.8 \times 1,279.8) +$
$(1,279.8 \times 1,279.8) + (1,279.8 \times 1,279.8) + (1,279.8 \times 1,279.8) +$
$(1,279.8 \times 1,279.8) = 16,378,880.4.$

This could also be written as $10(1,279.8)^2$.
For males:

$$IQV = \frac{OD}{MPD} \quad or \quad \frac{14,809,238}{16,378,880.4} = .904 \ or \ 90.4\%.$$

For females the same calculations (not given here) were made with the
following results:

$$IQV = \frac{OD}{MPD} \quad or \quad \frac{1,870,408}{2,440,360} = .766 \ or \ 76.6\%.$$

From the data above, it is clear that males were much more heterogeneous in type of offense (90.4%) than females (76.6%). In the case
of males, 90% of the possible variation that could exist does exist; for
females, nearly 77% of the possible variation that could exist does exist.

A formula can easily be programmed on a calculator or computer, and if repeated use of the calculation were required, it would be worthwhile to do so. Casting into a formula, as Leonard has done (1976, p. 87), simplifies programming for calculation by hand or by calculator or computer.

$$IQV = \frac{\Sigma n_i\, n_j}{\left[\dfrac{K(K-1)}{2}\right]\left[\dfrac{N}{K}\right]^2} \text{ or } \frac{1{,}870{,}408}{2{,}440{,}360} = .766 \text{ or } 76.6\%,$$

where

$\Sigma n_i\, n_j$ = the product of each category and each other category
K = number of categories
N = total number of observations (cases)
n = number of observations in the categories.

The subscripts n_i and n_j may be unfamiliar to the reader. The symbol n_i refers to the number of observations in each category and the symbol n_j refers to the number of observations in all other categories. The lower case n refers to the number in the category.

Index of Dispersion

Essentially the same type of index as the IQV, the Index of Dispersion, D, from Hammond and Householder (1962, pp. 136–142), provides an alternative to the Index of Qualitative Variation. The computation is less complicated and both yield the same index. The data on female probation offenders will provide an illustration of this calculation. The ingredients of the formula are essentially the same except for one term in the numerator, Σf^2.

Σf^2, our numerator, is calculated by adding the square of all five categories:

$$97^2 + 437^2 + 415^2 + 1{,}405^2 + 116^2 \text{ or } 9{,}409 + 190{,}969 + 172{,}225 +$$
$$1{,}974{,}025 + 13{,}456 = 2{,}360{,}084.$$

We square N and subtract the ΣF^2 term:

$$2{,}470^2 = 6{,}100{,}900; \;\; 6{,}100{,}900 - 2{,}360{,}084 = 3{,}740{,}816.$$

Now we can complete our calculation:

$$D = \frac{k(N^2 - \Sigma f^2)}{N^2(k - 1)} \text{ or } \frac{5(2,470^2 - 2,360,084)}{6,100,900\,(5 - 1)} \text{ or } \frac{5 * 3,740,816}{6,100,900 * 4}$$

$$\text{or } \frac{18,704,080}{24,403,600} = .766 \text{ or } 76.6\%$$

where

k = number of categories
N = number of values (cases) or observations
Σf^2 = frequency of cases in each category squared, then summed.

This equation is a ratio of the maximum number of unique combinations of offenses that could be made to the actual number of combinations that are observed.

The Index of Qualitative Variation and the Index of Dispersion are useful indices of variation for nominal-level data.

Interquartile Range

The interquartile range was used in Chapter 2 with data on the distribution of income. The IQR can be used with certain types of grouped ordinal data as a measure of spread or dispersion. It is necessary to obtain a frequency distribution with class intervals and to cumulate the frequencies in one direction or the other as in Table 6.11. In Table 6.11, the number of families is given in thousands (i.e., 52,711 families given in the table is actually 52,711,000 families). This convention occurs when large numbers are being used.

In calculating the interquartile range, the distribution is divided into quartiles (fourths). The range referred to is the distance from the bottom fourth to the top fourth. It establishes a point which divides the bottom fourth from the rest of the distribution and a point which divides the top fourth from the rest of the distribution. The distance between these two points is the interquartile range. You will recall that the median divides a distribution in two equal parts. The computation of the interquartile range and the computation of the median are essentially the same procedures but establish different points in the distribution.

Table 6.11

Total Money Income by Race, Families, United States, 1980

Total Money Income	White Families Frequency	White Families Cumulative Frequency	Black Families Frequency	Black Families Cumulative Frequency
Under $ 2,500	864	864	337	337
$ 2,500–$ 4,999	1,719	2,583	713	1,050
5,000– 7,499	2,814	5,397	845	1,895
7,500– 9,999	3,150	8,547	656	2,551
10,000– 12,499	3,725	12,272^F	574	3,125
12,500– 14,999 ←	3,589^f	15,861 ←	485	3,610
15,000– 17,499	3,840	19,701	434	4,044
17,500– 19,999	3,606	23,307	374	4,418
20,000– 22,499	4,003	27,310	373	4,791
22,500– 24,999	3,456	30,766	272	5,063
25,000– 27,499	3,519	34,285	240	5,303
27,500– 29,999	2,701	36,986^F	181	5,484
30,000– 32,499 ←	2,776^f	39,762 ←	195	5,679
32,500– 34,999	1,984	41,746	129	5,808
35,000– 37,499	1,949	43,695	123	5,931
37,500– 39,999	1,367	45,062	90	6,021
40,000– 44,999	2,332	47,394	118	6,139
45,000– 49,999	1,501	48,895	69	6,208
50,000– 59,999	1,843	50,738	72	6,280
60,000– 74,999	1,065	51,803	24	6,304
75,000 and over	908	52,711	13	6,317
TOTAL	52,711		6,317	
Median	21,903		12,673	
Mean	24,939		15,806	
IQR	19,162		15,577	

SOURCE: U.S. Bureau of the Census (1980, table 5, 1980)
[1]This means that the figures representing families should read as if they had three zeros added on; e.g. 864 in the second column, signifies 864,000 families, etc. The income intervals in the left-hand column, however, should be read as the amounts given.

The four quartiles are designated Q_1, Q_2, Q_3, and Q_4. To compute the interquartile range, it is necessary to establish where Q_1 and Q_3 are located, so we have a formula for each of the two points.

Locating Q_1	Locating Q_3
$Q_1 = LQ_1 + \left[\dfrac{N/4 - F}{f} \right] i$	$Q_3 = LQ_3 + \left[\dfrac{3N/4 - F}{f} \right] i$
Q_1 = 1st quartile	Q_3 = 3rd quartile
LQ_1 = lower exact limit of class interval containing family income at 25th percentile ($N/4$)	LQ_3 = lower exact limit of class interval containing family income at 75th percentile ($3N/4$)
F = cumulative frequency below interval containing $N/4$	F = cumulative frequency up to but not including interval containing $3N/4$
f = frequency of class interval containing $N/4$	f = frequency of class interval containing $3N/4$
i = width of class interval containing $N/4$	i = width of class interval containing $3N/4$
N = total number of families in distribution	N = total number of families in distribution

These formulas can be easily programmed in a calculator or computer. The distribution of income and the use of the interquartile range was discussed in Chapter 2. Dividing N (52,711 families) by 4 yields a value of 13,177.75. The 13,178th family would fall in the income range of $12,500–$14,999. The *exact* lower limit of the income range is considered to be $12,499.5 ($LQ_1$). Note that the 13,178th family would not fall in the group of 3,725 families in income range $10,000–$12,499, but would fall in the group of 3,589 (f) families in income ranges $12,500–$14,999. There are 12,272 (F) families below the range of income containing the 13,178th family. The formula interpolates what the income of the 13,178th family would be.

Substituting the data from Table 2.9 in Chapter 2, we can see how the index is derived:

$$Q_1 = \$12,499.5 + \left[\frac{52,711 / 4 - 12,272}{3,589} \right] 2,499 = \$13,130.17.$$

To obtain Q_3, we take three-fourths of N ($3 N/4$) which yields a figure of 39,533.25. The 39,533rd family would fall in the income range of $30,000–$32,499. The *exact* lower limit of the income range is considered to be $29,999.5 ($LQ_3$). Note that the 39,533rd family would not fall in the group of 2,701 families in income ranges $27,500–$29,999 but would fall in the group of 2,776 (f) families in income range $30,000–$29,999. There are 36,986 (F) families below the range of income containing the 39,533rd family. The formula again interpolates what the income of this family would be:

$$Q_3 = \$29,999.5 + \left[\frac{39,533.25 - 36,986}{2,776} \right] 2,499 = \$32,292.58$$

and

$$IQR = Q_3 - Q_1 \text{ or } \$32,292.58 - 13,130.17 = \$19,162.41.$$

The interquartile range for the White families is \$19,162.41. This can be thought of as an index of inequality (although there are several others more commonly used). The calculation for Black families results in an IQR of \$15,577.04, showing considerably less heterogeneity. It was noted that White and Black families differ considerably in dispersion of income with Black families clustering in the lower income ranges. From Table 6.11, note the difference in median and mean incomes of the two categories.

The Standard Deviation

Although the standard deviation was illustrated in Chapter 2, we did not discuss its formula or its computation for grouped data. We can use data from Chapter 2 to demonstrate these calculations (see Table 2.10).

The reader will recall that we use the mean as a starting point in computing the average deviation, the variance, and the standard deviation. We then compute the deviation from the mean, and the sum of the squared deviations provides the variance; from the variance we can extract the standard deviation (see Table 6.12).

In computing the average deviation we have taken the absolute value of the deviations, thus the symbol $|$ on either side of the summation symbol. In calculating the average deviation we are concerned with the absolute deviations from the mean. Note also that we have used s and s^2 instead of σ and σ^2 because these are sample data, not population data.

The formulas are the following.

Average Deviation (AD)	Variance	Standard Deviation (s)
$AD = \dfrac{\|\Sigma\|}{N}$	$s^2 = \dfrac{\Sigma d^2}{N}$	$s = \sqrt{\dfrac{\Sigma d^2}{N}} \quad s = \sqrt{\dfrac{754}{N}}$
$AD = \dfrac{76}{10} = 7.6$	$s^2 = \dfrac{754}{10} = 75.4$	$s = \sqrt{75.4} \quad s = 8.68$

Table 6.12
Computation Table for Standard Deviation, Average Deviation, and Variance
(from Table 2.5 in Chapter 2)

Age of Students (X)	Deviation from the Mean[1] (d)	Deviation from the Mean Squared (d^2)	The mean
21	−8	64	
22	−7	49	$\mu = \dfrac{\Sigma X}{N}$
22	−7	49	
22	−7	49	$\mu = \dfrac{294}{10}$
22	−7	49	
31	2	4	$\mu = 29.4$
33	4	16	
33	4	16	
42	13	169	
46	17	289	
Σ = 294	|Σ| = 76	Σ = 754	

[1]The mean here is rounded to 29 for convenience of calculation and demonstration.

To calculate the standard deviation from grouped data the formulas are similar but the computation tables are a bit more complicated. In fact there are three methods for calculating the standard deviation from grouped data: *the deviation method, the raw score method,* and *the coded* or *guessed mean method.* The first computation table is for the deviation method (see Table 6.13).

The formula and computation are:

$$s = \sqrt{\frac{\Sigma f d^2}{N}} \quad \text{or} \quad \sqrt{\frac{6{,}051.96}{102}} \quad \text{or} \quad \sqrt{59.33} = 7.70.$$

The necessary data for computation of the raw score method and the coded or guessed mean method is included in Table 6.14. The mean of the distribution was given earlier in the chapter, 27.98 (calculated from grouped data as in Table 6.14). The raw score formula requires that we square the mean ($27.98^2 = 782.88$). Using the raw score method,

$$s = \sqrt{\frac{\Sigma f d^2}{N} - \bar{X}^2} \quad \text{or} \quad \sqrt{\frac{85{,}908}{102} - 782.88} \quad \text{or}$$

$$\sqrt{842.24 - 782.88};$$

Table 6.13

Computation Table for the Standard Deviation with Grouped Data, Using the Deviation Method (from Table 2.1 in Chapter 2)

Class Interval (Age Groups)	Frequency (f)	Midpoint (X)	Deviation (d)	Deviation Squared (d^2)	Deviation Squared X Frequency ($f*d^2$)
15–19	2	17	−10.98	120.56	241.12
20–24	47	22	− 5.98	35.76	1,680.74
25–29	18	27	− .98	.96	17.29
30–34	16	32	4.02	16.16	258.57
35–39	8	37	9.02	81.36	650.88
40–44	6	42	14.02	196.56	1,179.36
45–49	4	47	19.02	361.76	1,447.04
50–54	1	52	24.02	576.96	576.96
	$\Sigma = 102$				$\Sigma = 6,051.96$

to continue,

$$s = \sqrt{59.36} = 7.70.$$

Using the coded or guessed mean method (guessing that the mean is the midpoint in the 20–24 year-old-age group),

$$s = i \sqrt{\frac{\Sigma(d*fd)}{N} - \left[\frac{\Sigma fd}{N}\right]^2} \quad \text{or} \quad i \sqrt{\frac{388}{102} - \left[\frac{122}{102}\right]^2};$$

to continue,

$$s = i \sqrt{3.80 - (1.20)^2} \quad \text{or} \quad i \sqrt{3.80 - 1.43} \quad \text{or} \quad 5 \sqrt{2.37}, \text{ or}$$

$$s = 5 * (1.54) = 7.70.$$

Regardless of the method, we come out with the same standard deviation, so the choice is really a matter of preference for different methods of computation. The coded method requires less computation than the other methods.

Table 6.14

Computation Table for the Standard Deviation with Grouped Data,
Using the Raw Score Method and the Coded or Guessed Mean Method
(from Table 2.3 in Chapter 2)

Class Interval (Age Groups)	Frequency (f)	Midpoint (X)	For Raw Score Method		For Coded Mean Method		
			Midpoint Squared (X^2)	Midpoint Squared X Frequency (fX^2)	Deviation d	fd	d(fd)
15–19	2	17	289	578	−1	− 2	2
20–24	47	22	484	22,748	0	0	0
25–29	18	27	729	13,122	1	18	18
30–34	16	32	1,024	16,384	2	32	64
35–39	8	37	1,369	10,952	3	24	72
40–44	6	42	1,764	10,584	4	24	96
45–49	4	47	2,209	8,836	5	20	100
50–54	1	52	2,704	2,704	6	6	36
$\Sigma = 102$				$\Sigma = 85,908$		122	388

$\mu = 27.98$ (calculated from grouped data)

NOTES: Coded mean = midpoint.
The deviation is from the class interval, not the midpoint.

TESTS OF SIGNIFICANCE FOR ONE VARIABLE

We noted in Chapter 2 that a test of significance can be computed on a sample to determine whether or not a univariate distribution might be due to chance alone. We used as an illustration the gender difference in the admissions of students to a social work program. There are two such measures of particular interest for one-variable distributions.

Chi Square Test of Goodness of Fit

On the basis that about one-third of the students completing social and behavioral science degrees in Australia are males and that most of the students admitted to social work programs are from the social and

Table 6.15

Number of Students in a 15% Random Sample of Those Admitted to the University of Melbourne Social Work Program in 1984, by Gender, Showing Chi Square Goodness of Fit Computation

Frequencies: Observed and Expected		Computations				
Observed(O)	Expected(E)	O	E	(O − E)	(O − E)^2	$\dfrac{(O-E)^2}{E}$
Males 3	5	3	5	-2	4	.80
Females 12	10	12	10	2	4	.40
Total 15	15					$\chi^2 = 1.20$
						p. = .27

NOTE: We determine probability (*p.*) by examining a Chi square probability table (Table C in Appendix B). In this case we had to interpolate because the table does not provide all the points on the probability curve. The table indicated that a χ^2 of 1.07 would have yielded a p. of .30; a χ^2 of 1.64 would have yielded a p. of .20 (see Table C in Appendix B).

behavioral sciences, one would expect about one-third of the admissions into social work to be males. What we want to do is to test the actual number of admissions against this expectation. The observed (actual) and expected (hypothetical) frequencies are presented in Table 6.15.

There are 15 students in the sample, and we assume that one-third or five of the 15 students in the hypothetical distribution will be males. What we observe, however, is that only one-fifth are males. Is this statistically significant or could it be a chance occurrence?

The calculation of a goodness of fit test will help us make this decision. Note that it is a test of significance for nominal variables. The Chi Square Goodness of Fit Test should not be confused with the Chi Square Test of Independence that we use with bivariate distributions, although the basic idea and the calculation are essentially the same. The purpose, however, is somewhat different.

The calculation is uncomplicated. We derive the difference between the observed and expected frequencies $(O - E)$, we square the result and obtain a ratio of the difference (Δ) and the expected frequency. We obtain this ratio for each category and add the ratios of all categories to obtain the Chi square figure. In and of itself, it does not tell us much because it is not standardized. However, it does provide the information

Table 6.16

Fathers' Support for Top-Level Female Administrators

| Occupation | Fathers' Support Level | | | |
	Low	Moderate	High	Total
Social work	7	9	13	29

SOURCE: Collins (1984).

we need when we consult a Chi square table to determine the probability of obtaining this result (see Table C in Appendix B).

In this case we find we have to interpolate because the table does not provide all the points on the probability curve. The table indicated that a χ^2 of 1.07 would have yielded a probability of .30; a χ^2 of 1.64 would have yielded a probability of .20; 1.20 is somewhere in between, probably about .27. We decided in Chapter 2 that 27 out of 100 is not significant. The conventional .05 (5 out of 100) would have been considered significant. We would have had to obtain a Chi square of about 3.85 to reach a probability of .05. Thus, we conclude that the difference between our hypothetical distribution and the actual distribution may be a chance occurrence.

Kolmogorov-Smirnov Test of Goodness of Fit

There is one potentially useful test of significance for univariate situations with ordinal data, the Kolmogorov-Smirnov Test (KS). The Kolmogorov-Smirnov Test can be considered a goodness of fit approach and is an index of the differences between a theoretical and observed set of values. To illustrate the KS Test, we draw on the data presented in Chapter 3 (reproduced in part in Table 6.16) on father's support for top-level administrators (see Collins, 1984).

Using these data, we start by assuming that father's support for top-level administrators is fairly evenly divided between a low, high, and moderate rating, as it was for all of the social workers, educators, and nurses when combined into one group. Fathers of social workers differed considerably from this pattern, however. Is the variation from the general pattern with fathers of social workers significant? Let us use the KS Test to help us determine this, setting a level of .05 as our cutoff point.

Table 6.17

Fathers' Support for Top-Level Female Administrators

| Frequency | Fathers' Support Level | | | |
	Low	*Moderate*	*High*	*Total*
Observed	7	9	13	29
Theoretical (expected)	9.7	9.7	9.7	29
Cumulative observed	7/29	16/29	29/29	29
Cumulative theoretical (expected)	9.7/29	19.4/29	29.1/29	29
Absolute difference (D)	2.7/29[1]	3.4/29[2]	1.0/29[3]	
Ratio	.09	.12	.03	

[1] $9.7 - 7 = 2.7$
[2] $19.4 - 16 = 3.4$
[3] $29.1 - 29 = .1$

If our expectation is that social workers would follow the pattern of other professions, we would anticipate that nearly 10 (9.66) of the fathers would fall into each category: low, moderate, and high. We actually find quite a different pattern. The computation of a significance level will help us decide whether or not the difference is statistically significant and, therefore, whether or not to pursue possible reasons for this difference. Table 6.17 illustrates the computation of the Kolmogorov-Smirnov Test.

The computation requires a determination of the difference between the cumulative observed and theoretical (expected) frequencies. Leonard (1976) terms this difference D. This is set out in Table 6.17 as the absolute difference.

The largest absolute difference between the cumulative observed and expected frequency is 3.4/29 or .12. Consulting a probability table (Table E, Appendix B), we find that D does not reach .24, which would be required if it were to satisfy the .05 level of significance. In other words, we cannot make too much of the difference between our observed and hypothetical expectations. This test can be used with a small number of cases in instances where a random sample has been drawn from a population.

SUMMARY

In this chapter, we have examined statistical procedures used with one-variable distributions. In some instances, we have used these measures to compare two different single-variable distributions, but we have not looked at the computation of those statistical procedures that enable us to examine the relationships between two or more variables to see how they co-vary in values with each other. We will do so in the next chapter.

Chapter 7

COMPUTATIONS AND ILLUSTRATIONS: BIVARIATE DISTRIBUTIONS — NOMINAL DATA

CROSS-TABULATIONS

Cross-tabulation is the conventional term for tables constructed to present data on two or more variables in a grid format. The usual source of data for a cross-tabulation is a questionnaire, interview schedule, direct observation, file, or recording sheet. From this original source, tabulations can be made, as in Table 7.1, using tally marks to designate values for each case and organizing the data in columns and rows in the categories of each variable.

Once we have tabulated the data, we can obtain the row and column totals and the total number of cases in the distribution. There are a number of conventions associated with cross-tabulations that assist in comprehending tables and avoiding confusion. Note that each variable in Table 7.1 has two categories. Where columns and rows intersect we have a *cell*. The number of cells in a table depend on the number of categories in each variable. In Table 7.1 we have four cells. We also refer to this as a 2 by 2 (2 × 2) table (i.e., two columns and two rows). Cross-tabulations like this are also referred to as contingency tables.

The cells are given a letter designation so that we can refer to them or identify them in a formula. The convention is to designate the cell in the first column, first row as *a*, the second column in the first row as *b*,

Table 7.1

Political Party Affiliation of Fathers and Political Party Affiliation of
Students Entering the La Trobe University School of Social Work Program in
1979, Showing Tallies

| Political Affilia- tion of Students | Political Affiliation of Fathers | | |
	Labor Party	Liberal/National Coalition Party	Total
Labor Party	~~TH~~ ~~TH~~ ~~TH~~ I	~~TH~~ I	22
Liberal/National Coalition Party	I	IIII	5
Total	17	10	27

and so on alphabetically until we have designated all cells in the first
row. Then we continue alphabetically with the second row. In this table
cells *a* and *b* are in the first row, and cells *c* and *d* are in the second row.

Row totals and column totals are called *marginals*. Thus we can
define the marginals by using cell letter designations. The first row total
(marginal) can be designated as $a + b$; the second row total (marginal)
as $c + d$. Table 7.2 shows these designation as well as the total. Note
that the independent variable is across the top of the table and the
dependent variable categories are on the left margin of the table. This
is the convention when the distinction is made between dependent and
independent variables in an asymmetric relationship. It is one of the
conventions that helps us interpret the meaning of a table. The use of
these designations will become apparent as we discuss some of the
formulas and as we discuss the tables.

One of the most convenient and meaningful statistical procedures for
analyzing nominal data in a cross-tabulation is the use of percentages
to determine how the categories of one variable are related to the
categories of a second variable. The procedure is essentially a comparison of the total distribution along one variable with the distributions
in the category of the other variable. To make this comparison, we
compute the percentages of each column and then compare across the
columns as in Table 7.3.

First we look at the totals in the right-hand column and we see that
81.5% of the students are affiliated with the Labor party and that 18.5%

Table 7.2
Political Party Affiliation of Fathers and Political Party Affiliation of
Students Entering the La Trobe University School of Social Work Program in
1979, Showing Dependent and Independent Variables and Cell Designations

Political Affilia- tion of Students (Dependent Variable)	Political Affiliation of Fathers (Independent Variable)		
	Labor Party	Liberal/National Coalition Party	Total
Labor Party	16a	6b	22 a + b
Liberal/National Coalition Party	1c	4d	5 c + d
Total	17 a + d	10 b + d	27 a + b + c + d

are affiliated with the Coalition party. If the father's affiliation was
irrelevant to the affiliation of the student, we would expect to find these
same percentages in each of the columns under the independent variable. Instead we find that only 60% of the offspring of fathers with a
Coalition affiliation are themselves affiliated with Labor, and con-
versely we find that 94% of the offspring of fathers with a Labor
affiliation are affiliated with Labor.

Thus we can see that there is an association between the two variables, and we can describe it in a straightforward manner: the offspring
of Labor-affiliated fathers are quite likely to be affiliated with the Labor
party (94%); the offspring of Coalition-affiliated fathers are less likely
to be affiliated with the Coalition parties (40%), and assuming strong
parental influences, many of them are defectors to the Labor party
(60%). This is a simple and effective way of analyzing contingency
tables with nominal data. The convention is to place the independent
variable on the top of the table, the dependent variable on the side of
the table, and percentage by columns; then we can compare categories
across the table in the direction of causation.

We may wish to test the significance of the distribution if the data
come from a random sample, or we may wish to determine with more
precision and with a standardized index just how strongly the two
variables are associated; but, using percentages is an acceptable and

Table 7.3

Political Party Affiliation of Fathers and Political Party Affiliation of
Students Entering the La Trobe University School of Social Work Program in
1979 Showing Numbers and Percentages

| Political Affiliation of Students (Dependent Variable) | Political Affiliation of Fathers (Independent Variable) | | | | | |
| | Labor Party | | Liberal/National Coalition Party | | Total | |
	No.	Percentage	No.	Percentage	No.	Percentage
Labor Party	16	94.1	6	60.0	22	81.5
Liberal/National Coalition Party	1	5.9	4	40.0	5	18.5
Total	17	100.0	10	100.0	27	100.0

useful way of examining the relationship between two variables in the
first instance. In the opinion of the author, this should be the first step
in analyzing nominal-level data in a contingency table because it provides a more intuitive sense of the relationship between two variables
than does computing a test of significance or a measure of association.
In the following paragraphs, we see how tests of significance and
measures of association are derived from contingency tables.

DELTA MEASURES: TEST OF SIGNIFICANCE AND DERIVED MEASURES OF ASSOCIATION

The term *Delta measure* is applied to those measures derived from
computing and summing the differences between the observed frequency in a distribution and a hypothetical expected frequency based
on the notion that there is no relationship between two variables. In this
instance Δ is the symbol for difference. The most well-known delta
measure is the Chi Square Test of Significance, but it is not the only one.
Measures of association can also be derived from the delta computation.

We will first discuss the Chi square computation and some of the
related concepts the reader needs to be familiar with in order to complete a test of significance and to interpret it properly. Then we will
discuss the measures of association derived from Chi square and an-

other family of measures of association—proportionate reduction of error (PRE) measures.

The Chi Square Computation

Using data from Table 7.3 we can demonstrate how delta measures and their derivative measures of association are computed. In Table 7.3 we computed the percentages vertically so that all columns add to 100%. We noted that there is some association between the two variables, but we did not have an index of the probability (perhaps it is just a chance occurrence), and we did not have an index of the degree of association. In the following paragraphs we will see what else we can say about this distribution.

It is an interesting question to ask what kind of distribution would have been obtained if no association existed between the two variables. In other words, if we take the null hypothesis that there is no association between the affiliation of fathers and the affiliation of offspring, what distribution would we expect?

By using the marginals and the total we can work this out. Let us look at cell *d*. Given the marginals, if political affiliations were not associated, we would expect to find 5/27ths of the 10 cases in cell *d* or 1.9; we would expect to find 5/27ths of 17 in cell *c* or 3.1; we would expect to find 22/27ths of 10 in cell *b* or 8.1; and we would expect to find 22/27ths of 17 in cell *a*, or 13.9. If that does not make sense to you, just remember this rule of thumb: to compute the expected frequency in a cell, obtain the product of the marginals of that cell (each cell has two marginals, a row total and a column total) and divide that by N. In other words, for cell *a*, multiply 17 by 22 and divide by 27, or $17 * 22/27 = 13.9$. This computation will provide the expected frequency for each cell. Note that the marginals will be the same for both expected and observed frequencies.

In Table 7.4 we have incorporated the expected frequencies (in parentheses), assuming no association between the two variables. Now we can compare the expected and the observed (actual) frequencies and we can see the discrepancies between them. Whereas we expected to find about two cases in cell *d*, we actually found four, and whereas we expected to find three in cell *c*, we found only one, and so on. There is a difference between observed and expected frequencies in each cell. It is from these differences (Δ) that we derive a Chi square figure.

Table 7.4

Political Party Affiliation of Fathers and Political Party Affiliation of
Students Entering the La Trobe University School of Social Work Program in
1979, Showing the Expected Frequency in Each Cell

Political Affiliation of Students (Dependent Variable)	*Political Affiliation of Fathers (Independent Variable)*		
	Labor Party	*Liberal/National Coalition Party*	*Total*
Labor Party	16 (13.9)	6 (8.1)	22
Liberal/National Coalition Party	1 (3.1)	4 (1.9)	5
Total	17 (17.0)	10 (10.0)	27

The Chi square figure in turn is useful in providing a confidence level
if we are generalizing to a population from the sample drawn from that
population; it will provide a basis for estimating the probability of
obtaining an observed frequency, given the marginals; and it can provide a means of constructing measures of association.

Here is how we compute Chi square for a 2 × 2 table. The formula is:

$$\chi^2 = \Sigma \; \frac{(O - E)^2}{E}$$

where

O = observed frequencies
Σ = summation (sigma)
E = expected frequencies
χ^2 = Chi square

You will also see the observed and expected frequencies written as f_o
and f_e, the subscripts referring to observed and expected frequencies.

To put it into words, we sum the ratio of the expected frequencies to
the squared differences between the observed and expected frequencies.
Although Δ is the symbol for differences, it is not used in the above
formula. However, as you consult various textbooks you will find that

Table 7.5

Computation of Chi Square for a 2 × 2 Table

Cell	O	E	$O - E$	$(O - E)^2$	$\dfrac{(O - E)^2}{E}$
a	16	13.9	2.1	4.4	.317
b	6	8.1	−2.1	4.4	.543
c	1	3.1	−2.1	4.4	1.419
d	4	1.9	2.1	4.4	2.316
					$\Sigma = 4.595$
					$\chi^2 = 4.595$

the formula can be written in a variety of ways, using Δ and other symbols:

$$\chi^2 = \Sigma \left[\frac{\Delta^2}{E} \right] \quad \text{or} \quad \chi^2 = \Sigma \left[\frac{\Delta^2}{f_e} \right].$$

The computation can be seen in Table 7.5, using the data from Table 7.3. Chi square is 4.595. Note that each cell contributes something to the Chi square, some cells more than others. In a 2 × 2 table, the numerical difference between expected and observed frequencies is always the same for all four cells. This is not true in tables with more categories.

The use and interpretation of Chi square is complex. It is a versatile measure and worth the trouble of understanding how to use it properly. It is often misused in the literature. To use it without a proper understanding, one runs the risk of misinterpreting data, making claims that are unjustified, or failing to see the strength of a relationship because additional procedures were not followed. To get the most out of Chi square, one needs to understand something about probability tables, degrees of freedom, one-tailed and two-tailed tests, and corrections for continuity as well as the assumptions about its use.

For purposes of illustration above, we computed the expected frequencies for all four cells; this was not necessary. In a 2 × 2 table, once you have computed the expected frequency for one cell, the others can be determined by subtraction. If 1.9 cases are expected in cell d, then there can only be 3.1 in cell c (5 − 1.9) and if there are 3.1 in cell c, there could only be 13.9 in cell a, and so on.

The degree of freedom is the number of expected frequencies that are free to vary. Thus we have only one degree of freedom in this table once the expected frequencies for one cell are established, all the others are fixed. The degrees of freedom are important in entering the Chi square table of probabilities because these probabilities are different for each size table (or for each degree of freedom).

The degree of freedom can be computed for any size table by a simple formula. It is the product of the number of rows less one and the number of columns less one or $(r-1)(c-1)$. The symbol for degrees of freedom is df. The parenthetic quantities are multiplied as indicated by their proximity. It could be written $(2-1) * (2-1)$ or $(2-1) \times (2-1)$ but the usual and simplest way is: $(2-1)(2-1)$. In this case, $df = 1$.

We can enter a Chi square table with one degree of freedom to determine the probability of obtaining the observed frequencies or, if the data are from a sample, in determining the level of confidence we can have in generalizing to a population. In this instance we are concerned with the former because these data were not derived from a sample. To put it in the positive, we are attempting to respond to the cynic who says that eye color of the fathers would have been just as powerful a variable in explaining the offsprings' political affiliation as using parental affiliation. To do this, we test the null hypothesis which states that there is no relationship between the two variables.

However, before we enter the probability table, we need to decide whether we consider this to be a symmetric or an asymmetric distribution (see Chapter 1). The reason for making this determination is that in entering a Chi square probability table we must use either a two-tailed or a one-tailed test. If it is symmetric (nondirectional hypothesis), we would use the two-tailed test. Two-tailed and one-tailed tests will be discussed below.

Let us assume that this distribution is asymmetric (i.e., the parental affiliation has some causative effect on the political affiliation of the offspring). Therefore we will use a one-tailed test. Turn now to Chi square probability Table C in Appendix B.

The degrees of freedom are given in the left-hand column. We find 1, which is our degree of freedom, and proceed along that row to see where our Chi square figure would fall. The table actually gives only points on a curve, and in this case, we must interpolate. The figure 4.595 would fall between 3.841 and 5.412. If we look above these two figures (points on a curve), we see that they correspond to .05 and .02, respectively. The actual probability is likely to be about .04. The convention

Table 7.6

Illustration of the Effect on Chi Square of Doubling the Size of Sample with Cell Proportions Remaining Constant

Example 1 Variable B	Variable A Low	High	Example 2 Variable B	Variable A Low	High	Example 3 Variable B	Variable A Low	High
High	7	3	High	14	6	High	28	12
Low	5	10	Low	10	20	Low	20	40
Total	12	13	Total	24	26	Total	48	52

N = 25 χ^2 = 3.23 $p.$ = .07 V = .36

N = 50 χ^2 = 6.46 $p.$ = .02 V = .36

N = 100 χ^2 = 12.93 $p.$ = .001 V = .36

is to consider .05 or less to be significant. If that is the case, then we would say that this distribution is not likely to have occurred by chance. The probability of obtaining a distribution like this, given the marginals, is 4 out of 100. However, we must accept this figure with caution because of the small number of cases in the distribution. Below we will discuss why this is so and suggest an alternative procedure.

To illustrate the fact that the level of significance obtained from Chi square computations is related directly to sample size, let us examine three sets of hypothetical data in which the relative magnitude of cells is the same (Table 7.6).

Assume we have a symmetric distribution and will use a two-tailed test. Note that as the magnitude of the table increases, Chi square increases and the level of confidence increases, even though the relative proportions in the four cells remains the same. Note also that the measure of association, V, remains the same. This illustrates the importance of the size of the sample in using a test of significance.

Probability Curves and Tables

Each size table (each degree of freedom) has its own probability curve, and each is quite different in shape ranging from a curve that closely resembles a flattened dome (10 *df*) to a curve that is sharply skewed to the left (4 *df*). When we examine the Chi square probability table, we are consulting points on these curves that correspond to the various levels of significance (e.g., .10, .05, .01, 001).

One-tailed and Two-tailed Tests

The reader will undoubtedly be familiar with a normal curve. The normal curve has two tails, one at either end. These tails contain that portion of the curve which reflects decreasing probabilities. If we are testing a directional hypotheses (asymmetric), we are concerned only with one end of the curve because we are predicting in one direction. In such a case, we use a one-tailed test for level of significance. If we are testing a nondirectional hypotheses (symmetric), we are concerned with both ends of the curve because we are predicting an association without regard to a particular direction, and therefore, we use a two-tailed test for significance levels. One should be clear, therefore, in determining the probability of obtaining a given Chi square result from the probability table whether it is an asymmetric or symmetric hypothesis that is being tested.

Corrections for Continuity

When the Chi square computation is applied to samples that are large, it is a versatile and dependable measure. When the number of cases in the sample is small, the Chi square computation is less stable and may give inflated results. The remedy for this for 2 × 2 tables is to correct for continuity. Blalock discusses the commonly used corrective method (Yates's correction for continuity) which, in his opinion, should be applied when the expected frequency in any cell falls below 10. He observes that with small samples even the correction may provide misleading results (Blalock, 1981, p. 290ff.).

Blalock also suggests that when there is a relatively large number of cells and only one or two cells have expected frequencies of five or less, it is advisable to go ahead with Chi square tests without concern for correction (1981, p. 292).

The expected frequencies in Table 7.4 are less than ten in three of the cells. We correct for continuity by adding or subtracting .5 from each of the observed frequencies, the addition or subtraction depending upon whether or not the expected frequency is greater than or less than the observed frequency. Because, in cell a, the observed frequency is larger than the expected frequency, we subtract .5 from the observed frequency and designate the frequency in cell a as 15.5. We note the same situation in cell d so we reduce that cell frequency to 3.5. In the other two cells the expected frequency is greater than the observed frequency, so we add .5 to each. Now we have a new computation, Table

Table 7.7

Computation of Chi Square for a 2 ×2 Table, with Correction for Continuity

Cell	O	E	O – E	$(O-E)^2$	$\dfrac{(O-E)^2}{E}$
a	15.5	13.9	1.6	2.56	.184
b	6.5	8.1	–1.6	2.56	.316
c	1.5	3.1	–1.6	2.56	.826
d	3.5	1.9	1.6	2.56	1.347

$$\Sigma = 2.673$$
$$\chi^2 = 2.673$$

7.7, corrected for continuity. Note that our Chi square figure was 4.595 in the previous table, now it is 2.673. When we enter the Chi square probability table, we find that this falls between 1.642 and 2.706, close to the latter. Above these two points on the curve, we see the probability figures of .20 and .10. In other words the probability does not quite reach the .10 level. We would not ordinarily consider this to be a significant difference. By correcting for continuity we take a more conservative decision, which we should do given the small number of cases and the fact that so many of the cases fall in one cell. For a brief discussion on correction for continuity and the necessity for it, see Blalock (1981, pp. 290–292). If, because of a small number of cases, we want to try an alternative, we can use Fisher's Exact Test, which is a more appropriate test for a distribution with a small number of cases.

Fisher's Exact Test

For nominal data, given a 2 × 2 table, Fisher's Exact Test is a preferred index of probability. It does not require a probability table because the computation itself provides the exact probability of obtaining the cell values given the marginals and size of sample or population. It has been infrequently used, perhaps because it is cumbersome to compute by hand. With modern calculators and computers this need not trouble us. Also note that it is generally limited to 2 × 2 tables (for extension beyond the 2 × 2 table, see Pierce, 1969, chap. 8).

The formula looks complicated but is really simple. It requires a new symbol, the factorial !. The symbol ! is used in mathematics to denote the multiplication of a number successively by each number of less quantity. The quantity 4! means $4 \times 3 \times 2 \times 1$ or 24. 4! = 24. The formula for Fisher's Exact Test (P) looks like this:

One-tailed test: $P = \dfrac{(a + b)!(c + d)!(a + c)!(b + d)!}{N!a!b!c!d!}$,

and

Two-tailed test: $P = 2\,\dfrac{(a + b)!(c + d)!(a + c)!(b + d)!}{N!a!b!c!d!}$.

Keeping in mind that ! is the factorial sign, we can put the one-tailed test into words: P is the ratio of the product of the factorials of the cells and N to the product of the factorials of the marginals.

The computation is not difficult with a calculator if the calculator has a factorial key. One can compute a Fisher's Exact Test in about 30 seconds with the calculator, whereas by hand, it becomes tedious and subject to error. If we apply Fisher's Exact Test to the data in the table above, we obtain an exact probability of .044 (one-tailed test). This suggests that applying the correction for continuity was too stringent, and the initial probability derived from Chi square was close to the exact probability. To obtain a two-tailed test, we would multiply the probability by two and the probability becomes .09. If we are predicting that political party affiliations of parents and offspring are associated, the probability is .09; if we are predicting that political party affiliation of parents determines the affiliation of offspring, a more rigorous proposition, the probability is .04. In other words, the chances of obtaining this distribution, given the directional hypothesis, is 4 out of 100; the chances of obtaining this distribution, given the nondirectional hypothesis, is 9 out of 100.

McNemar Test of Significance

We noted in Chapter III that if we make observations on an individual or group at two or more points in time, we cannot use Chi square as a test of significance. In statistical jargon this is called a related sample because the observations in the first instance are *ipso facto* related to the second instance, which confounds the evaluation of the significance of difference. With interval data, there is a t test for related samples. We also noted that there is a useful and simple one for nominal data, called the McNemar Test.

We will use the hypothetical data from Table 3.13 to illustrate the computation of the McNemar Test because I was unable to find an actual example in the education, social work and nursing literature (see Leonard, 1976, for an example). Nevertheless, it is an important test of significance and one that could readily be applied in these three fields when dichotomous variables are employed in the examination of change in attitude or behavior following a seminar, workshop, or training sessions in the pretest, posttest situation.

The formula is simple and makes use of the data on changes in attitude or behavior from the pretest to the posttest. I will use the symbol M^2 for McNemar's Test. The test is the ratio between the squared absolute difference (less 1) between those respondents whose attitudes changed in either direction and the sum of the respondents that changed between the pretest and posttest. Thus we have the formula:

$$M^2 = \frac{[\,|a - d| - 1\,]^2}{a} + d$$

Out of 16 smokers in the pretest, 10 were nonsmokers in the post-test. Out of 20 nonsmokers in the pretest, one was a smoker in the post-test:

Status Before Seminar	Status After Seminar		
	Smoker	Nonsmoker	Total
Nonsmoker	1	19	20
Smoker	6	10	16
Total	7	29	36

Substituting the figures in the formula, we have the following calculation:

$$M^2 = \frac{(\,|1 - 10| - 1)^2}{1 + 10} \quad \text{or} \quad \frac{(9 - 1)^2}{11} \quad \text{or} \quad \frac{64}{11} = 5.82.$$

The McNemar Test makes use of the Chi square probability table to determine probability. Thus we consult Table C in Appendix B to find that our hypothetical M^2 reaches the .02 level of confidence. Had we considered this a one-tailed test, it would have reached the .01 level of confidence. We can see that more than half the smokers gave up smoking following the seminar, and only one out of 20 took up smoking following the seminar. As a cautionary note, it should be pointed out that, without a control group, it would be unwarranted to assume that such a change, if it occurred, could be attributed solely to the seminar because we can never be certain what other variables could have influenced the results.

The McNemar Test is limited to the 2 × 2 situation using dichotomous nominal categories in the pretest, posttest situation in which data from a random sample have been obtained and in which the subjects are used as their own controls in the pretest and posttest situation. Leonard notes that this test should not be used with small samples and suggests that the minimum size of sample required should be determined by halving the sum of the respondents who changed from pretest to posttest: $(a + d)/2$. If the resulting figure is less than five, the test should not be used. In our hypothetical sample, we have met this requirement, $(10 + 1)/2 = 5.5$, but just barely. Leonard also notes that the formula has a correction for continuity built into it (Leonard, 1976, pp. 197–200).

MEASURES OF ASSOCIATION DERIVED FROM DELTA

As we noted in Chapter 3, there are several important measures of association derived from Δ. Cramer's V, one of the measures derived from Δ, and another measure, the uncertainty coefficient (UC), are the most versatile for the symmetric situation. There are other measures of association derived from Δ that have undesirable limitations or idiosyncracies, but because they are sometimes used in the literature and usually discussed in statistical texts, the calculations are presented along with a reminder of their limitations. The uncertainty coefficient is not a delta measure, and the reader is referred to the SPSS literature for information about, and computation of, this measure (Nie, 1983; Nie et al., 1975; and Norusis, 1986).

Phi Coefficient

The phi coefficient (Φ) is mentioned in some of the older statistical texts (Freeman, 1965; Siegel, 1956) as well as recent ones. It is a measure used with nominal data when at least one of the variables is dichotomous. It is a delta measure, but it can also be computed directly from the cell frequencies without using the Chi square value. The latter method is practical when both variables are dichotomous.

The Φ coefficient can be used with $2 \times k$ tables (k meaning any number) but it cannot be used with 3×3 or other tables without at least one variable being dichotomous. This limits its utility if one has larger tables or wishes to compare associations in different size tables. From the Chi square value it can be computed easily for the data from Table 7.3.

$$\Phi = \sqrt{\frac{\chi^2}{N}} \qquad \Phi = \sqrt{(4.595 / 27)} = \sqrt{.17018} = .413.$$

It can also be computed for a 2×2 table from cell frequencies:

$$\Phi = \frac{ad - bc}{\sqrt{(a + b)(c + d)(b + d)(a + c)}} \quad \text{or} \quad \frac{64 - 6}{\sqrt{18,700}}$$

$$\text{or} \quad \frac{58}{136.75} = .424.$$

In this instance, we obtained a slightly different coefficient using the two different methods. If we correct for continuity and use the delta formula, we obtain a Φ coefficient of .315.

If you realize that the letters a, b, c, and d are symbols for the four cells in a 2×2 contingency table, it is apparent that Φ is the ratio of the square of the product of the marginals and the difference between the product of the diagonal cells. It is an index of the concentration of values (cases) in the diagonal cells. This is a useful index of association, particularly for 2×2 tables but also for $2 \times k$ tables. Some texts (Leonard, 1976, p. 290) limit Φ to the 2×2 table, but authors of several other texts advocate its use with $2 \times k$ tables (as long as one variable is dichotomous). There is also a Φ^2 version of Φ which will be discussed below under proportionate reduction of error measures.

Contingency Coefficient (C and C~)

The calculation of the contingency coefficient appeared in Siegel's 1956 edition of *Nonparametric Statistics for the Behavioral Sciences*, a popular book in use at that time by social workers, sociologists, educators, and psychologists. This was the only measure of association for nominal data discussed in that text and was, therefore, adopted by many researchers analyzing nominal data. More recent textbooks (Blalock, 1960, and later editions; Leege & Francis, 1974; Leonard,

1976; Loether & McTavish, 1974, and later editions) discuss additional and more versatile and useful measures for nominal variables.

The contingency coefficient could be used with all sizes of tables, but the drawback is that each size table has its own upper limit. In other words, it is not standardized on a unity scale. The upper limit of a 2 × 2 table is .707, not 1.00, as it would be on a unity scale. It can be put on a unity scale by dividing the coefficient by its upper limit, but even then, it appears to be inflated compared with other measures, such as Cramer's V and the uncertainty coefficient.

The computation of the contingency coefficient is straightforward. As a delta measure, it is calculated from Chi square. The calculation is illustrated below using the data from Table 7.3:

$$C = \sqrt{\frac{\chi^2}{\chi^2 + N}} \quad \text{or} \quad \sqrt{\frac{4.595}{4.595 + 27}} \quad \text{or} \quad \sqrt{\frac{4.595}{31.595}}$$

$$\text{or} \quad \sqrt{.1455} = .3814.$$

Leonard (1976, p. 283) provides the upper limits of C for various size tables (from 2 × 2 to 10 × 10). Because it has been used for nominal data in the literature, possibly more than any other measure of association, it is important to know about it, but there are other preferred measures for nominal data.

Tschuprow's T

Tschuprow's T is another delta index, more versatile than the Φ coefficient but not as versatile as Cramer's V. It is standardized on a unity scale for all square tables, that is, when the number of rows and the number of columns are equal ($r = c$). The computation is similar to that of Φ, C, and V but it makes use of the degree of freedom as well as Chi square and N. Here is the calculation using the data from Table 7.3.

$$T = \sqrt{\frac{X^2}{N(df)}} \quad \text{or} \quad \sqrt{\frac{4.595}{27(1)}} \quad \text{or} \quad \sqrt{.17019} \quad \text{or} \quad .413.$$

Note that in a 2 × 2 table, T will be the same as phi computed from Chi square because the equation has the same numerator. We will also see that this is the case with Cramer's V with a 2 × 2 table. Tschuprow's T is limited by the fact that it cannot be used when the number of columns and rows in a contingency table are unequal (i.e., when the tables are not square).

Cramer's V

Cramer's V is a versatile measure, can be used on all sizes of tables, and is standardized on a unity scale. Therefore, it overcomes the limitations of Φ, C, and T. The computation of V makes use of the number of columns and rows as well as Chi square and N. Using the data from Table 7.3, it is computed as follows (note the denominator):

$$V = \sqrt{\frac{\chi^2}{Nt}} \quad \text{or} \quad \sqrt{\frac{4.595}{27}} \quad \text{or} \quad \sqrt{.17019} \quad \text{or} \quad .413$$

where $t = r - 1$ or $c - 1$ whichever is smaller.

T is identical to V in square tables (i.e., when $r = c$) and Φ and V are identical when one of the variables is dichotomous. Therefore, V can be used to replace both Φ and T and is more versatile in that it can be used with any size table. While infrequently used in the past, it is certainly a preferred measure. It is included in the repertoire of the SPSS programs.

PRE MEASURES OF ASSOCIATION

Yule's Q

Yule's Q was thoroughly discussed in Chapter 3. The computation of Yule's Q makes use of the diagonal products as does the denominator in the Φ coefficient formula. But it derives an index somewhat differently. The data from Table 3.8 in Chapter 3 will be used to illustrate the computation. This is the data on worker's assessment of attachment and the placement decision (home or foster care). The reader may wish to review the discussion of Yule's Q in Chapter 3 before proceeding.

Computing Yule's Q may result in a negative correlation but if it does, this should be ignored. It is a relatively simple formula, easily calculated:

Data

1	12
7	7

$$Q = \frac{ad - bc}{ad + bc} \quad \frac{(1)(7) - (12)(7)}{(1)(7) + (12)(7)} \quad \frac{7 - 84}{7 + 84} \quad \frac{-77}{91} = -.846,$$

ignoring the minus sign, Q becomes .846 or .85.

The reader should be aware that the index is larger than one would expect if the restrictive version of perfect association were used and may recall that the distribution approximates the necessary condition using a less restrictive measure of association. Yule's Q can only be used with a 2 × 2 table, which makes it less versatile than one might wish, but on the other hand, many of the variables used in examining necessary and sufficient conditions would be dichotomous variables. Yule's Q has a proportionate reduction of error interpretation (Leonard, 1976, p. 279).

Phi Squared

Leonard points out that if we square Φ we have a proportionate reduction in error measure (1976, p. 289–290). When an index is squared, the squared index is a lower number than the original. From Table 7.3, Φ was calculated as .413; if we square this figure, we get .171. But of course Φ^2 has a different interpretation than Φ. Phi is an index of the diagonal concentration of values; Φ^2 is an index of how much of the variation in one variable you can predict by knowing the values of the categories in the other variable.

Guttman's Coefficient of Predictability: Lambda

This measure must be used with caution. The reason for caution is that in certain distributions with values concentrated in either one row or one column, the formula yields a coefficient of zero (.00) when, in fact, there is at least an appreciable correlation. If this feature of lambda (λ) is kept in mind, it can be a useful measure with many distributions. It has the versatility of a symmetric and an asymmetric version, and it can be used on tables of all sizes. The SPSS, SPSS-X, and SPSS/PC readouts provide both the symmetric and asymmetric index of λ.

Lambda is a PRE measure and is known as Guttman's coefficient of predictability. The calculation is simple but tedious by hand. Table 7.8, taken from a study by Marshall (1982), will be used to illustrate the computation of asymmetric λ. Later we will use the data from Table 3.10 in Chapter 3 to illustrate a major problem with its use.

The PRE measures are about prediction of errors and how those errors can be reduced if values of a second variable are known. Let us assume that we know the parole board decision on parole: we know that 327 have been paroled and 313 have not been paroled. At this point we do not know the parole officer's recommendation. If we pick up a case

Table 7.8

Parole Officer's Recommendation and Parole Board Decision in Cases
Coming Before the New South Wales Parole Board

| | Parole Officer's Recommendation | | | |
Parole Board Decision	Positive	Neutral	Negative	Total
Yes	299	19	9	327
No	43	51	219	313
Total	342	70	228	640

SOURCE: Abstracted from Marshall (1982, table 6, p. 21).
NOTE: Marshall has three additional categories in the independent variable that have been excluded here to simplify the computation.

file, without immediately looking at the contents our best guess would be that the offender was paroled, based on the fact that more people are paroled than not. If we consistently made this guess, we would be right more times than we would be wrong; that is, we would be wrong 313 times, and we would be right 327 times. If we knew the recommendation of the parole officer, would that improve our prediction? Obviously it would in this case.

Supposing we find that the color of the file folders indicate the recommendation of the parole officer and from the color we know the proportion of positive, negative, and neutral recommendations in each of the categories. If it is a positive recommendation, we would predict parole; if it is negative one, we would predict no parole; if it is neutral, we would predict no parole. How much has this improved our prediction rate? In these three predictions we would be wrong 71 times (43 + 19 + 9). We have reduced our error by 242 (313 – 71); our original error was 313. We have reduced our guessing error by .77 or 77%.

Lambda is an index of the number of errors in prediction made when only the values of one variable are known, to the number of errors in prediction when the values of a second variable are known. The best prediction when the value of only one variable is known is the modal value (for which we use the symbol, Fd). In words, the formula becomes:

$$\lambda_a = \frac{\text{amount of reduction in error}}{\text{amount of original error}}$$

The computation of the original error is N, less the modal value ($N - Fd$); the computation of the reduction in error is the amount of the original error less the sum of the modal values in the categories of the other variable (Σfi). The formula then becomes:

$$\lambda_a = \frac{\mid \Sigma fi - Fd \mid}{N - Fd},$$

where

λ_a = the asymmetric version of Lambda
Fd = modal value of the row totals
Σfi = the sum of the modal values in the columns.

The vertical lines, $\mid$, surrounding the numerator indicate that the absolute value is to be taken.

From the table above:

$$\lambda_a = \frac{(299 + 51 + 219) - 327)}{640 - 327} = \frac{242}{313} = .773 \text{ or } .77.$$

The interpretation of this index is that 77% of the errors in predicting the modal value of the dependent variable can be reduced by knowing the values of the categories in the independent variable.

There is an alternative use of symbols with λ that employs the use of the subscript symbols $_x$ and $_y$. We have predicted the modal value of y, the dependent variable, from our knowledge of the values of x, the independent variable; thus the symbol is not simply λ, but λ_{yx}. We can also make the prediction in the other direction, predicting x from y. In other words, we can predict the modal value of x from information about y in the same manner and the prediction will not ordinarily be identical. In this case we obtain an index of .59 when we compute λ_{xy}. The formula has the same characteristics but would be written as follows (followed by the calculation on the data above):

$$\lambda_{xy} = \frac{\mid \Sigma fi - Fd \mid}{N - Fd} \quad \text{or} \quad \lambda_{xy} = \frac{(299 + 219) - 342}{640 - 342} = \frac{176}{298} = .59.$$

Note that our prediction is better in one direction than the other.

The symmetric version of λ (λ_n) can be computed by combining our two asymmetric coefficients:

$$\lambda_n = \frac{\text{amount of reduction in error in both variables}}{\text{amount of original error in both variables}}.$$

The computation becomes

$$\lambda_n = \frac{\Sigma fr + \Sigma fc - (Fr + Fc)}{2N - (Fr + Fc)} \quad \text{or} \quad \frac{(569 + 518) - (327 + 342)}{2(640) - (327 + 342)};$$

to continue,

$$\lambda_n = \frac{1,087 - 669}{1,280 - 669} \quad \text{or} \quad \frac{418}{611} = .684$$

where

λ_n = nondirectional lambda (symmetric)
f_r = maximum frequency within each row
f_c = maximum frequency within each column
F_f = maximum frequency in a row total
F_c = maximum frequency in a column total.

Thus knowing the values of each of these variables reduces our prediction error by 68%. Knowing the parole officer's recommendation is more useful in guessing the board's decision than knowing the board's decision is for guessing the recommendation of the parole officer.

Several standard texts describe λ (Blalock, 1981, and earlier editions; Freeman, 1965; Leonard, 1976; Loether & Mctavish, 1980, and earlier editions; Mueller, Schuessler, & Costner, 1970). Lambda is useful because it can be used for both directional and nondirectional hypotheses, but it must be used with caution. When applied to the data in Table 3.1, for instance, the λ_a yields .00 when in fact there is a slight correlation between the two variables. Because of the concentration of cases in one column, λ breaks down.

Goodman and Kruskal's Tau$_y$

Another index that can be used in directional hypotheses with nominal level variables is Goodman and Kruskal's Tau$_y$ (τ_y). Tau$_y$ has a different interpretation from λ, although the basic notion of proportional reduction of errors is the same. Stated in words, it is an index of the proportional reduction in error when one predicts from the marginal values of one variable as compared with predicting from the knowledge of the marginal values in the second variable. However, it predicts the distribution of the values of the dependent variable, whereas λ predicts the modal value of the dependent variable.

Goodman and Kruskal's Tau$_y$ (τ_y) is standardized on a unity scale. The subscript $_y$ symbolizes that we are predicting the value of the dependent variable y from the values of the independent variable x. As with λ one could also predict in the other direction and the symbol would then be τ_x.

The calculation of τ_y is more complicated than the calculation of λ, but it can be easily programmed on calculators and computers. It has a more complicated explanation than λ and requires some preliminary calculations before applying the formula. Several authors provide discussions of τ_y and present more or less complicated formulas (Blalock, 1981, and earlier editions; Loether & McTavish, 1980, and earlier editions; Mueller, Schuessler, & Costner, 1970, 2nd ed.). I prefer my own symbols.

The calculation requires the computation of expected errors by random assignment to categories of the dependent variable. We compute the expected errors first for the dependent variable and then for each category of the independent variable. The calculation of the expected category error by random assignment is made by multiplying the proportion not in a given category by that category's frequency (Loether & McTavish, 1980, p. 225).

The marginal expected errors in the dependent variable are computed as follows:

$$E_1 = \Sigma \left[\frac{N - M_1}{N} \, (M_1) \right] + \left[\frac{N - M_2}{N} \, (M_2) \right] \text{ and so on.}$$

where

E_1 = expected errors in predicting column category from observed cases in columns

N = total number of cases in the table

M_1 = marginal for row 1

M_2 = marginal for row 2

Σ = summation symbol.

The marginal expected errors in the independent variable are computed as follows:

$$E_2 = \Sigma \left[\frac{n - C_1}{n} (C_1) \right] + \left[\frac{n - C_2}{n} (C_2) \right] \text{ and so on,}$$

where

E_2 = expected errors in predicting column category from knowledge of the row category

n = total number of cases in the column

C_1 = value of first cell

C_2 = value of second cell

Σ = summation symbol.

With E_1 and E_2, the formula for Goodman and Kruskal's τ_y now becomes:

$$\tau = \frac{E_1 - E_2}{E_1}.$$

From the data in Table 7.8 above, we can now make the calculations for τ.

For the dependent variable,

$$\left[\frac{640 - 327}{640} (327) \right] = 159.92 + \left[\frac{640 - 313}{640} (313) \right] = 159.92 = 319.84.$$

We add the two sums to obtain our expected error in the dependent variable without knowledge of the independent variable. This is E_1.

For the independent variable,

$$\left[\frac{342 - 299}{343}(299)\right] = 37.59 + \left[\frac{342 - 43}{342}(43)\right] = 37.59 = 75.18,$$

$$\left[\frac{70 - 19}{70}(19)\right] = 13.84 + \left[\frac{70 - 51}{70}(51)\right] = 13.84 = 27.68,$$

and

$$\left[\frac{228 - 9}{288}(9)\right] = 8.64 + \left[\frac{288 - 219}{228}(219)\right] = 8.64 = 17.28.$$

We add the three sums to obtain the expected error when knowledge of the independent variable is taken into account (75.18 + 27.68 + 17.28 = 120.14). The expected error is E_2. Now we can make the final calculation:

$$\tau = \frac{E_1 - E_2}{E_1} \quad \text{or} \quad \frac{319.84 - 120.14}{319.84} \quad \text{or} \quad \frac{199.70}{319.84} = .62.$$

We interpret this by saying that 62% of the error in prediction is reduced when we know the values of the second variable. Mueller, Schuessler, and Costner (1970, p. 263) state it in this way: τ_y

. . . indicates the relative reduction in error made possible by replacing random assignment of marginal categories with random assignment to cells within subclasses.

In comparing the relative advantages of τ_y and λ, it is important to see what happens when a distribution has a concentration of values in one column or one row. Table 7.3 is a good example with a concentration of cases in one row. When we calculate λ, τ_y, and Cramer's V, we obtain the following results: $\lambda = .00$, $\tau = .18$, and $V = .41$.

In spite of the fact that there is an appreciable correlation between the two variables, the calculation for λ yields .00, whereas τ is .18, a not insubstantial correlation with an asymmetric assumption. Note that Cramer's V, which we would use if it were considered a symmetric relationship, is larger than τ. This is because V is an index of a nondirectional relationship between the two variables, while τ is an index of a directional relationship, a more stringent procedure. You might note also that $\tau = V^2$. As has been noted, this frequently occurs but is not always the case.

If we make the prediction that fathers' political party affiliations determines the political party affiliation of offspring, we would want to use τ, but if we simply predict that the two variables will be associated, without an assumption of cause and effect, we would use V. We would not use λ because the values are concentrated in one category of the dependent variable. If a calculation yields .00 for λ, it is worthwhile to question the result unless another measure, such as τ, also yields .00.

Tests of Significance for Nominal/Nominal Distributions

We have already discussed the Chi square computation and how to determine the probability by consulting the Chi square table. When using delta measures, Chi square is the appropriate route for determining significance levels or probability. We also noted that Fisher's Exact Test could be used with 2 × 2 tables. In the case of τ_y, the uncertainty coefficient, and λ, Chi square could also be used. However, Harshbarger (1977, p. 481) provides another test of significance that can be used with λ, providing the sample size is large (N is at least 50) and assuming a normal distribution. It is a formula for calculating a z index which can then be used in a standard z table to determine probability. The formula is a bit complicated, and I will not attempt to discuss it here.

SUMMARY

In this chapter we have discussed the computations for two-variable, nominal-level distributions in which we desired to determine the level of association between two variables. We also examined some of the nuances of Chi square as well as its computation and explored some of the concepts necessary for interpreting the results of a Chi square computation: degrees of freedom, one- and two-tailed tests, and the correction for continuity. In addition to the Chi Square Test of Independence, we looked at the computation of two other tests of significance for the bivariate situation: Fisher's Exact Test and McNemar's Test of Significance.

In Chapter 8 we will examine the computations for bivariate distributions in which the two variables are ordinal. We will also examine computations for bivariate distributions in which two variables with different levels of measurement are employed: nominal/ordinal and nominal/interval combinations.

Chapter 8

COMPUTATIONS AND ILLUSTRATIONS: COMBINATIONS OF BIVARIATE DISTRIBUTIONS – NOMINAL, ORDINAL, AND INTERVAL DATA

NOMINAL, ORDINAL, AND INTERVAL COMBINATIONS

In this chapter we examine the statistical procedures and computations used with various combinations of variables: nominal/ordinal, nominal/interval, ordinal/ordinal, and ordinal/interval. We first present the computation of the measures of association and then the computation of the associated tests of significance.

Nominal/Ordinal Combinations: Theta

In Chapter 4 we looked at data from a study by Jayaratne and Ivey (1983) in which age and gender of clinical social workers were analyzed. Theta (Θ) was the appropriate measure of association for this distribution. The computation of Θ is not complex; we compare the rank in age of each group of females with the rank in age of each group of males. From this analysis, we obtain a ratio of the total possible comparisons to the difference between those males ranking below and those ranking above the females in age.

Thus, the first step is to determine the frequency of rankings above and below for each pair of classes in the nominal categories. By pair of

Table 8.1

Number of Clinical Social Workers by Gender and Age

| | Age | | | | |
Gender	35 & Under	36–45	46–55	56 & Over	Total
Female workers	57a	91b	130c	88d	366
Male workers	23e	66f	58g	20h	167
Total	80	157	188	108	533
Cumulative Column totals	80	237	425	533	
Mean rank	40.5	159	331.5	479.5	

$V = .18$ $\chi^2 = 16.87$ $(p. = .001)$.
$\Theta = .14$ $U = 2.75$ $(p. = .0001)$

SOURCE: Raw data from Jayaratne & Ivey (1983, table 1).

classes, we mean each pair of cells, that is, cell a with each of the cells in the other category (or row): $e, f, g,$ and h; cell b with each of the cells in the other category, and so on. Because of the placement of some cells, there are no other cells from the other category above or below them in rank; these cells are not included in the calculation. The calculation for the data in Table 8.1 could be considered tedious, but it is straightforward and can easily be programed for calculator or computer.

The formula as set forth by Freeman (1965, p. 10ff) is as follows:

$$\Theta = \frac{\Sigma D_i}{T_2},$$

or in words,

$$\Theta = \frac{|\text{ total ranked below } - \text{ total ranked above }|}{\text{total number of comparisons}}.$$

ΣD_i is the absolute sum of the differences from one category to another in the ranking above and below of respective cells. T_2 is the total number of possible comparisons, and Θ is the ratio between ΣD_i and T_2.

The horizontal lines enclosing the numerator signify that the absolute difference is taken. In other words, it does not matter whether or not the difference is negative or positive. The | signifies absolute value.

Our calculation is as follows:

$$57 * (66 + 58 + 20) + 91 * (58 + 20) + 130 * 20 = 17,906$$
$$91 * 23 + 130 * (23 + 66) + 88 * (23 + 66 + 58) = 26,599.$$

D is the absolute difference between these two products. Thus,

$$D = \mid 26,599 - 17,906 \mid = 8,693$$

In this case we have only one D because we have only two categories in the nominal variable. When the nominal variable has more than two categories, there is more than one D. In the calculation above, the sum of D "ΣD" is D_i.

Now we must compute the total number of comparisons. In a two-category variable, this is simply the product of the row totals of each category: $366 * 167 = 61,122$. Now we have the ingredients for our calculation:

$$\Theta = \frac{\Sigma D_i}{T_2} \quad \text{or} \quad \frac{8,693}{61,122} \quad \text{or} \quad \Theta = .14.$$

The result can be interpreted as indicating that females rank higher than males in age in 14% more cases than they rank lower.

Note the value of Cramer's V which does not take order into account (see Table 8.1). It would not be appropriate to use it with these data, but it is given here to illustrate the fact that a stronger association is possible when order is not considered. If data have been collected on an ordinal scale, ordinality would usually be considered important in the analsis of data, and therefore Θ is the appropriate measure. Two possible tests of significance for this important index are described here: the Mann-Whitney U Test and the Kruskal-Wallis H Test.

Mann-Whitney U Test of Significance

Of the two significance tests available for the distribution in Table 8.1, we will first discuss the Mann-Whitney U Test. If there were more than two categories in the nominal variable, we would use the Kruskal-Wallis H Test of significance, to be discussed below.

The calculation of U for large samples or populations is complex and tedious if done by hand, but there are ready-made programs for both calculators and computers for this index. Unfortunately some of these are based on the assumption that all cases in the distribution can be ranked in order between the various categories. This assumption often is not justified in the type of distributions we work with in the human services. In Table 8.1 we cannot rank each individual case. We only know that a certain proportion of the sample is under 35, 55 and over, and so on. Therefore we have to use a formula that computes a mean rank for the cases in each category.

In more than half a dozen statistical texts for social science (Blalock, various eds.; Freeman, 1965; Harshbarger, 1977; Jacobson, 1976; Leonard, 1976; Mueller, Schuessler & Costner, 1970; Siegel, 1956; Turney & Robb, 1973), I found only one that did not make the assumption that all cases could be ranked (Leege & Francis, 1974, p. 324ff). As a matter of fact all except the latter actually converted interval data to ordinal data to provide an example of a combination of nominal and ordinal data. In the human services it is not at all difficult to find tables with nominal and ordinal variables where the ordinal data have been gathered or obtained as ordinal data, not as interval data. A common example of this type of data is low, moderate, and high categories or scales.

In reading about the Mann-Whitney U Test or the Kruskal-Wallis H Test, keep in mind that most statistical texts do not provide the formula needed (i.e., one that includes computation of a mean rank for each ordinal category). Leege and Francis do so but there is a typographical error in the standard deviation formula in that text (1974, p. 326).

In computing the Mann-Whitney U Test there are actually several different calculations that need to be made. Mean ranks for each ordinal category must be computed, the standard deviation must be determined, the number of ties must be determined, and the expected value of U calculated. Finally a z value is derived to enable us to consult a z table for the probability level.

A computation table is useful once the mean rank for each category is determined. To determine the mean rank for each category, we must add all the ranks in a category and divide by the total number of cases in that category. From the data in Table 8.1, we can apply this somewhat tedious procedure. Starting at one end of the distribution, we take the oldest age group, with 108 cases. These cases share 108 ranks:

$$1 + 2 + 3 + 4 + \ldots + 106 + 107 + 108 = 5{,}886; \quad 5{,}886/108 = 54.5.$$

In the next category, 188 cases share the ranks between 108 and 296:

$$109 + 110 + \ldots + 294 + 295 + 296 = 38{,}070; \quad 38{,}070/188 = 202.5.$$

We would make this calculation for each of the four columns. However, the mean rank can be computed in another simpler, though less intuitive, way. Note that in Table 8.1 we have a row of figures that cumulates the frequencies of the columns. By using these cumulated frequencies we can calculate the average rank in each column:

$$MR = \frac{Cf + Cf_p + 1}{2},$$

where

MR = mean rank of the category
Cf = cumulative frequency of the column
Cf_p = frequency of previous column

Two examples are the following:

Column 1: $\frac{80 + 0 + 1}{2} = 40.5$;   Column 2: $\frac{237 + 80 + 1}{2} = 159$.

Once we have calculated the mean ranks, we can prepare a calculation table to obtain the ingredients needed for determining the difference between an expected U value and the observed U value of each of our nominal categories. From these values we then obtain a z value so we can enter a probability table to determine the significance of the distribution.

Thus several steps are required, and we start with a computation:

Age	Mean Rank	Females (f)	Wf for Females	Males (f)	Wf for Males	Total
35 & under	40.5	57	2,308.5	23	931.5	80
36–45	159	91	14,469	66	10,494	157
46–55	331.5	130	43,095	58	19,227	188
55 & over	479.5	88	42,196	20	9,590	108
Total		Σ = 366	102,068.5	167	40,242.5	533

NOTE: Each cell is weighted by multiplying its frequency by the mean rank (Wf). Then we sum the weighted cell frequencies for each nominal category (ΣWf).

The calculation in the computation table is to determine the weighted frequency (Wf) for each category. Once the weighted frequencies are summed, we can calculate the U for each category.

Actually we can compute a U for each category or we can compute it for one category and subtract one-half of the product of the two category totals $[(n_1)(n_2)]$.

Now we are ready to calculate U for females using the formula:

$$U = \Sigma Wf - \frac{n(n + 1)}{2}$$

$$U_F = \Sigma Wf_F - \frac{n_1(n_1 + 1)}{2} \quad \text{or} \quad U_F = \Sigma Wf_F - \frac{366(366 + 1)}{2}$$

$$U_F = 102,068.5 - 67,161 = 34,907.5.$$

And for the males:

$$U_M = \Sigma Wf_M - \frac{n_2(n_2 + 1)}{2} \quad \text{or} \quad U_M = \Sigma Wf_M - \frac{167(167 + 1)}{2}$$

$$U_M = 40,242.5 - 14,028 = 26,214.5$$

where

U_F = U for females
U_M = U for males
ΣWf = sum of mean rank x frequency
n_1 = total in female category
n_2 = total in male category

The expected value of U (U_E) is easily determined:

$$U_E = \frac{(n_1)(n_2)}{2} \quad \text{or} \quad \frac{(366)(167)}{2} = 30,561.$$

We could also determine this by using the sum of the weighted frequencies: $(34,907.5 + 26,214.5)/2 = 30,561$.

Because we have a large sample we will use a z table; if we had a small sample, we would use a U table (see Leonard, 1976, pp. 379–382 for U table). In order to use a z table, we must convert the difference between the expected and observed values to a z score with the formula:

$$\frac{U_E - U_F}{SD} \quad \text{and} \quad \frac{U_E - U_M}{SD}$$

where

U_E = expected U
SD = standard deviation
U_F = U for females
U_M = U for males

We have two additional steps before we can refer to the z table, however. We must calculate the sum of the tied values in each ordinal category (or for each ordinal rank), then compute a standard deviation of U.

The formula for determining ties for each ordinal category is:

$$T = \frac{t^3 - t}{12}$$

where t is the total in each ordinal category.
Thus each category contributes to the sum of T (ΣT).

$T_1 = (108^3 - 108) / 12$ or   104,976
$T_2 = (188^3 - 188) / 12$ or   553,707
$T_3 = (157^3 - 157) / 12$ or   322,478
$T_4 = (\ 80^3 - \ 80) / 12$ or   42,660
The sum of T (ΣT) =   1,023,812

Now we are ready to compute the standard deviation:

$$S_U = \sqrt{\left[\frac{(n_1)(n_2)}{N(N-1)}\right]\left[\frac{N^3 - N}{12} - \Sigma T\right]}$$

$$S_U = \sqrt{\left[\frac{(366)(167)}{533(533-1)}\right]\left[\frac{533^3 - 533}{12} - 1,023,812\right]}$$

$$S_U = \sqrt{\left[\frac{61,122}{283,556}\right][\,12,618,242 - 1,023,812\,]}$$

$$S_U = \sqrt{[.216]\,[\,11,594,430\,]} \quad \text{or} \quad \sqrt{2,499,240.89} \quad \text{or} \quad 1,580.90.$$

At last we have the ingredients to determine the z value for each of the categories. The formula is:

$$z_F = \frac{U_F - U_E}{S_U} \quad \text{or} \quad \frac{34,907.5 - 30,561}{1,580.90} \quad \frac{4,346.5}{1,580.90} \quad \text{or} \quad 2.75$$

$$z_M = \frac{U_M - U_E}{S_U} \quad \text{or} \quad \frac{26,214.5 - 30,561}{1,580.90} \quad \frac{-4,346.5}{1,580.90} \quad \text{or} \quad -2.75.$$

Note that the z for females and males is the same, one positive and one negative. We ignore the negative and consult a z table to find that the probability is .0004 (see Fitz-Gibbon & Morris, 1978, pp. 56–69 for alternative calculation method).

We can have considerable confidence in generalizing to the population from this sample, and we can be certain that the relationship is not due to chance alone; however, we note from the value of Θ that the degree of association between gender and age level is not a strong one ($\Theta = .14$).

Kruskal-Wallis H Test

When employing Θ with distributions that have three or more nominal categories (and any number of ordinal categories), we cannot use the Mann-Whitney U Test of Significance. The Kruskal-Wallis H Test can be used for distributions with two or more nominal categories and any number of ordinal categories. Thus, the Kruskal-Wallis H Test is the more versatile of the two tests. The two tests are calculated in much the same way. Like the U test, the computation for H is a bit tedious and time-consuming but can easily be programmed for calculators or computers. To illustrate its use, the data from Sheila Collins' study (1984) discussed in Chapter 4 (see Table 8.2) will be employed.

The formula requires the computation of mean ranks and the sum of tied values for the ordinal variable. In fact the Kruskal-Wallis H is an extension of U, and it is feasible to program them together because the formulas use many of the same ingredients.

Table 8.2

Fathers' Support for Top Level Administrators

| Occupation | Fathers' Support Level | | | |
	Low No.	Moderate No.	High No.	Total No.
Social Work	7	9	13	29
Nursing	21	10	13	44
Education	5	13	6	24
Total	33	32	32	97

H = 3.63   p. = .17 (approximately)   Θ = .16

SOURCE: Collins (1984).

All of the texts mentioned in relation to the Mann-Whitney U Test also provide formulas for computing H, although they use somewhat different symbols. I have adopted my own symbols in order to simplify the presentation of the formula. Perhaps the best explanation of the procedures is contained in Leege and Francis (1974, p. 327ff), although there is a typographical error in the formula presented.

We turn now to actual data to see what is involved in the computation of H. Unlike the Mann-Whitney U Test, we need not compute a standard deviation of H because the values of H approximate the distribution of Chi square, and we can use that table to determine the probability of H. A computation table is useful:

| Occupation | Fathers' Support Level | | | |
	Low	Moderate	High	Total
Social work	7	9	13	29
Nursing	21	10	13	44
Education	5	13	6	24
Total	33	32	32	97
Cumulative f	97	64	32	
Mean rank	81	48.5	16.5	

	Social Work		Nursing		Education	
Low	7 × 81 =	567	21 × 81 =	1,701	5 × 81 =	405
Moderate	9 × 48.5 =	436.5	10 × 48.5 =	485	13 × 48.5 =	630.5
High	13 × 16.5 =	214.5	13 × 16.5 =	214.5	6 × 16.5 =	99
Sum of weighted cell frequencies		= 1,218		2,400.5		1,134.5

Two preliminary calculations are necessary, the mean rank and the sum of the tied values for each of the ordinal categories. First, it is necessary to determine the sum of the ties on the ordinal variable:

$$T_1 = \frac{33^3 - 33}{12} \quad \frac{35,937 - 33}{12} \quad \frac{35,904}{12} = 2,992$$

$$T_2 = \frac{32^3 - 32}{12} \quad \frac{32,768 - 32}{12} \quad \frac{32,736}{12} = 2,728$$

$$T_3 = \frac{32^3 - 32}{12} \quad \frac{32,768 - 32}{12} \quad \frac{32,736}{12} = 2,728$$

$$\Sigma T \qquad\qquad\qquad\qquad\qquad\qquad = 8,448$$

The reader will recall that we computed the mean rank with the formula:

$$MR = (Cf + Cf_p + 1)/2.$$

The formula for H and computation for these data follows:

$$H = \frac{\left(\dfrac{12}{N(N+1)} \sum \dfrac{W^2}{n}\right) - 3(N+1)}{1 - \Sigma T/N^3 - N}$$

where

W = the weighted cell frequencies (W_1, W_2, and W_3 for each of the categories in the ordinal variable)
ΣT = the sum of the ties on the ordinal variable
N = the total number of cases
n = the total number of cases in the category.

The computation:

$$H = \frac{\left[\dfrac{12}{97(97+1)}\left(\dfrac{1,218^2}{29} + \dfrac{2,400.5^2}{44} + \dfrac{1,134.5^2}{24}\right)\right] - 3(97+1)}{1 - (8,448)/97^3 - 97}$$

$$H = \frac{\left[\dfrac{12}{9,506}(51,156 + 130,963.64 + 53,628.76) \right] - 3(98)}{1 - (8,448 / 912,673 - 97)}$$

$$H = \frac{[.001262361(235,748.4)] - 294}{1 - (8,448 / 912,576)}$$

$$H = \frac{297.599 - 294}{1 - .0092573} \quad \text{or} \quad \frac{3.599}{.99074} = 3.63$$

When we consult the Chi square table we find that 3.63 falls somewhere between .10 and .20, making it necessary to interpolate the probability. The probability for this distribution is approximately .17. At any rate it does not reach the .05 level which we would ordinarily consider to be the critical point for this type of data. One can have little confidence in generalizing to the population from this sample, and in spite of a modest correlation between the two variables ($\Theta = .16$), we cannot be certain that the correlation itself may not be one of chance.

NOMINAL/INTERVAL MEASURES

Eta and the Correlation Ratio

Although Pearson's r can be used with the combination of nominal and interval variables when the nominal variable is dichotomous, eta (η) and the correlation ratio are more appropriate and, in some ways, more useful procedures designed for this combination. Eta is the square root of the correlation ratio (η^2). Eta and the correlation ratio are not limited to relationships that are linear, a distinct advantage in determining the strength of association between variables reflecting attributes of human behavior.

In spite of the potential usefulness of the correlation ratio and eta in human service research, it is difficult to find an example of its use in the social work and human services literature, even though several texts on statistics for social science provide a description of the measure: Freeman (1965, p. 120ff), Harshbarger (1977, p. 455ff), Jacobson (1976, p. 464ff), Leege and Francis (1974, p. 294ff), Loether and

Table 8.3

Ideological Orientation and Change in Per Capita Energy Consumption,
1950 to 1974, Nine Nations

Ideological Orientation	Change in Per Capita Energy Consumption
Situational	
El Salvador	2.44
Haiti	.82
Iraq	5.43
Syria	5.02
Traditional	
Afghanistan	15.75
Ethiopia	14.50
Jordon	4.99
Saudi Arabia	4.95
Thailand	12.64

$\eta = .69$
Correlation ratio $(\eta^2) = .48$
$F = 8.33$ $p. = .05$

SOURCE: Author's data, drawing from categorical data on ideological orientation provided by Adelman and Morris (1971).

McTavish (1980, p. 261ff, Mueller, Schuessler, and Costner (1970, p. 325ff) and Nie et al (1975, p. 230).

Table 4.5 in Chapter 4 provides the data for an illustration of the computation of the correlation ratio (see Table 8.3). The formula for computing η and the correlation ratio looks complex but it is relatively simple.

Essentially the computation involves a number of steps in simple arithmetic: computing the means for each category and for the total distribution, squaring each value and summing the squares, squaring the grand mean and the categorical means, and multiplying this product by the totals. The equation ends up being a ratio of (1) the difference between the sum of the categorical values squared and the squared means weighted by respective totals and (2) the difference between the sum of the categorical values squared and the product of the grand mean squared weighted by the total number of cases in the distribution.

The procedure resembles the computation of Pearson's correlation coefficient and, in fact, will be identical to Pearson's r if the relationship between two variables happens to be linear. However, a major advantage of the correlation ratio is that the index reflects nonlinear relationships as well as linear ones.

Eta (η) is asymmetric and the correlation ratio (η^2) indicates the proportionate reduction of error (it is a PRE measure) in the dependent variable by using the means of the categories. In other words, the correlation ratio is an index of the variation in the dependent variable that can be predicted from knowing the means of the categories of the independent variable. The procedure is initiated by first squaring, then adding, figures in each category of the nominal variable, then adding the summed values for both categories:

Category 1 (Situational)		Category 2 (Traditional)		Both Categories	
Y	Y^2	Y	Y^2	Y	Y^2
2.44	5.95	15.75	248.06		
.82	.67	14.50	210.25		
5.43	29.48	4.99	24.90		
5.02	25.20	4.95	24.50		
		12.64	159.77		
13.71	61.30	52.83	667.48	66.54	728.78
ΣY	ΣY^2	ΣY	ΣY^2	ΣY	ΣY^2

where Y = values of dependent variable (change in per capita energy consumption).

The next step:

Category 1	Category 2	Total Distribution
$\mu = 13.71/4$ or 3.43	$\mu = 52.83/5$ or 10.57	$\mu = 7.39$
$\mu^2 = 11.75$	$\mu^2 = 111.64$	$\mu^2 = 54.66$
$\mu^2 * 4 = 46.99$	$\mu^2 * 5 = 558.20$	$\mu^2 * N = 491.95$

Sum of $\mu^2 * n$ for each category: $(\Sigma \mu^2 * n) = 605.19$

where

N = total number of cases in the distribution
n = total number of cases in the categories
μ = mean.

After summing the values in each category and the squared values in each category, we obtain the mean, the mean squared, and the product of the number of cases in the category and the squared mean. This is carried out for each category and for the distribution as a whole.

We now have the ingredients for computing η^2: the sum of the values of all cases in the two categories (ΣY^2), the sum of the categorical means squared, weighted by the total number of cases in the categories $(\Sigma\mu^2 * n)$, and the product of the grand mean squared and the total number of cases. The numerator is the sum of squares between groups, and the denominator is the sum of squared differences for the total distribution; η^2 is the ratio of the two sums.

$$\eta^2 = 1 - \frac{\Sigma Y^2 - \Sigma\mu^2 * N}{\Sigma Y^2 - \mu^2 * N} \quad \text{or} \quad 1 - \frac{728.80 - 605.19}{728.80 - 491.95}$$

$$\text{or} \quad 1 - \frac{123.61}{236.85};$$

and to continue;

$$\eta^2 = 1 - .52 \quad \text{or} \quad .48,$$

and

$$\eta = .69.$$

The interpretation of the two indices is that eta (η) provides an asymmetric index of the strength of relationship between the two variables, in this case relatively strong, and the correlation ratio, η^2, is an index of the amount of variability that can be predicted in the dependent variable from knowledge of the independent variable (48%), also relatively strong.

F Statistic for the Correlation Ratio and Eta

Probability is determined by use of the F statistic, which is computed by using the correlation ratio, η^2, the total number of values in the distribution, N, and the number of categories in the nominal variable, Σn. Using the data from Table 8.3, we compute F as follows:

$$F = \frac{\eta^2 * (N - \Sigma n) + (\Sigma n - 1)}{(1 - \eta^2)(\Sigma n - 1)} \quad \text{or} \quad F = \frac{.48(9 - 2) + (2 - 1)}{(1 - .48)(2 - 1)};$$

to continue,

$$F = \frac{3.36 + 1}{.52 * 1} \quad \text{or} \quad \frac{4.36}{.52} = 8.38; \quad F = 8.38.$$

Because the data are not from a sample, we are not trying to generalize to a population, but the skeptic might suggest that the finding is due to chance. We can consult an F table to determine that the probability of obtaining this result is .05. However, the population is small, so we must view the result with some uneasiness and, although perhaps not due to chance, the relationship may be spurious (i.e., other factors may be exerting an effect on the change in energy consumption which we have erroneously attributed to ideological orientation). Obviously more data are needed and additional variables need to be taken into account.

In consulting the F table (Table D, Appendix B), we note that we need to have two different degrees of freedom: one on the vertical axis and one on the horizontal axis. The vertical axis is the one we are most familiar with and is simply $N - 1$ or 8. On the horizontal scale we take as the degree of freedom the number of pairs of variables in the distribution, in this case one pair, so we consult the column under 1. An F of 5.32 would reach the .05 level of probability, but it would take an F of 11.26 to reach the .01 level of probability so we take the former as the probability in this instance. We can conclude that the relationship is not simply due to chance, but it may be spurious.

ORDINAL/ORDINAL COMBINATIONS

Ranked Data: Spearman's Rho

Spearman's rho (ρ or r_s) is a frequently used measure of association in human services research when ranks have been assigned to attributes associated with two or more individuals or groups. The table from Chapter 4 on McGrath's study (1986) of family functioning after heart attacks will be used to illustrate the computation of ρ.

Table 8.4

Comparison of Family Functioning Level by Areas of Functioning for
Husbands and Wives After Heart Attack

Area of Functioning	Rank Order of Level of Functioning Husband	Wife
Family relationships	8	8
Individual behavior	4.5	7
Care of children	4.5	3.5
Social activities	7	5.5
Economic conditions	3	2
Home and household	1	5.5
Health conditions	2	1
Use of community resources	6	3.5

$r_s = .55$ $t = 1.60$ $p. = .15$

SOURCE: McGrath (1986, table E.20, p. 368).

Spearman's Rho (ρ or r_s) establishes the degree of association between two sets of ranks. In Table 8.4 the various functions are derived by each spouse separately scaling their own perceptions. The scale results were then ranked and a Spearman's ρ calculated. The formula for Spearman's ρ is an uncomplicated one:

$$\rho = 1 - \frac{6(\Sigma D^2)}{N(N^2 - 1)},$$

where D = difference in rank.

In ranking categories for each case, you must remember that if there are ties, the ties must be given the same rank. In the computation table that follows, you will note that because "individual behavior" and "care of children" were given the same rank, they are given the value of 4.5, and there is no rank of 4 or 5 in the column. Actually there are more ties in this distribution than is desirable for the use of Spearman's ρ.

The following computation table will be useful in understanding how the calculations are made:

Area of Functioning	Husband's Rank	Wife's Rank	Difference in Rank (D)	D^2
Family relationships	8	8	0	—
Individual behavior	4.5	7	2.5	6.25
Care of children	4.5	3.5	1	1
Social activities	7	5.5	1.5	2.25
Economic conditions	3	2	1	1
Home and household	1	5.5	4.5	20.25
Health conditions	2	1	1	1
Use of community resources	6	3.5	2.5	6.25

$\Sigma D^2 = 38.00$

With the sum of the differences in rank, the calculation is readily made:

$$\rho = 1 - \frac{6(\Sigma D^2)}{N(N^2 - 1)} \quad \text{or} \quad 1 - \frac{6(38)}{8(8^2 - 1)} \quad \text{or} \quad 1 - \frac{6(38)}{8(63)};$$

to continue,

$$\rho = 1 - \frac{228}{504} \quad \text{or} \quad 1 - .45 = .55.$$

The correlation is fairly high, although one would expect a considerable amount of congruence on this variable. The data are from a population, not a sample; therefore, we are not concerned with generalizing to a larger group of patients. In anticipation of skepticism, however, we might want to determine the probability of obtaining this distribution, given the number of cases. With this in mind we would employ the t statistic to determine probability. If we had a larger population we would have used the z test. The computation is straightforward:

$$t = \rho \sqrt{\frac{N-2}{1-(\rho)^2}} \quad \text{or} \quad \rho \sqrt{\frac{8-2}{1-.300}} \quad \text{or} \quad \rho \sqrt{\frac{6}{.700}};$$

to continue,

$$t = \rho \sqrt{8.570} \quad \text{or} \quad \rho * 2.927 = 1.60.$$

We now enter the t table to determine probability and find that with seven degrees of freedom (8-1), the t statistic does not reach the .10 level of 1.895, but it does reach the .20 level of 1.415 (two-tailed test).

By interpolation we can estimate that the probability was about .15, not a good basis for assuming that the correlation is anything other than chance.

Ordinal Categories: Concordant, Discordant, and Tied Pairs

Often data are not ranked case by case or attribute by attribute but are obtained in categorical order. In such instances several measures of association can be used. The most useful are γ, Kendall's τ_b, and Somer's d. To determine the extent to which the ranking of one variable is useful in predicting the rank on a second variable, it is necessary to identify pairs of cases that are ranked in the same order, ranked in reverse order, or are tied. An example, using a small number of hypothetical cases, will illustrate these patterns (Table 8.5).

Six individuals, ranked on two variables in categories of low, medium, and high, are represented by the letters A, B, C, D, E, and F. The cells are lettered in lower-case italics in the conventional mode. Our goal is to identify pairs of cases that are ranked in the same order (concordant) (i.e., highs with highs and lows with lows), those ranked in reverse order (discordant) (i.e., highs with lows); and cases in which pairs are tied. They can be tied on both variables (C and F), tied on the independent variable (A and B, C and E, and E and F) or tied on the dependent variable (B and E, C and D, and D and F). There are 15 combinations or 15 pairs that we need to classify by pattern. The number of pairs to be compared can be determined by the formula $N(N - 1)/2$. There are conventional symbols for each of these patterns, identified as follows:

		pairs
N_s = concordant (ranked in same order): AD AC AE AF DE		(5)
N_d = discordant (ranked in reverse order): BD BC BF		(3)
T_x = ties on independent variable: AB CE EF		(3)
T_y = ties on dependent variable: BE CD DF		(3)
T_{xy} = ties on both variables: CF		(1)

These are the elements used to compute measures of association for ordinal categories. From these ingredients we can compute ratios to reflect the prediction value in ranking one ordinal variable from knowledge of another.

Table 8.5

Relationship Between Hypothetical Independent and Dependent Ordinal
Variables

Dependent Variable	Independent Variable		
	Low	Medium	High
High	B a	b	E c
Medium	d	D e	F C f
Low	A g	h	i

$\tau_b = .18$

$N_s = AD\ AC\ AE\ AF\ DE \quad (5)$ $N_d = BD\ BC\ BF \quad (3)$

$T_x = AB\ CE\ EF \quad (3)$ $T_y = BE\ CD\ DF \quad (3)$

$T_{xy} = CF \quad (1)$

The various ratios discussed in this chapter for ordinal/ordinal combinations take into account concordant and discordant pairs and, in
some instances, ties on one or the other variable: Kendall's τ_a and τ_b, γ
and Somer's d. The formulas are presented here for comparative pur-
poses:

τ_a	τ_b	γ	Somer's d
$\dfrac{N_s - N_d}{N(N-1)/2}$	$\dfrac{N_s - N_d}{\sqrt{(N_s + N_d + T_y)(N_s + N_d + T_x)}}$	$\dfrac{N_s - N_d}{N_s + N_d}$	$\dfrac{N_s - N_d}{N_s + N_d + T_y}$

Note that all four equations have the same numerator and that τ_a is a
ratio of the difference between concordant and discordant cases to the
total number of combinations in the distribution. Neither τ_a nor γ takes
ties into consideration. Three of these measures are for relationships
considered to be symmetric or nondirectional, τ_a, τ_b and γ; only Somer's
d is used for relationships in which the distinction is to be made between
dependent and independent variables (i.e., asymmetric or directional
relationships).

Symmetric Measures for Ordinal Data: Kendall's Tau$_a$ and Tau$_b$, and Gamma

Selecting one of the measures (τ_b) for illustration, we apply it to our hypothetical data from Table 8.5:

$$\tau_b = \frac{N_s - N_d}{\sqrt{(N_s + N_d + T_y)(N_s + N_d + T_x)}} \quad \text{or}$$

$$\frac{5 - 3}{\sqrt{(5 + 3 + 3)(5 + 3 + 3)}} \quad ;$$

to continue

$$\tau_b = \frac{2}{\sqrt{(11)(11)}} \quad \text{or} \quad \frac{2}{\sqrt{121}} \quad \text{or} \quad \frac{2}{11} = .18.$$

This can be interpreted as the proportionate reduction in errors in predicting the order of one variable when the order of the other variable is known (i.e., by 18%).

If the hypothetical data are re-organized so that there is greater concentration in the diagonal, we obtain a quite different result and by only shifting one case. Thus the measure is sensitive to order. This is illustrated in Table 8.6.

Now we compute the τ_b for this distribution:

$$\tau_b = \frac{N_s - N_d}{\sqrt{(N_s + N_d + T_y)(N_s + N_d + T_x)}} \quad \text{or}$$

$$\frac{7 - 0}{\sqrt{(7 + 0 + 4)(7 + 0 + 2)}} \quad ;$$

to continue,

$$\tau_b = \frac{7}{\sqrt{(11)(9)}} \quad \text{or} \quad \frac{7}{\sqrt{99}} \quad \text{or} \quad \frac{7}{9.95} = .70.$$

With this distribution, the index of association shows a proportionate reduction in error of 70% when the order of the second variable is known.

One more illustration will demonstrate a negative correlation with highs associated with lows in the ranking of the ordinal categories

Table 8.6

Relationship Between Hypothetical Independent and Dependent Ordinal
Variables

Dependent Variable	Independent Variable		
	Low	Medium	High
High	a	b	E c
Medium	d	B D e	F C f
Low	A g	h	i

$\tau_b = .70$

$N_s = AB\ AD\ AC\ AF\ AE\ BE\ DE$ (7) $N_d = (0)$
$T_x = CE\ EF$ (2) $T_y = BC\ BF\ CD\ DF$ (4)
$T_{xy} = BD\ CF$ (2)

(Table 8.7). Once the number of cases falling in each category is
determined from Table 8.7, we can calculate τ_b:

$$\tau_b = \frac{N_s - N_d}{\sqrt{(N_s + N_d + T_y)(N_s + N_d + T_x)}} \quad \text{or}$$

$$\frac{1 - 9}{\sqrt{(1 + 9 + 2)(1 + 9 + 2)}};$$

to continue,

$$\tau_b = \frac{-8}{\sqrt{(11)(12)}} \quad \text{or} \quad \frac{-8}{\sqrt{144}} \quad \text{or} \quad \frac{-8}{12} = -.67.$$

In this instance, the proportionate reduction in error is 67% when the order
of a second variable is known, but the direction of the association is
negative (i.e., highs are associated with lows).

These examples are given to provide a more intuitive understanding
of these measures. In actually computing them, even with just a few
more cases, the process becomes tedious, and an alternative computa-

Table 8.7

Relationship Between Hypothetical Independent and Dependent Ordinal Variables

Dependent Variable	Independent Variable		
	Low	Medium	High
High	A B a	b	c
Medium	d	C e	E f
Low	g	D h	F i

$\tau_b = -.67$

N_s	$=$	DE	(1)	N_d	$=$ AC AE AD AF BC BD BE BF CF	(9)
T_x	$=$	CD EF	(2)	T_y	$=$ CE DF	(2)
T_{xy}	$=$	AB	(1)			

tion method is used to make it less so. In using the alternative method, some of the intuitive understanding of the measure is lost.

The data from McGrath's study (1986) on adjustment and the number of days in the hospital (Table 4.10 from Chapter 4) can be used to illustrate the computation of the ordinal measures (see Table 8.8).

There are 78 pairs to compare in this distribution $(N(N-1)/2)$, and it would be tedious to locate all of them as we did when we only had 15 pairs to compare. There is a simpler way to locate the number of different patterns than the one we used above. Assigning cell designations in the conventional fashion enables us to construct a computation formula for each of the patterns.

Working from the lower left-hand cell, g, we identify all cases ranked higher than the cases in g on either the dependent or independent variable (i.e., cases in cells b, c, e, and f). We obtain the product of these cases in the formula $g(b + c + e + f)$. This has to be calculated for the other cells as well: $h(c + f)$; $e(c)$; and $d(b + c)$. This total product gives us N_s, the number of concordant pairs (see Table 8.9 for cell designations).

$$N_s = g(b + c + e + f) + h(c + f) + e(c) + d(b + c)$$
$$4(0 + 1 + 2 + 0) + 1(1 + 0) + 2(1) + 2(0 + 1)$$

Table 8.8

Relationship Between Days in Hospital and Individual Behavior and
Adjustment After the Heart Attack

Level of Individual Behavior and Adjustment	Number of Days in Hospital			
	1–10	11–20	21+	Total
Most	3	0	1	4
In between	2	2	0	4
Least	4	1	0	5
Total	9	3	1	13

$\gamma = .21$	$z = .32$	$p. = .37$
$d = .15$	$z = .23$	$p. = .41$
$\tau_a = .08$	$z = .38$	$p. = .35$
$\tau_b = .13$	$z = .37$	$p. = .36$

SOURCE: McGrath (1985, p. 362).
NOTE: Indices for measures of association, z, and probabilities have been added.

or
$$4(3) + 1 + 2 + 2$$
or
$$12 + 5 = 17$$

$$N_d = a(e + f + h + i) + b(f + i) + e(i) + d(h + i).$$
$$3(2 + 0 + 1 + 0) + 0(0 + 0) + 2(0) + 2(1 + 0)$$
or
$$3(3) + 2(1)$$
or
$$9 + 2 = 11$$

$$T_y = a(d + g) + d(g) + b(e + h) + e(h) + c(f + i) + f(i)$$
$$3(0 + 1) + 0(1) + 2(2 + 0) + 2(0) + 4(1 + 0) + 1(0)$$
or
$$3(1) + 2(2) + 4(1)$$
or
$$3 + 4 + 4 = 11$$

Table 8.9

Relationship Between Days in Hospital and Individual Behavior and
Adjustment After the Heart Attack

Level of Individual Behavior and Adjustment	Number of Days in Hospital			Total
	1–10	*11–20*	*21+*	
Most	3 a	0 b	1 c	4
In between	2 d	2 e	0 f	4
Least	4 g	1 h	0 i	5
Total	9	3	1	13

$\tau_b = .13$

$$T_x = a(b + c) + b(c) + d(e + f) + e(f) + g(h + i) + h(i)$$
$$3(2 + 4) + 2(4) + 0(2 + 1) + 2(1) + 1(0 + 0) + 0(0)$$

or

$$3(6) + 2(4) + 2(1)$$

or

$$18 + 8 + 2 = 28$$

Now we have the ingredients to compute τ_b, τ_a, γ, or Somer's d. For the data in McGrath's study (1986), we will first compute τ_b, then the other measures.

$$\tau_b = \frac{N_s - N_d}{\sqrt{(N_s + N_d + T_y)(N_s + N_d + T_x)}} \quad \text{or}$$

$$\frac{17 - 11}{\sqrt{(17 + 11 + 28)(17 + 11 + 11)}} \; ;$$

to continue,

$$\tau_b = \frac{6}{\sqrt{(39)(56)}} \quad \text{or} \quad \frac{6}{\sqrt{2,184}} \quad \text{or} \quad \frac{6}{46.73} = .13.$$

In this instance knowing the order of the second variable only reduces the proportionate error by 13%. τ_b accounts for ties in both the independent and the dependent variable; ties on both variables are considered to be trivial because they fall in the same cell in the contingency table. On a square table (if $r = c$), τ_b is standardized on a unity scale but cannot reach unity (1.00) if the table is not square.

τ_a is a less preferred measure because it does not take ties into account, and in the type of data we are dealing with here, there are usually a good many ties. In addition, it cannot reach a magnitude of 1.00 (unity) if there are ties. Otherwise, it is applicable to all size tables.

$$\tau_a = \frac{N_s - N_d}{N(N-1)/2} \quad \text{or} \quad \frac{17 - 11}{13(13-1)/2} \quad \text{or} \quad \frac{6}{156/2} \quad \text{or} \quad \frac{6}{78};$$

to continue,

$$\tau_a = \frac{6}{78} = .08.$$

Goodman and Kruskal's gamma (G or γ) ignores ties as well, but it will reach unity regardless of the number of ties. Gamma yields the same coefficient as Yule's Q when the variables are dichotomous. However, γ can be used with all sizes of tables. Like Yule's Q, γ also takes the less restrictive meaning of a perfect association (see Chapter 3 for discussion of Yule's Q and the meaning of a perfect association).

$$\gamma = \frac{N_s - N_d}{N_s + N_d} \quad \text{or} \quad \frac{17 - 11}{17 + 11} \quad \text{or} \quad \frac{6}{28} = .21.$$

Gamma, τ_a, and τ_b are all symmetric measures of association. It may seem curious that with three measures of association, we have produced three different coefficients, using measures that are specifically for nondirectional relationships: .13, .08, and .21. You may recall that γ takes the less restrictive meaning of perfect association, and the other two measures do not. Thus it yields a larger index than τ_a or τ_b. τ_a does not take ties into consideration, and there are a number of ties in this distribution. τ_b is, therefore, the most appropriate measure if we assume this is a nondirectional relationship and we want the more restrictive version of perfect association. In any case, the level of association is not strong.

Asymmetric Measure for Ordinal Data: Somer's d

If a distribution is considered to be asymmetric, Somer's d is an appropriate statistical procedure for ordinal variables. Somer's d takes account of which variable is the predictor and takes account of ties on the predicted variable. Ties on the predictor variable are not included in the formula. However, the variables can be reversed, and the denominator would then be $N_s + N_d + T_x$. Thus two d's can be computed on the same distribution. In this case (Table 8.8), logic dictates that the number of days in hospital would be the independent variable because it precedes the adjustment after hospitalization. Nevertheless, for purposes of demonstration we will run the correlation both ways:

$$d_{xy} = \frac{N_s - N_d}{N_s + N_d + T_y} \quad \text{or} \quad \frac{17 - 11}{17 + 11 + 11} \quad \text{or} \quad \frac{6}{39} = .14;$$

$$d_{yx} = \frac{N_s - N_d}{N_s + N_d + T_x} \quad \text{or} \quad \frac{17 - 11}{17 + 11 + 28} \quad \text{or} \quad \frac{6}{56} = .11.$$

You will note that if we take an average of the two coefficients, it will be identical with the τ_b coefficient; in fact, τ_b is the square root of the product of two d's run either way:

$$\tau_b = \sqrt{d_{yx} * d_{xy}} \quad \sqrt{(.11)(.15)} \quad \sqrt{.017} = .13.$$

The symbol d_{yx} indicates that x is the predictor variable, and the symbol d_{xy} indicates that y is the predictor variable.

Because Somer's d is asymmetric and therefore can provide an index of predictability in each direction and τ_b is asymmetric and provides an index of predictability in both directions, it makes sense that τ_b is an average of two Somer's d coefficients on the same distribution.

Somer's d is clearly a useful and versatile measure. It is an asymmetric measure with a proportionate reduction of error (PRE) interpretation. It can be used on any size table. The reader should not be discouraged by the tediousness of the computation for Somer's d. It can be easily programmed in BASIC or on the more sophisticated electronic calculators. The SPSS programs include Somer's d in their repertoire.

TESTS OF SIGNIFICANCE FOR ORDINAL MEASURES OF ASSOCIATION

Tests of Significance for Tau$_b$, Tau$_a$, Gamma and Somer's d

The test of significance for τ_a and τ_b requires the computation of a standard error:

For τ_a	*For* τ_b
$z = \dfrac{\tau_a}{\tau_{SE}}$	$z = \dfrac{N_s - N_d}{N_s - N_{dSE}}$
The term τ_{SE} is computed by:	The term $N_s - N_{dSE}$ is computed by:
$\tau_{SE} = \sqrt{\dfrac{2(2N+5)}{9N(N-1)}}$	$N_s - N_{dSE} = \sqrt{1/18N(N-1)(2N+5)}$
$\tau_{SE} = \sqrt{\dfrac{2(31)}{117(12)}}$	$N_s - N_{dSE} = \sqrt{.056(13)(12)(31)}$
$\tau_{SE} = \sqrt{\dfrac{62}{1,404}}$	$N_s - N_{dSE} = \sqrt{.056(4,836)}$
$\tau_{SE} = \sqrt{.04}$	$N_s - N_{dSE} = \sqrt{268.667}$
$\tau_{SE} = .21$	$N_s - N_{dSE} = 16.39$

Aside from that computation, it is a straightforward use of z, although the terms of the formula are different for each of the measures.

We can now compute z for τ_a and τ_b :

For τ_a —	*For* τ_b —
$z = \dfrac{.08}{.21} = .38$	$z = \dfrac{6}{16.39} = .37$

Entering the z table, we find that these two z quantities for τ_a and τ_b have probabilities of .35 and .36, respectively. The z test can also be used with γ and Somer's d using the same formula for the two measures.

For γ	*For Somer's* d
$z = \gamma \sqrt{\dfrac{N_s + N_d}{N(1 - \gamma^2)}}$	$z = d \sqrt{\dfrac{N_s + N_d}{N(1 - d^2)}}$
$z = \gamma \sqrt{\dfrac{17 + 11}{13(.96)}}$	$z = d \sqrt{\dfrac{17 + 11}{13(.99)}}$
$z = \gamma \sqrt{\dfrac{28}{12.43}}$	$z = d \sqrt{\dfrac{28}{12.84}}$
$z = \gamma \sqrt{2.25}$	$z = d \sqrt{2.18}$
$z = .21 * 1.50 = .32$	$z = .15 * 1.48 = .23$

Consulting the z table we find that the probability of obtaining γ is .37 and for Somer's d .41, neither of which inspires great confidence in the findings; they could well be due to chance.

SUMMARY

The computation of several unique measures of association were presented in this chapter, for ordinal/ordinal distributions (Spearman's rho, τ_a, τ_b, γ, and Somer's d) and for distributions with mixed levels of measurement: nominal/ordinal (Q) and nominal/interval (h and the correlation ratio). We also looked at two specialized tests of significance, the Mann-Whitney U Test and the Kruskal-Wallis H Test). In the next chapter, we will explore the computations of some of the measures used for interval/interval distributions.

Chapter 9

COMPUTATIONS AND ILLUSTRATIONS: INTERVAL- AND NOMINAL-LEVEL VARIABLES

MEASURES OF ASSOCIATION AND DERIVATIVE INDICES: PEARSON'S r, r², α, AND β

In Chapter 5 we examined the relationship between two interval variables and discussed the correlation coefficient (r), the coefficient of determination (r²), and the regression coefficient (ß). We will use data from Table 5.3 in Chapter 5 to illustrate the derivation of these indices and will include the original table here as Table 9.1. Note that it contains the indices and prediction formula along with the raw data. Because we want to demonstrate the complete prediction formula, we will also illustrate the computation of alpha (α).

By now the reader will be aware of the use of X to stand for the independent variable and Y to stand for the dependent variable. If there is more than one independent variable, we designate them as X_1, X_2, and so on.

CALCULATING THE CORRELATION COEFFICIENT

To calculate Pearson's correlation coefficient, r, we must obtain the sum of the values of X, the sum of the values of Y, the sum of the values

Table 9.1

Compensation of Employees as Proportion of National Income and the Share
of the National Income Received by the Top Decile in the Following Year,
United Kingdom, 1953–1967

Year	Compensation on Employees (%) (X)	Year	Share of Top Decile (%) (Y)
1953	70.0	1954	30.6
1954	70.6	1955	30.2
1955	72.5	1956	29.8
1956	72.8	1957	29.6
1957	72.5	1958	29.4
1958	72.1	1959	29.4
1959	71.9	1960	28.6
1960	72.6	1961	27.2
1961	73.3	1962	28.2
1962	73.9	1963	28.0
1963	72.8	1964	29.8
1964	73.2	1965	27.6
1965	74.4	1966	28.0
1966	75.4	1967	26.4

(linear assumption)

$r = -.79$ $r^2 = .63$ $\alpha = 80.3$ $\beta = -.71$ $F = 19.9$ $p. = .001$

SOURCE: Pilcher (1981).
NOTES: The regression equation for two variables is $Y = \alpha + \beta X$. The equation for this distribution is
$Y = 80.3 - .71X$. Using this equation, if $X = 70$, $Y = 30.69$; if $X = 75$, $Y = 27.15$. This establishes two
points to enable us to fix the regression line on a graph.

of both X and Y squared, and the sum of the product of X and Y for each
case. In this instance, each case is a pair of years (e. g., 1953 and 1954).

The formula for r can be put in different forms, depending on whether
you want to use it for calculating or programming or for intuitive
understanding (see Blalock, 1981, p. 398; Freeman, 1965, p. 102;
Harshbarger, 1977, p. 428; Johnson, 1977, p. 106; Leege & Francis,
1974, p. 310; Leonard, 1976, p. 320; Loether & McTavish, 1980,
p. 253; Mueller, Schuessler, & Costner, 1970, p. 319; Turney & Robb,
1973, p. 110). The most common formula given for calculation of the
correlation coefficient is the raw score formula:

$$r = \frac{N\Sigma XY - (\Sigma X)(\Sigma Y)}{\sqrt{[N\Sigma X^2 - (\Sigma X)^2][N\Sigma Y^2 - (\Sigma Y)^2]}}$$

where

ΣXY = sum of the product of X and Y values
ΣX^2 = all X values squared and summed
ΣY^2 = all Y values squared and summed
$(\Sigma X)^2$ = the sum of all X's squared
$(\Sigma Y)^2$ = the sum of all Y's squared
ΣX = sum of X values
ΣY = sum of Y values
N = total number of cases.

What the calculation is designed to do is to provide a ratio of the covariance of the two variables (the extent to which X and Y vary together) to the product of the standard deviations of X and Y. The product of the standard deviations of the two variables provides a measure of the total amount of variation in the data. It is thus an index of the proportion of the total variation that consists of covariation. Looking at the formula above, it can be described somewhat more elaborately as a ratio of the covariation to the square root of the product of the variation in the two variables.

A second formula provides us with an alternative way of computing the coefficient of correlation and may also give the reader a better intuitive understanding of what is being done. There are only two symbols used in this formula that are not defined for the raw score formula above: $\overline{X}$ is the mean of the independent variable; $\overline{Y}$ is the mean of the dependent variable. We will use this formula to compute r for the distribution from Table 9.1:

$$ r = \frac{\Sigma(X - \overline{X})(Y - \overline{Y})}{\sqrt{[\Sigma(X - \overline{X})^2][\Sigma(Y - \overline{Y})^2]}} $$

In the equation, $\Sigma(X - \overline{X})(Y - \overline{Y})$ in the numerator is an index of the covariance of the two variables, the extent to which they vary together. In the denominator you may recognize that in the equation, $[\Sigma(X - \overline{X})^2]$ is the standard deviation of X and $[\Sigma(Y - \overline{Y})^2]$ is the standard deviation of Y. Thus it is a ratio of the covariance to the square of the product of the two standard deviations:

$$ r = \frac{\text{covariance}}{(\text{standard deviation of } X)(\text{standard deviation of } Y)} . $$

Table 9.2

Computation Table for Correlation Coefficient Using the Covariance and Standard Deviation Formula

Years	(X) (1)	(Y) (2)	$X - \bar{X}$ (3)	$Y - \bar{Y}$ (4)	$(X-\bar{X})^2$ (5)	$(Y-\bar{Y})^2$ (6)	$(X-\bar{X})(Y-\bar{Y})$ (7)	$(Y*Y)$ (8)
1953–4	70.0	30.6	−2.71	1.83	7.34	3.35	− 4.96	2,142.0
1954–5	70.6	30.2	−2.11	1.43	4.45	2.04	− 3.02	2,132.1
1955–6	72.5	29.8	− .21	1.03	.04	1.06	− .22	2,160.5
1956–7	72.8	29.6	.09	.83	.01	.69	.07	2,154.9
1957–8	72.5	29.4	− .21	.63	.04	.40	− .13	2,131.5
1958–9	72.1	29.4	− .61	.63	.37	.40	− .38	2,119.7
1959–0	71.9	28.6	− .81	− .17	.66	.03	.14	2,056.3
1960–1	72.6	27.2	− .11	−1.57	.01	2.46	.17	1,974.7
1961–2	73.3	28.2	.59	− .57	.35	.32	− .34	2,067.1
1962–3	73.9	28.0	1.19	− .77	1.42	.59	− .92	2,069.2
1963–4	72.8	29.8	.09	1.03	.01	1.06	.09	2,169.4
1964–5	73.2	27.6	.49	−1.17	.24	1.37	− .57	2,020.3
1965–6	74.4	28.0	1.69	− .77	2.86	.59	− 1.30	2,083.2
1966–7	75.4	26.4	2.69	−2.37	7.24	5.62	− 6.38	1,990.6
$\Sigma =$	1,018.0	402.8			25.04	19.99	−17.73	29,271.6

μ of $X = \Sigma X/N$ or 1,018/14 or $\mu = 72.71$;
μ of $Y = 402.8/14$ or $\mu = 28.77$
$N = 14$

NOTE: Column (7) is obtained by multiplying columns (3) and (4) for each year; column (7) is then summed, Column (5) is obtained by squaring column (3); column (6) is obtained by squaring column (4); each column is then summed.

See computation Table 9.2 for the compilation of the data using the standard deviation formula. We can easily compute r from the data provided:

$$r = \frac{-17.73}{\sqrt{(25.04)(19.99)}} \text{ or } \frac{-17.73}{\sqrt{500.55}} \text{ or } \frac{-17.73}{22.37} = -.79.$$

When using a hand calculator, the *raw score* formula is more commonly used and computation Table 9.3 is sufficient for this purpose and is, perhaps, less complicated. Note that the formula makes use of both the sum of the squared value of each case in each variable (ΣX^2 and ΣY^2) and also the sum of all values in each variable squared [$(\Sigma X)^2$ and $(\Sigma Y)^2$]. The novice may find this a subtle distinction but it is important in computing indices.

Table 9.3
Computation Table for Correlation Coefficient Using the Common
Computation Formula (raw score formula)

Years	(X)	(Y)	X^2	Y^2	XY
1953–4	70.0	30.6	4,900.0	936.4	2,142.0
1954–5	70.6	30.2	4,984.4	912.0	2,132.1
1955–6	72.5	29.8	5,256.3	888.0	2,160.5
1956–7	72.8	29.6	5,299.8	876.2	2,154.9
1957–8	72.5	29.4	5,256.3	864.4	2,131.5
1958–9	72.1	29.4	5,198.4	864.4	2,119.7
1959–0	71.9	28.6	5,169.6	818.0	2,056.3
1960–1	72.6	27.2	5,270.8	739.8	1,974.7
1961–2	73.3	28.2	5,372.9	795.2	2,067.1
1962–3	73.9	28.0	5,461.2	784.0	2,069.2
1963–4	72.8	29.8	5,299.8	888.0	2,169.4
1964–5	73.2	27.6	5,358.2	761.8	2,020.3
1965–6	74.4	28.0	5,535.4	784.0	2,083.2
1966–7	75.4	26.4	5,685.2	697.0	1,990.6

$\Sigma X = 1,018.0$ $\Sigma Y = 402.8$ $\Sigma X^2 = 74,048.2$ $\Sigma Y^2 = 11,609.1$ $\Sigma XY = 29,271.6$

Thus $\Sigma X = 1,018$; $\Sigma Y = 402.8$; $\Sigma X^2 = 74,048.2$; $\Sigma Y^2 = 11,609.1$ and $\Sigma XY = 29,271.6$.
$N = 14$ $(\Sigma X)(\Sigma Y) = 410,050.4$

Either formula can be readily programmed for calculator or computer. An appropriate computational formula for the coefficient of correlation is in the repertoire of SPSS, SPSS-X, and SPSS-PC and other statistical programs designed for computers and calculators.

We also have the ingredients for the computation of the coefficient of correlation for our data, using the raw score formula:

$$r = \frac{N\Sigma XY - (\Sigma X)(\Sigma Y)}{\sqrt{N\Sigma X^2 - (\Sigma X)^2][N\Sigma Y^2 - (\Sigma Y)^2]}}$$

$$= \frac{14(29,271.6) - (1,018 * 402.8)}{\sqrt{[14(74,048.2) - 1,918^2][14(11,609.1) - 402.8^2]}}$$

$$= \frac{409,802.4 - 410,050.4}{\sqrt{(1,036,674.8 - 1,036,324.0)(162,527.4 - 162,247.8)}}$$

$$= \frac{-248}{\sqrt{(350.8)(279.6)}} \text{ or } \frac{-248}{\sqrt{98,083.7}} \text{ or } \frac{-248}{\sqrt{313.2}} = -.79.$$

We find a strong and negative correlation between the two variables, compensation of employees as a proportion of national income and the share of the top income decile for the following year (see Table 9.1).

THE COEFFICIENT OF DETERMINATION

The coefficient of determination is obtained by squaring r, thus $r^2 = (-.79)^2$ or .63. Note that r^2 will always be positive. In words, we can interpret the coefficient of determination in terms of proportionate reduction of error (PRE):

$$\frac{\text{amount of reduction in error}}{\text{amount of original error}}$$

The PRE interpretation can be made with the coefficient of determination but not with the correlation coefficient. We can explain or, perhaps more accurately, predict that 63% of the variation in Y, the dependent variable, can be determined from the values of X, the independent variable. Comparatively speaking, given this type of data, predicting 63% of the variation in the dependent variable from the independent variable is a substantial result. This leaves 37% $(1 - r^2)$ of the variation unexplained, attributed to other variables not in the equation or to measurement error, usually both. This is called the *coefficient of alienation*.

COMPUTING ALPHA AND BETA

It remains now to compute α and β. The formula for β uses the ingredients from the first computation table:

$$\beta = \frac{N\Sigma XY - (\Sigma X)(\Sigma Y)}{N\Sigma X^2 - (\Sigma X)^2}$$

$$= \frac{14(29,271.58) - (1,018)(402.8)}{14(74,048.18) - 1,036,324}$$

$$= \frac{409,802.12 - 41,005.4}{1,036,674.52 - 1,036,324}$$

$$= \frac{-248.28}{350.52} = -.71.$$

Our functional form will be complete when we compute α, which is derived by the following formula:

$$\alpha = |\beta(\overline{X})| + \overline{Y}$$

$$= |-.71(72.71)| + 28.77$$

$$= 51.50 + 28.77 = 80.27 \text{ or } 80.3$$

Note that we take the absolute product of βX as symbolized by the vertical bars, $|$, ignoring the negative sign.

With these calculations we now have the complete functional form for this distribution: $Y = \alpha + \beta X$ or $Y = 80.3 .71X$. Using this equation we can predict (with some error) the value of Y from a value of X. It also enables us to fix two points on a scattergram in order to draw the regression line. Refer to Chapter 5 if you have forgotten that β provides an index of the impact of one variable on another and is called the regression coefficient (or slope).

TEST OF SIGNIFICANCE: THE F TEST

Although these data are not from a sample, we may want to anticipate the skeptic by determining the probability of obtaining this result given the N, the coefficient of determination, and the coefficient of alienation. The F Test is the usual means of doing so and can be calculated readily from the following formula:

$$F = \frac{r^2(N-2)}{1-r^2}$$

where r^2 = coefficient of determination or the proportion of explained variation and $1 - r^2$ = coefficient of alienation or unexplained variation.

Substituting our data from the distribution above:

$$F = \frac{.63(14-2)}{1-.63} \text{ or } \frac{7.52}{.37} = 20.17.$$

Using the F table in Appendix B (Table D), we determine that an F value of 20.17 is significant at the .01 level. Note that the table has two degree-of-freedom decisions to make. We take $N - 1$ as the degree of freedom for the vertical columns, and the number of associations (one association, two variables) as the degree of freedom for the horizontal columns. Consequently we look in column 1 and at row 13 to find a value of 9.07 as the critical value for a probability of .01. Because our F value is much larger than 9.07, we take .01 as the probability for this distribution. However, if we had consulted a more elaborate table with the values of .001, we could have found that 20.17, given the N, actually reaches the .001 level of confidence. Some statistical texts provide probabilities for the .001 level of significance.

SUMMARY

In the first five chapters, we examined the guiding principles essential for understanding the use of statistical procedures. This enabled us to make more logical decisions about using various statistical procedures and to know when they are appropriate to a given set of data. It also provided guidance on planning the observation and data-gathering stage of research in anticipation of using statistical procedures. These five chapters provided an introduction to various statistical procedures appropriate for research in the human services.

In the last four chapters we looked, in detail, at how data are manipulated and processed in the analysis stage of research. This enabled the reader to understand how various indices are obtained and how to prepare data for analysis and, to some extent, for input and manipulation by calculators and computers.

The approach used in this book is based on two convictions and assumptions: (1) that knowledge of the guiding principles for use of statistical procedures can be readily understood and (2) if the purpose of the research enterprise is clearly in mind, the use of statistics becomes useful, practical, and enjoyable to the student and practitioner. The purpose of the research enterprise must be to assess and interpret findings in a reasonable and logical fashion and to use statistical procedures to make sound decisions about characteristics of variables, the relationship(s) between variables, and the probabilities associated with collection of data, that is, the results of observations, interviews, surveys, or the analysis of records or files. If the readers of this book have arrived at these convictions, I have succeeded in my mission.

REFERENCES

Adelman, Irma, & Morris, Cynthia Taft. (1971). *Society, politics, and economic development.* Baltimore, MD: Johns Hopkins Press.

Andrews, Frank M., Klem, Laura, Davidson, Terrence N., O'Malley, Patricia M., & Rodgers, Willard L. (1981). *A guide for selecting statistical techniques for analyzing social science data* (2nd ed.). Ann Arbor: The University of Michigan, Survey Research Center.

Andrews, Frank M., Morgan, James N., & Sonquist, J.A. (1969). *Multiple classification analysis.* Ann Arbor: The University of Michigan, Survey Research Center.

Baer, Donald M. (1977a). Perhaps it would be better not to know everything. *Journal of Applied Behavior Analysis, 10.*

Baer, Donald M. (1977b). Reviewer's comment: Just because it's reliable doesn't mean that you can use it. *Journal of Applied Behavior Analysis, 10.*

Baird, John S. (1987). Perceived learning in relation to student evaluation of university instruction. *Journal of Educational Psychology, 79*(1).

Benbenishty, Rani. (1988). Assessment of task-centered interventions with families in Israel. *Journal of Social Service Research, 11*(4).

Benbenishty, Rani, & Ben-Zaken, Anat. (1988). Computer-aided process of monitoring task-centered family interventions. *Social Work Research and Abstracts, 24*(1).

Berlin, Sharon. (1985). Maintaining reduced levels of self-criticism through relapse-prevention treatment. *Social Work Research and Abstracts, 21*(1).

Berlin, Sharon, & Jones, Linda E. (1983). Life after welfare: AFDC termination among long-term recipients. *Social Service Review, 57*(3).

Blalock, Hubert M. (1964). *Causal inferences in non-experimental research.* Chapel Hill: The University of North Carolina Press.

Blalock, Hubert M. (1960). Social statistics (2nd ed.). New York: McGraw-Hill.

Blalock, Hubert M. (1972). *Social statistics.* (rev. 2nd ed.). New York: McGraw-Hill.

Blalock, Hubert M. (1981). *Social Statistics.* (rev. 2nd ed.). New York: McGraw-Hill.

Bloom, Martin, & Block, Stephen P. (1977a). Evaluating one's own effectiveness and efficiency. *Social Work, 22*(2).

Bloom, Martin, & Block, Stephen P. (1977b). Bloom and Block reply. *Social Work, 22*(6).

Bloom, Martin, & Fischer, Joel. (1982). *Evaluating practice*. Englewood Cliffs, NJ: Prentice-Hall.

Bronson, Denise E., & Blythe, Betty J. (1987). Computer support for single-case evaluation of practice. *Social Work Research and Abstracts, 23*(3).

Caty, Suzanne, & Tamlyn, Deborah. (1984). Positive effects of education on nursing students' attitudes toward death and dying. *Nursing Papers, 16*(4).

Challis, David, & Shepherd, Richard. (1983). An assessment of the potential for community living of mentally handicapped patients in hospital. *British Journal of Social Work, 13*(5).

Clark, Carlton F. (1988). Computer applications in social work. *Social Work Research and Abstracts, 24*(1).

Close, Mary M. (1983). Child welfare and people of color: Denial of equal access. *Social Work Research and Abstracts, 19*(4).

Cocozzelli, Carmelo. (1988). Understanding canonical discriminant function analysis: Testing typological hypotheses. *Journal of Social Service Research, 11*(2/3).

Collins, Sheila K. (1984). A comparison of top and middle level women administrators in social work, nursing and education: Career supports and barriers. *Administration in Social Work, 8*(2).

Cowger, Charles D. (1984). Statistical significance tests: Scientific ritualism or scientific method? *Social Service Review, 58*(3).

Crane, John. (1976). The power of social intervention experiments to discriminate differences between experimental and control groups. *Social Service Review, 50*(2).

Craft, John L., Epley, Stephen W., & Clarkson, Cheryl D. (1980). Factors influencing legal disposition in child abuse investigations. *Journal of Social Service Research, 4*(1).

de Anda, Diane. (1984). Informal support networks of Hispanic mothers: A comparison across age groups. *Journal of Social Service Research, 7*(3).

De Prospero, Anthony, & Cohen, Stanley. (1979). Inconsistent visual analysis of intrasubject data. *Journal of Applied Behavior Analysis, 12*(4).

Dillon, William R., & Goldstein, Matthew. (1984). Multivariate analysis: Methods and applications. New York: John Wiley.

Dolan, Sister Nuala. (1987). The relationship between burnout and job satisfaction in nurses. *Journal of Advanced Nursing, 12*.

Duggan, Thomas J., & Dean, Charles W. (1968). Common misinterpretations of significance levels in sociological journals. *The American Sociologist, 3*(1).

Dunster, J. J. P. (1978). *Municipal social work: A study of social work practice in local government settings*. Unpublished master's thesis. The University of Melbourne, Australia.

Edgington, Eugene S. (1967). Statistical inference from N = 1 experiments. *Journal of Psychology, 65*.

Edgington, Eugene S. (1975a). Randomization tests for predicted trends. *Canadian Psychological Review, 16*.

Edgington, Eugene S. (1975b). Randomization tests for one-subject operant experiments. *Journal of Psychology, 90*.

Edgington, Eugene S. (1980). *Randomization tests*. New York: Marcel Dekker.

Edleson, J. L. (1985). Rapid assessment instruments for evaluating practice with children and youth. *Journal of Social Service Research, 8*(3).

Edwards, Allen L. (1967). *Statistical methods* (2nd ed.). New York: Holt, Rinehart & Winston.

Feather, N. T. (1986). Employment importance and helplessness about potential unemployment among students in secondary schools. *Australian Journal of Psychology*, *38*(1).

Feitler, Fred C., & Tokar, Edward B. (1986). School administrators and organizational stress: Matching theory, hunches and data. *The Journal of Educational Administration*, *24*(2).

Finn, Jerry. (1988). Microcomputers in private, non-profit agencies: A survey of trends and training requirements. *Social Work Research and Abstracts*, *24*(1).

Fisher, R. A. & Yates, F. (1963). *Statistical tables for biological agricultural, and medical research* (6th ed.). New York: Hafner Publishing Co. (Now published by Longman Group Ltd., London).

Fitz-Gibbon, Carol Taylor, & Morris, Lynn Lyons. (1978). How to calculate statistics. Beverly Hills, CA: Sage.

Freeman, Linton C. (1965). *Elementary applied statistics*. New York: John Wiley.

Gambrill, Eileen. (1983). *Casework: A competency based approach*. Englewood Cliffs, NJ: Prentice-Hall.

Gockel, Galen L. (1966). *Silk stockings and blue collars*. (Report No. 114). University of Chicago, National Opinion Research Center.

Gold, David. (1969). Statistical tests and substantive significance. *The American Sociologist*, *4*(1).

Gottman, J.M., & Leiblum, S.R. (1974). *How to do psychotherapy and how to evaluate it*. New York: Holt, Rinehart & Winston.

Greene, Roberta. (1983). Ageism, death anxiety and the caseworker. *Journal of Social Service Research*, *7*(1).

Grinnell, Richard M., Jr. (1985). *Social work research and evaluation* (2nd ed.). Itasca, MN: F. E. Peacock.

Hammond, K. R., & Householder, J. E. (1962). *Introduction to the statistical method*. New York: Knopf.

Harshbarger, Thad R. (1977). *Introductory statistics: A decision map* (2nd ed.). New York: Macmillan.

Hattie, John, & Fitzgerald, Donald. (1987). Sex differences in attitudes, achievement and use of computers. *Australian Journal of Education*, *31*(1).

Hawkins, J. David, & Fraser, Mark W. (1985). Social networks of street drug users: A comparison of two theories. *Social Work Research and Abstracts*, *21*(1).

Hawley, Willis D. (1987). The high costs and doubtful efficacy of extended teacher-preparation programs: An invitation to more basic reforms. *American Journal of Education*, *95*(2).

Haynes, Karen S. (1983). Sexual differences in social work administrators' job satisfaction. *Journal of Social Service Research*, *6*(3/4).

Henkel, Ramon E. (1976). Tests of significance. Beverly Hills, CA: Sage.

Himle, D. P., Jayaratne, S. R., & Chess, W. A. (1987). Gender differences in work stress among clinical social workers. *Journal of Social Service Research*, *10*(1).

Hirschi, Travis, & Selvin, Hanan C. (1967). *Delinquency research: An appraisal of analytic methods*. New York: Free Press.

Hudson, Walter W. (1977). Elementary techniques for assessing single-client/single-worker interventions. *Social Service Review, 51*(2).

Hudson, Walter W. (1982). Behavioral mismeasurement. *Social Work Research and Abstracts, 18*(2).

Hudson, Walter W., Thyer, B. A., & Storks, J. T. (1985). Assessing the importance of experimental outcomes. *Journal of Social Service Research, 8*(4).

Iversen, Gudmund R., & Norpoth, Helmut. (1976). *Analysis of variance.* Beverly Hills, CA: Sage.

Jacobson, Perry E. (1976). *Introduction to statistical measures for the social and behavioural sciences.* Orlando, FL: Dryden Press.

Jayaratne, Srinika. (1978). Analytic procedures for single-subject designs. *Social Work Research and Abstracts, 14*(3).

Jayaratne, Srinika, & Ivey, Karen V. (1983). The world view of clinical social workers and some related gender differences. *Journal of Social Service Research, 6*(3/4).

Johnson, Allan G. (1977). *Social statistics without tears.* New York: McGraw-Hill.

Kazdin, Alan E. (1979). Data evaluation for intrasubject-replication research. *Journal of Social Service Research, 3*(1).

Keogh, B. K. (1984). *Advances in special education.* (Vol. 4). Greenwich, CT: JAI Press.

Kim, Jae-on, & Mueller, Charles W. (1978a). *Introduction to factor analysis.* Beverly Hills, CA: Sage.

Kim, Jae-on, & Mueller, Charles W. (1978b). *Factor Analysis.* Beverly Hills, CA: Sage.

Kratochwill, T. R. (1978). *Single subject research: Strategies for evaluating change.* San Diego, CA: Academic Press.

Labovitz, Sanford. (1968). Criteria for selecting a significance level: A note on the sacredness of .05. *The American Sociologist, 3*(3).

Le Croy, C. W., & Rose, A. D. (1986). Evaluation of preventive interventions for enhancing social competence in adolescents. *Social Work Research and Abstracts, 22*(2).

Leege, David C., & Francis, Wayne L. (1974). *Political research: Design, measurement and analysis.* New York: Basic Books.

Leonard, Wilbert M. (1976). *Basic social statistics.* St. Paul, MN: West Publishing Co.

Loether, Herman J., & McTavish, Donald G. (1974). *Descriptive statistics for sociologists: An introduction.* Boston, MA: Allyn & Bacon.

Loether, Herman J., & McTavish, Donald G. (1980). *Descriptive and inferential statistics: An introduction.* (2nd ed.). Boston, MA: Allyn & Bacon.

Loftus, Geoffrey L., & Levy, Rona L. (1977). Statistical evaluation of clinical effectiveness. *Social Work, 22*(6).

Marjoribanks, Kevin. (1987). Gender/social class, family environments and adolescents' aspirations. *Australian Journal of Education, 31*(1).

Marsh, Jeanne, & Shibano, Matsujiro. (1984). Issues in the statistical analysis of clinical time-series data. *Social Work Research and Abstracts, 20*(4).

Marshall, Colin. (1982). Parole decisions and justice. *Australian Social Work, 35*(4).

Massey, Jr., F. J. (1951) The Kolmogorov-Smirnov Test of Goodness of Fit, *Journal of the American Statistical Association, 46,* p. 70.

Merry, Gordon. (1986). *Retinitis pigmentosa —Evaluating a counselling treatment using anxiety measures.* Unpublished master's thesis. University of Melbourne, Australia.

MacRae, Isabel, & Johnson, Barbara A. (1986). Influences of age and gender on self-perceived components of health, health concerns, and health ratings. *Nursing Papers, 18*(2).

McGrath, Frances. (1986). *The family and illness: Changes in family functioning following a myocardial infarction in one family member.* Unpublished master's thesis. University of Melbourne, Australia.

Mueller, John H., Schuessler, Karl F., & Costner, Herbert L. (1970). *Statistical reasoning in sociology.* (2nd ed.). Boston: Houghton Mifflin.

Nelson, Judith. (1984). Intermediate treatment goals as variables in single-case research. *Social Work Research and Abstracts, 20*(3).

Nie, Norman H. (1983). *SPSS-X user's guide.* New York: McGraw Hill.

Nie, Norman H., Hull, C. Hadlai, Jenkins, Jean G., Steinbrenner, Karin, & Bent, Dale H. (1975). *Statistical package for the social sciences.* (2nd ed.). New York: McGraw-Hill.

Norusis, Marija J. (1986). *SPSS/PC+ for the IBM PC/XT/AT.* Chicago: SPSS, Inc.

Nurius, Paula S. (1984). Utility of data synthesis for social work. *Social Work Research and Abstracts, 20*(3).

Orme, John G., & Combs-Orme, Terri D. (1986). Statistical power and type II errors in social work research. *Social Work Research and Abstracts, 22*(3).

Parry, Joan K., & Smith, Michael J. (1987). A study of social workers' job satisfaction as based on an optimal model of care for the terminally ill. *Journal of Social Service Research, 11*(1).

Pascarella, Ernest T., Smart, John C., Ethington, Corinna A., & Nettles, Michael T. (1987). The influence of college on self-concept: A consideration of race and gender differences. *American Educational Research Journal, 24*(1).

Philip, Alistair E. (1969). A method of analyzing assessments of symptom change. *British Journal of Psychiatry, 115*(13).

Pierce, Albert. (1969). *Fundamentals of nonparametric statistics: A sample space approach.* Dickenson Publishing.

Pilcher, Ann J. (1982). Australian students in social work education. *Contemporary Social Work Education, 5*(2 & 3).

Pilcher, Donald M. (1981). *The sociology of income distribution: A theoretical and empirical study.* Unpublished manuscript.

Pilcher, Donald M., Ramirez, Charles J., & Swihart, Judson J. (1968). Some correlates of normal pensionable age. *International Social Security Review, No. 3.,* International Social Security Association.

Pinkston, Elsie M., Howe, Michael W., & Blackman, Donald K. (1986). Medical social work management of urinary incontinence in the elderly: A behavioral approach. *Journal of Social Service Research, 10*(2/3/4).

Pope, Carl E. & Feyerherm, William H. (1982). Gender bias in juvenile court distributions. *Journal of Social Service Research, 6*(1/2).

Poulin, John E. (1985). Long term foster care, natural family attachment and loyalty conflict. *Journal of Social Service Research, 9*(1).

Resnick, Gary. (1984). The short and long-term impact of a competency-based program for disadvantaged women. *Journal of Social Service Research, 7*(4).

Rosenblatt, Aaron, & Waldfogel, Diana. (Eds.) (1983). *Handbook of clinical social work.* San Francisco: Jossey-Bass.

Rubin, Allen, & Conway, Patricia G. (1985). Standards for determining the magnitude of relationships in social work research. *Social Work Research and Abstracts, 21*(1).

Runyon, R. P., & Haber, A. (1971). *Fundamentals of behavioral statistics* (2nd ed.). Reading, MA: Addison-Wesley.

Sampson, Shirley N. (1987). Equal opportunity, alone, is not enough or why there are more male principals in schools these days. *Australian Journal of Education, 31*(1).

Schinke, S. P., Schilling, R. F., & Gilchrist, L. D. (1986). Prevention of drug and alcohol abuse in American Indian youths. *Social Work Research and Abstracts, 22*(4).

Schilling, R. F., Schinke, S. P., Kirkham, Maura A., Metzer, Nancy J., & Norelius, Kristine L. (1988). Social work research in social service agencies: Issues and guidelines. *Journal of Social Service Research, 11*(4).

Schuerman, John R. (1983a). *Research and evaluation in the human services.* New York: Free Press.

Schuerman, John R. (1983b). *Multivariate analysis in the human services*. Amsterdam: Kluwer-Nijhoff.

Schwab, James A., Bruce, Michael E., & McRoy, Ruth G. (1985). A statistical model of child placement decisions. *Social Work Research and Abstracts, 21*(2).

Siddle, Sandra, & Wilson, Jill. (1984). Mapping murky waters: Describing content and techniques in student supervision. *Australian Social Work, 37*(1).

Siegel, Sidney. (1956). *Nonparametric statistics for the behavioral sciences*. New York: McGraw-Hill.

Smith, Catherine Begnoche, & Marcus, Philip M. (1984). Structural persistence in proactive organizations: The case of sexual assault treatment agencies. *Journal of Social Service Research, 7*(4).

Smith, Mieko Kotake, & Holland, Thomas P. (1982). Measurement of institutional resident management practices. *Journal of Social Service Research, 6*(1/2).

Stewart, Ruth. (1982). *Assessments and decisions: A study of professional decision-making about children*. Unpublished master's thesis, La Trobe University, Australia.

Thomas, Edwin J., Santa, Cathleen, Bronson, Denise, & Oyserman, Daphna. (1986). Unilateral family therapy with the spouses of alcoholics. *Journal of Social Service Research, 10*(2/3/4).

Turney, Billy L., & Robb, George P. (1968). *Statistical methods for behavioral science*. New York: Intext Educational Publishers.

U.S. Bureau of the Census. (1981). *Money income and poverty status of families and persons in the United States: 1980*. (Current Population Reports, Consumer Income, Series P-60, No. 127). Washington, DC: Government Printing Office.

Van Tran, Thanh, Wright, Roosevelt, Jr., & Mindel, Charles H. (1987). Alienation among Vietnamese refugees in the United States: A causal approach. *Journal of Social Service Research, 11*(1).

Weinberg, George H., & Schumaker, John A. (1962). *Statistics: An intuitive approach*. Belmont, CA: Wadsworth.

Wiehe, V. R. (1984). Self-esteem, attitude toward parents, and locus of control in children of divorced and non-divorced parents. *Journal of Social Service Research, 8*(1).

Wiehe, V. R. (1986). Empathy and locus of control in child abusers. *Journal of Social Service Research, 9*(2/3).

Williams, Antony (1985). The patients of private psychiatrists. *Australian Psychologist, 20*(3).

Winston, Craig, Le Croy, C. W., & Rank, Mark R. (1987). Factors associated with burnout in the social services: An exploratory study. *Journal of Social Service Research, 10*(1).

Wodarski, John S. (1986). Evaluating a social learning approach to teaching adolescents about alcohol and driving: A multiple variable evaluation. *Journal of Social Service Research, 10*(2/3/4).

Wong, S. E., Woolsley, J. E., & Gallegas, Estrella. (1986). Behavioral treatment of chronic psychiatric patients. *Journal of Social Service Research, 10*(2/3/4).

APPENDIX A: GLOSSARY

Asymmetrical Relationship A relationship in which a distinction is made between a dependent and independent variable with the assumption that changes in the dependent variable are effected by, "caused" by, or are brought about by one or more independent variables.

Bivariate Two variables.

Central Tendency In general refers to averages, such as the mean, median, or mode. It is an index that reflects a putative typical value of a distribution.

Constructs Usually used in research to identify a variable or characteristic that is constructed from observations made about sets of characteristics. It is not something that one measures or observes directly but something one constructs as a logical concept on the basis of measurable indicators.

Contingency Table A table in which the attributes or characteristics of one variable are related to the attributes or characteristics of another variable set out in the form of a grid. Often we are speculating that one variable is contingent on another. More than two variables can be included in contingency tables.

Correction for Continuity A correction applied to a Chi square distribution when there are a small number of cases and particularly when the expected frequencies in any cell are five or less. A correction is made to the Chi square computation by adding or subtracting .5 to the observed frequencies. This usually reduces the magnitude of Chi square and provides a more conservative estimate of probability.

Cross-Tabulation Tabulating or constructing a table that includes two or more variables on the X and Y axes so that cells are created in which a unit can be scaled on each variable, essentially a contingency table.

Degree of Association An index of how closely the categories of two or more variables are associated; often, but not always, on a scale of .00 to 1.00.

Degree of Freedom Used in determining probability in tests of significance best illustrated by the 2×2 Chi square distribution. When determining the expected frequencies in a 2×2 table, the marginals allow only one degree of freedom in computing a value; all others are given once this value is established (see text for elaboration).

Dependent Variable The variable assumed to be acted upon by another or other variables. Changes in a dependent variable are assumed to be brought about by one or more independent variables.

Descriptive Statistics Statistical procedures usually used with populations as opposed to samples (inferential statistics), although descriptive statistics may be applied to sample data.

Dichotomous Variable A two-category variable.

Directional Hypothesis A hypothesis that predicts changes in one variable (dependent) that can be predicted from another variable (independent). Sometimes referred to as an asymmetric assumption.

Independent Variable The variable(s) assumed to act upon another variable, the *causal* variable(s) that bring about changes in the dependent variable.

Inferential Statistics Statistical procedures in which properties (characteristics or attributes) from a sample are examined with the goal of inferring these properties to a population, as in tests of significance.

Level of Measurement Term used to distinguish between the relationship of categories in different types of variables, whether or not the categories are qualitatively different, ordered, and of equal or unequal units. In the context of statistics it distinguishes between nominal (named), ordinal, and cardinal categories.

Marginals The sums of the quantities in rows and columns.

Mean Usually refers to the arithmetic mean that is determined by summing all the values in a distribution and dividing by the total number of values.

Median The midpoint (50th percentile) in a distribution of values. The value which, in a crude sense, divides the distribution in half.

Modal Category The category with the greatest frequency of values.

Mode   The value in a distribution that occurs most frequently. Occasionally there will be two such values, a bimodal situation, and there can be more than two modal values or scores.

Multivariate   Used to describe distributions in which there are more than two variables.

Necessary Condition   A hypothetical distribution of two variables in which the occurrence of a case in the category of one variable is necessary for it to occur in the category of another variable. Actual distributions may or may not approach the hypothetical situation (see Chapter 3 for an illustration).

Nondirectional Hypothesis   A hypothesis that simply assumes than an association exists between the categories of one variable and another without attributing *causality* to the association. Also referred to as an asymmetric relationship.

Null Hypothesis   A hypothesis that deliberately states the negative proposition that two (or more) variables are not associated. If the null hypothesis does not hold up, this leaves the possibility that the alternative hypothesis may be true. Assuming you have used appropriate indicators and procedures, you can prove that two variables are not associated; you cannot prove that two variables are associated because you can never be certain that you have included all of the pertinent variables.

One-tailed Test   A test applied in the asymmetric or directional situation in which a prediction is made or an assumption is made that the changes in one variable bring about changes in another.

Population   The total number of units of concern in a study; the total number of cases about which one is generalizing, as distinguished from a sample of those cases.

Random Sample   A sample in which each unit in the sample has an equal chance of being selected, usually referred to as a probability sample.

Sample   A number of units selected on some basis from a population. The selection might be on a random or probability basis and it might not. Nonprobability sampling might include accidental, purposive, convenience, snowball, or quota sampling. When using a nonprobability sample, it is not possible to draw firm conclusions about the population from which it came with confidence because it is not possible to know whether or not there is a significant bias in the method of sampling itself.

Skewed   If a distribution is skewed, it means that cases or units or values are concentrated at one end of the distribution as opposed to a normal distribution with a bell-shaped curve that is symmetrical or balanced.

Sufficient Condition   A hypothetical distribution of two variables in which the occurrence of a case in the category of one variable is sufficient for it to occur in the category of another variable. Actual distributions may or may not approach the hypothetical situation (see Chapter 3 for an illustration).

Symmetrical Relationship   A balanced relationship in which no distinction is made between a dependent and an independent variable with the assumption that the two variables are simply associated without one or the other being the causal or a determining factor.

Test of Significance   A test to determine the probability that the association between two or more variables in a sample is significantly (in a statistical sense) different from the association in the population from which it was drawn. This provides a basis for determining the level of confidence one can have in generalizing to a population from a sample. It can also be used simply to determine the likelihood that a given distribution might be a chance occurrence given its size and the number of values in each cell or category (see Blalock, 1981, pp. 241–243 or Henkel, 1976, pp. 85–87).

Two-tailed Test   A test applied in the symmetric or nondirectional situation in which no assumption is made that one variable is dependent and the other is independent; neither variable is considered to be determinant.

Univariate   One variable distribution.

Variable   A concept or phenomenon that involves characteristics or attributes that can vary from unit to unit or case to case; a concept that can be described by various categories: nominal, ordinal, or cardinal. If you select all females for a study, then gender is not a variable, it is a constant; but if the characteristics or attributes of these females vary, then the characteristics or attributes become variables such as educational level, occupation, height, and weight.

APPENDIX B: THE USE OF PROBABILITY TABLES

STUDENT'S t DISTRIBUTION

It is important to know three things before entering the t distribution table (Table A) to determine probability: the t value from your calculation, the degree of freedom for your distribution, and whether or not you have a directional or nondirectional relationship.

When you have this information, locate the degrees of freedom (df) in the left-hand column, then read across that row until you find the number that most closely approximates your t value.

Supposing your degree of freedom is 2 and your t value is 7.01. Reading across row two, you see that 7.01 is just slightly greater than 6.965; at the top of that column are two probability figures, one for a nondirectional two-tailed test (.02) and one for a directional one-tailed test (.01). If your t value had been 5.87, it would not have reached these values, and you would have to record your probability as .05 or .025, depending on whether or not the relationship is directional or nondirectional. Directional relationships require a one-tailed test, a more rigorous test; nondirectional relationships require a two-tailed test.

Table A
Student's t Distribution

df	Level of Significance for One-tailed Test					
	.10	.05	.025	.01	.005	.0005
	Level of Significance for Two-tailed Test					
	.20	.10	.05	.02	.01	.001
1	3.078	6.314	12.706	31.821	63.657	636.619
2	1.886	2.920	4.303	6.965	9.925	31.598
3	1.638	2.353	3.182	4.541	5.841	12.941
4	1.533	2.132	2.776	3.747	4.604	8.610
5	1.476	2.015	2.571	3.365	4.032	6.859
6	1.440	1.943	2.447	3.143	3.707	5.959
7	1.415	1.895	2.365	2.998	3.499	5.405
8	1.397	1.860	2.306	2.896	3.355	5.041
9	1.383	1.833	2.262	2.821	3.250	4.781
10	1.372	1.812	2.228	2.764	3.169	4.587
11	1.363	1.796	2.201	2.718	3.106	4.437
12	1.356	1.782	2.179	2.681	3.055	4.318
13	1.350	1.771	2.160	2.650	3.012	4.221
14	1.345	1.761	2.145	2.624	2.977	4.140
15	1.341	1.753	2.131	2.602	2.947	4.073
16	1.337	1.746	2.120	2.583	2.921	4.015
17	1.333	1.740	2.110	2.567	2.898	3.965
18	1.330	1.734	2.101	2.552	2.878	3.922
19	1.328	1.729	2.093	2.539	2.861	3.883
20	1.325	1.725	2.086	2.528	2.845	3.850
21	1.323	1.721	2.080	2.518	2.831	3.819
22	1.321	1.717	2.074	2.508	2.819	3.792
23	1.319	1.714	2.069	2.500	2.807	3.767
24	1.318	1.711	2.064	2.492	2.797	3.745
25	1.316	1.708	2.060	2.485	2.787	3.725
26	1.315	1.706	2.056	2.479	2.779	3.707
27	1.314	1.703	2.052	2.473	2.771	3.690
28	1.313	1.701	2.048	2.467	2.763	3.674
29	1.311	1.699	2.045	2.462	2.756	3.659
30	1.310	1.697	2.042	2.457	2.750	3.646
40	1.303	1.684	2.021	2.423	2.704	3.551
60	1.296	1.671	2.000	2.390	2.660	3.460
120	1.289	1.658	1.980	2.358	2.617	3.373
∞	1.282	1.645	1.960	2.326	2.576	3.291

SOURCE: Adapted from Fisher & Yates (1963, 6th ed., table III, p. 46).

TEST FOR z UNDER A NORMAL CURVE

To determine the probability from a z table (Table B) all you need to know is the z value. Note that there are three columns: A, B, and C. The A column is the key to determining the probability — that is where you locate your z value — the C column provides the probability figure. Column B is blank.[1]

When you've computed your z value, find that value in the A column then read the probability under the C column in that row. For instance, supposing your z value is 1.94; find that figure under the A column then read in the C column that the probability is .0262. This is a one-tailed test. If you want to make a two-tailed test, multiply the probability figure by 2. In this case it would be .0524.

THE CHI SQUARE DISTRIBUTION

To enter the Chi square table (Table C) to determine probability, you must know the degree of freedom for your distribution, the Chi square figure, and whether or not the relationship you are examining is a directional or nondirectional one. Assume that your Chi square figure is 7.92, you have three degrees of freedom, and your hypothesis is nondirectional. Read across the columns from df 3 to find the figure that most closely approximates 7.92. You will find 7.815 which is very close. The probability figure above that column indicates that 7.815 has a probability of .05, given three degrees of freedom and a nondirectional hypothesis. Your Chi square figure is greater than 7.815, so you are safe in assuming a probability of .05. To obtain the probability figure for a directional hypothesis, you would divide by 2: .05/2 = .025.

THE DISTRIBUTION OF F

To enter the F table (Table D), you need two degree-of-freedom figures; one df is the number of cases, less one. So $N - 1$ puts you in the right row (df_2); df_1 is determined by the number of independent variables in your distribution. With the bivariate situation you have one

---

[1] A middle column is usually included which gives the area between the mean and z. To simplify the table it is not included here. If given, it would be the difference between unity (1.00) and the figure in column C.

Table B

Table of Areas Under a Normal Curve

(A) z	(B)[1] z	(C)[2] z	(A) z	(B)[1] z	(C)[2] z	(A) z	(B)[1] z	(C)[2] z
0.00		.5000	0.49		.3121	0.98		.1635
0.01		.4960	0.50		.3085	0.99		.1611
0.02		.4920	0.51		.3050	1.00		.1587
0.03		.4880	0.52		.3015	1.01		.1562
0.04		.4840	0.53		.2981	1.02		.1539
0.05		.4801	0.54		.2946	1.03		.1515
0.06		.4761	0.55		.2912	1.04		.1492
0.07		.4721	0.56		.2877	1.05		.1469
0.08		.4681	0.57		.2843	1.06		.1446
0.09		.4641	0.58		.2810	1.07		.1423
0.10		.4602	0.59		.2776	1.08		.1401
0.11		.4562	0.60		.2743	1.09		.1379
0.12		.4522	0.61		.2709	1.10		.1357
0.13		.4483	0.62		.2676	1.11		.1335
0.14		.4443	0.63		.2643	1.12		.1314
0.15		.4404	0.64		.2611	1.13		.1292
0.16		.4364	0.65		.2578	1.14		.1271
0.17		.4325	0.66		.2546	1.15		.1251
0.18		.4286	0.67		.2514	1.16		.1230
0.19		.4247	0.68		.2483	1.17		.1210
0.20		.4207	0.69		.2451	1.18		.1190
0.21		.4168	0.70		.2420	1.19		.1170
0.22		.4129	0.71		.2389	1.20		.1151
0.23		.4090	0.72		.2358	1.21		.1131
0.24		.4052	0.73		.2327	1.22		.1112
0.25		.4013	0.74		.2296	1.23		.1093
0.26		.3974	0.75		.2266	1.24		.1075
0.27		.3936	0.76		.2236	1.25		.1056
0.28		.3897	0.77		.2206	1.26		.1038
0.29		.3859	0.78		.2177	1.27		.1020
0.30		.3821	0.79		.2148	1.28		.1003
0.31		.3783	0.80		.2119	1.29		.0985
0.32		.3745	0.81		.2090	1.30		.0968
0.33		.3707	0.82		.2061	1.31		.0951
0.34		.3669	0.83		.2033	1.32		.0934
0.35		.3632	0.84		.2005	1.33		.0918
0.36		.3594	0.85		.1977	1.34		.0901
0.37		.3557	0.86		.1949	1.35		.0885
0.38		.3520	0.87		.1922	1.36		.0869
0.39		.3483	0.88		.1894	1.37		.0853
0.40		.3446	0.89		.1867	1.38		.0838
0.41		.3409	0.90		.1841	1.39		.0823
0.42		.3372	0.91		.1814	1.40		.0808
0.43		.3336	0.92		.1788	1.41		.0793
0.44		.3300	0.93		.1762	1.42		.0778
0.45		.3264	0.94		.1736	1.43		.0764
0.46		.3228	0.95		.1711	1.44		.0749
0.47		.3192	0.96		.1685	1.45		.0735
0.48		.3156	0.97		.1660	1.46		.0721

Table B
Table of Areas Under a Normal Curve (Continued)

(A) z	(B)[1]	(C)[2] z	(A) z	(B)[1]	(C)[2] z	(A) z	(B)[1]	(C)[2] z
1.47		.0708	1.97		.0244	2.47		.0068
1.48		.0694	1.98		.0239	2.48		.0066
1.49		.0681	1.99		.0233	2.49		.0064
1.50		.0668	2.00		.0228	2.50		.0062
1.51		.0655	2.01		.0222	2.51		.0060
1.52		.0643	2.02		.0217	2.52		.0059
1.53		.0630	2.03		.0212	2.53		.0057
1.54		.0618	2.04		.0207	2.54		.0055
1.55		.0606	2.05		.0202	2.55		.0054
1.56		.0594	2.06		.0197	2.56		.0052
1.57		.0582	2.07		.0192	2.57		.0051
1.58		.0571	2.08		.0188	2.58		.0049
1.59		.0559	2.09		.0183	2.59		.0048
1.60		.0548	2.10		.0179	2.60		.0047
1.61		.0537	2.11		.0174	2.61		.0045
1.62		.0526	2.12		.0170	2.62		.0044
1.63		.0516	2.13		.0166	2.63		.0043
1.64		.0505	2.14		.0162	2.64		.0041
1.65		.0495	2.15		.0158	2.65		.0040
1.66		.0485	2.16		.0154	2.66		.0039
1.67		.0475	2.17		.0150	2.67		.0038
1.68		.0465	2.18		.0146	2.68		.0037
1.69		.0455	2.19		.0143	2.69		.0036
1.70		.0446	2.20		.0139	2.70		.0035
1.71		.0436	2.21		.0136	2.71		.0034
1.72		.0427	2.22		.0132	2.72		.0033
1.73		.0418	2.23		.0129	2.73		.0032
1.74		.0409	2.24		.0125	2.74		.0031
1.75		.0401	2.25		.0122	2.75		.0030
1.76		.0392	2.26		.0119	2.76		.0029
1.77		.0384	2.27		.0116	2.77		.0028
1.78		.0375	2.28		.0113	2.78		.0027
1.79		.0367	2.29		.0110	2.79		.0026
1.80		.0359	2.30		.0107	2.80		.0026
1.81		.0351	2.31		.0104	2.81		.0025
1.82		.0344	2.32		.0102	2.82		.0024
1.83		.0336	2.33		.0099	2.83		.0023
1.84		.0329	2.34		.0096	2.84		.0023
1.85		.0322	2.35		.0094	2.85		.0022
1.86		.0314	2.36		.0091	2.86		.0021
1.87		.0307	2.37		.0089	2.87		.0021
1.88		.0301	2.38		.0087	2.88		.0020
1.89		.0294	2.39		.0084	2.89		.0019
1.90		.0287	2.40		.0082	2.90		.0019
1.91		.0281	2.41		.0080	2.91		.0018
1.92		.0274	2.42		.0078	2.92		.0018
1.93		.0268	2.43		.0075	2.93		.0017
1.94		.0262	2.44		.0073	2.94		.0016
1.95		.0256	2.45		.0071	2.95		.0016
1.96		.0250	2.46		.0069	2.96		.0015

Table B
Table of Areas Under a Normal Curve (Continued)

(A) z	(B)[1]	(C)[2] z	(A) z	(B)[1]	(C)[2] z	(A) z	(B)[1]	(C)[2] z
2.97		.0015	3.07		.0011	3.17		.0008
2.98		.0014	3.08		.0010	3.18		.0007
2.99		.0014	3.09		.0010	3.19		.0007
3.00		.0013	3.10		.0010	3.20		.0007
3.01		.0013	3.11		.0009	3.21		.0007
3.02		.0013	3.12		.0009	3.22		.0006
3.03		.0012	3.13		.0009	3.23		.0006
3.04		.0012	3.14		.0008	3.24		.0006
3.05		.0011	3.15		.0008	3.25		.0006
3.06		.0011	3.16		.0008	3.30		.0005

SOURCE: Adapted from Runyon & Haber (1971, table A, pp. 290-291).
NOTES: Probabilities beyond .0005 not given. Values above 3.30 can be given as .0005.
[1]For simplicity, the complete table is not reproduced from the source; a middle column, B, is usually included, which gives the area between the mean and z. If given, it would be the difference between unity (1.00) and the figure in column C.
[2]This is the area beyond z.

pair of variables, so you enter the first column. If you had a multivariate situation then the number of pairs would determine the column. Or, another way to think of it is the number of variables (dependent and independent) less one.

Assume that you have two variables and 27 cases. You would scan the left hand column to find 26 ($N-1$), and you would read the figure in the first column ($2-1$). You would have to have an F value of 4.23 to reach the .05 level of significance. Note that there are two pages of F tables, one for the .05 level and one for the .01 level of significance. Some texts carry additional tables for the .001 level of significance.

THE KOLMOGOROV-SMIRNOV ONE-SAMPLE TEST

Two pieces of information are required to determine the probability of the KS Test: the largest absolute difference between the cumulative observed frequency and expected frequency (D) and the size of the sample. Assuming a sample size of 20, and a D of .30, level of significance would be .05. If D is .290, it would not reach .05 and p. would have to be considered to be .10.

Table C

Distribution of χ^2

df	Probability (two-tailed) .30	.20	.10	.05	.02	.01	.001
1	1.074	1.642	2.706	3.841	5.412	6.635	10.827
2	2.403	3.219	4.605	5.991	7.824	9.210	13.815
3	3.665	4.878	6.251	7.815	9.837	11.345	16.268
4	4.878	5.989	7.779	9.488	11.668	13.277	18.465
5	6.064	7.289	9.236	11.070	13.388	15.086	20.517
6	7.231	8.558	10.645	12.592	15.033	16.812	22.457
7	8.383	9.803	12.017	14.067	16.622	18.475	24.322
8	9.524	11.030	13.362	15.507	18.168	20.090	26.125
9	10.656	12.242	14.684	16.919	19.679	21.666	27.877
10	11.781	13.442	15.987	18.307	21.161	23.209	29.588
11	12.899	14.631	17.275	19.675	22.618	24.725	31.264
12	14.011	15.812	18.549	21.026	24.054	26.217	32.909
13	15.119	16.985	19.812	22.362	25.472	27.688	34.528
14	16.222	18.151	21.064	23.685	26.873	29.141	36.123
15	17.322	19.311	22.307	24.996	28.259	30.578	37.697
16	18.418	20.465	23.542	26.296	29.633	32.000	39.252
17	19.511	21.615	24.769	27.587	30.995	33.409	40.790
18	20.601	22.760	25.989	28.869	32.346	34.805	42.312
19	21.689	23.900	27.204	30.144	33.687	36.191	43.820
20	22.775	25.038	28.412	31.410	35.020	37.566	45.315
21	23.858	26.171	29.615	32.671	36.343	38.932	46.797
22	24.939	27.301	30.813	33.924	37.659	40.289	48.268
23	26.018	28.429	32.007	35.172	38.968	41.638	49.728
24	27.096	29.553	33.196	36.415	40.270	42.980	51.179
25	28.172	30.675	34.382	37.652	41.566	44.314	52.620
26	29.246	31.795	35.563	38.885	42.856	45.642	54.052
27	30.319	32.912	36.741	40.113	44.140	46.963	55.476
28	31.391	34.027	37.916	41.337	45.419	48.278	56.893
29	32.461	35.139	39.087	42.557	46.693	49.588	58.302
30	33.530	36.250	40.256	43.773	47.962	50.892	59.703

SOURCE: Abridged table from Fisher & Yates (1963, 6th ed., Table IV, p. 47).
NOTE: For one-tailed test, simply halve the probabilities shown (i.e., .10 — two-tailed — becomes .10/2, or .05 for a one-tailed test). The computed Chi square is significant if it is equal to or larger than the table Chi square.

Table D

Distribution of F

$p. = 0.05$

df_2	1	2	3	4	5	6	8	12
1	161.4	199.5	215.7	224.6	230.2	234.0	238.9	243.9
2	18.51	19.00	19.16	19.25	19.30	19.33	19.37	19.41
3	10.13	9.55	9.28	9.12	9.01	8.94	8.85	8.74
4	7.71	6.94	6.59	6.39	6.26	6.16	6.04	5.91
5	6.61	5.79	5.41	5.19	5.05	4.95	4.82	4.68
6	5.99	5.14	4.76	4.53	4.39	4.28	4.15	4.00
7	5.59	4.74	4.35	4.12	3.97	3.87	3.73	3.57
8	5.32	4.46	4.07	3.84	3.69	3.58	3.44	3.28
9	5.12	4.26	3.86	3.63	3.48	3.37	3.23	3.07
10	4.96	4.10	3.71	3.48	3.33	3.22	3.07	2.91
11	4.84	3.98	3.59	3.36	3.20	3.09	2.95	2.79
12	4.75	3.89	3.49	3.26	3.11	3.00	2.85	2.69
13	4.67	3.81	3.41	3.18	3.03	2.92	2.77	2.60
14	4.60	3.74	3.34	3.11	2.96	2.85	2.70	2.53
15	4.54	3.68	3.29	3.06	2.90	2.79	2.64	2.48
16	4.49	3.63	3.24	3.01	2.85	2.74	2.59	2.42
17	4.45	3.59	3.20	2.96	2.81	2.70	2.55	2.38
18	4.41	3.55	3.16	2.93	2.77	2.66	2.51	2.34
19	4.38	3.52	3.13	2.90	2.74	2.63	2.48	2.31
20	4.35	3.49	3.10	2.87	2.71	2.60	2.45	2.28
21	4.32	3.47	3.07	2.84	2.68	2.57	2.42	2.25
22	4.30	3.44	3.05	2.82	2.66	2.55	2.40	2.23
23	4.28	3.42	3.03	2.80	2.64	2.53	2.37	2.20
24	4.26	3.40	3.01	2.78	2.62	2.51	2.36	2.18
25	4.24	3.39	2.99	2.76	2.60	2.49	2.34	2.16
26	4.23	3.37	2.98	2.74	2.59	2.47	2.32	2.15
27	4.21	3.35	2.96	2.73	2.57	2.46	2.31	2.13
28	4.20	3.34	2.95	2.71	2.56	2.45	2.29	2.12
29	4.18	3.33	2.93	2.70	2.55	2.43	2.28	2.10
30	4.17	3.32	2.92	2.69	2.53	2.42	2.27	2.09
40	4.08	3.23	2.84	2.61	2.45	2.34	2.18	2.00
60	4.00	3.15	2.76	2.53	2.37	2.25	2.10	1.92
120	3.84	3.07	2.68	2.45	2.29	2.17	2.02	1.83
∞	3.84	3.00	2.60	2.37	2.21	2.10	1.94	1.75

Table D

Distribution of F (continued)

$p. = 0.01$

df_2	df_1 1	2	3	4	5	6	8	12
1	4052	4999.5	5403	5625	5764	5859	5982	6106
2	98.50	99.00	99.17	99.25	99.30	99.33	99.37	99.42
3	34.12	30.82	29.46	28.71	28.24	27.91	27.49	27.05
4	21.20	18.00	16.69	15.98	15.52	15.21	14.80	14.37
5	16.26	13.27	12.06	11.39	10.97	10.67	10.29	9.89
6	13.75	10.92	9.78	9.15	8.75	8.47	8.10	7.72
7	12.25	9.55	8.45	7.85	7.46	7.19	6.84	6.47
8	11.26	8.65	7.59	7.01	6.63	6.37	6.03	5.67
9	10.56	8.02	6.99	6.42	6.06	5.80	5.47	5.11
10	10.04	7.56	6.55	5.99	5.64	5.39	5.06	4.71
11	9.65	7.21	6.22	5.67	5.32	5.07	4.74	4.40
12	9.33	6.93	5.95	5.41	5.06	4.82	4.50	4.16
13	9.07	6.70	5.74	5.21	4.86	4.62	4.30	3.96
14	8.86	6.51	5.56	5.04	4.69	4.46	4.14	3.80
15	8.68	6.36	5.42	4.89	4.56	4.32	4.00	3.67
16	8.53	6.23	5.29	4.77	4.44	4.20	3.89	3.55
17	8.40	6.11	5.18	4.67	4.34	4.10	3.79	3.45
18	8.29	6.01	5.09	4.58	4.25	4.01	3.71	3.37
19	8.18	5.93	5.01	4.50	4.17	3.94	3.63	3.30
20	8.10	5.85	4.94	4.43	4.10	3.87	3.56	3.23
21	8.02	5.78	4.87	4.37	4.04	3.81	3.51	3.17
22	7.95	5.72	4.82	4.31	3.99	3.76	3.45	3.12
23	7.88	5.66	4.76	4.26	3.94	3.71	3.41	3.07
24	7.82	5.61	4.72	4.22	3.90	3.67	3.36	3.03
25	7.77	5.57	4.68	4.18	3.85	3.63	3.32	2.99
26	7.72	5.53	4.64	4.14	3.82	3.59	3.29	2.96
27	7.68	5.49	4.60	4.11	3.78	3.56	3.26	2.93
28	7.64	5.45	4.57	4.07	3.75	3.53	3.23	2.90
29	7.60	5.42	4.54	4.04	3.73	3.50	3.20	2.87
30	7.56	5.39	4.51	4.02	3.70	3.47	3.17	2.84
40	7.31	5.18	4.31	3.83	3.51	3.29	2.99	2.66
60	7.08	4.98	4.13	3.65	3.34	3.12	2.82	2.50
120	6.85	4.79	3.95	3.48	3.17	2.96	2.66	2.34
∞	6.63	4.61	3.78	3.32	3.02	2.80	2.51	2.18

SOURCE: Adapted from Fisher & Yates (1963, 6th ed., table V, p. 53).

If you have a sample larger than 35, extract the square root of N and divide the indicated figure by that number to obtain the appropriate level of significance. For instance, if your N was 49, you would extract the square root (7) and divide the indicated figures by 7. This would yield the following indices for determining probability:

$$1.07 \div 7 = .15; \quad 1.14 \div 7 = .16; \quad 1.22 \div 7 = .17$$

$$1.36 \div 7 = .19 \quad 1.63 \div 7 = .23$$

Now we can create an addition to Table E that would look like this:

Sample size (N)	Level of Significance for D				
	.20	.15	.10	.05	.01
49	.15	.16	.17	.19	.23

In this instance, you would have to have a D of at least .19 to reach the .05 level of significance. You would have to have a D of .23 to reach the .01 level of significance.

Table E

Critical Values of D in the Kolmogorov-Smirnov One-Sample Test[1]

Sample size (N)	Level of Significance for D [2]				
	.20	.15	.10	.05	.01
1	.900	.925	.950	.975	.995
2	.684	.726	.776	.842	.929
3	.565	.597	.642	.708	.828
4	.494	.525	.564	.624	.733
5	.446	.474	.510	.565	.669
6	.410	.436	.470	.521	.618
7	.381	.405	.438	.486	.577
8	.358	.381	.411	.457	.543
9	.339	.360	.388	.432	.514
10	.322	.342	.368	.410	.490
11	.307	.326	.352	.391	.468
12	.295	.313	.338	.375	.450
13	.284	.302	.325	.361	.433
14	.274	.292	.314	.349	.418
15	.266	.283	.304	.338	.404
16	.258	.274	.295	.328	.392
17	.250	.266	.286	.318	.381
18	.244	.259	.278	.309	.371
19	.237	.252	.272	.301	.363
20	.231	.246	.264	.294	.356
25	.21	.22	.24	.27	.32
30	.19	.20	.22	.24	.29
35	.18	.19	.21	.23	.27
Over 35	$\dfrac{1.07}{\sqrt{N}}$	$\dfrac{1.14}{\sqrt{N}}$	$\dfrac{1.22}{\sqrt{N}}$	$\dfrac{1.36}{\sqrt{N}}$	$\dfrac{1.63}{\sqrt{N}}$

SOURCE: Abridged from Massey (1951, p. 70).

[1] Two-tailed values.

[2] D, the maximum absolute observed-theoretical cumulative frequency difference, is statistically significant if it is equal to or larger than the table value.

AUTHOR INDEX

SUBJECT INDEX

ABOUT THE AUTHOR

DON PILCHER (Ph.D., University of California, San Diego) is Senior Educational Specialist with the Council on Social Work Education in Washington, D.C. He previously held the professorial chair in social work at the University of Melbourne in Australia. He has worked with several social service agencies and had taught research methodology and statistics for more than twenty years at the University of Melbourne, and La Trobe University in Australia, and San Diego State University in California. His most recent publications include "A Pragmatic Look at Income Inequality" which appeared in the *California Sociologist*.

NOTES

NOTES

NOTES

NOTES

NOTES